A Theatre for Cannibals

A Theatre for Cannibals

Rodolfo Usigli and the Mexican Stage

Peter Beardsell

Rutherford • Madison • Teaneck
Fairleigh Dickinson University Press
London and Toronto: Associated University Presses

Associated University Presses
440 Forsgate Drive
Cranbury, NJ 08512

Associated University Presses
25 Sicilian Avenue
London WC1A 2QH, England

Associated University Presses
P.O. Box 39, Clarkson Pstl. Stn.
Mississauga, Ontario,
L5J 3X9 Canada

The paper used in this publication meets the requirements
of the American National Standard for Permanence of Paper
for Printed Library Materials Z39.48-1984.

Library of Congress Cataloging-in-Publication Data

Beardsell, Peter R., 1940–
  A theatre for cannibals : Rodolfo Usigli and the Mexican stage /
Peter Beardsell.
      p.   cm.
  Includes bibliographical references and index.
  ISBN 0-8386-3436-2 (alk. paper)
  1. Usigli, Rodolfo, 1950– —Criticism and interpretation.
I. Title.
PQ7297.U85Z59   1992
863—dc20   90-56174
                                                           CIP

PRINTED IN THE UNITED STATES OF AMERICA

Contents

Preface

Lo que . . . he pretendido realizar en toda mi carrera . . . es un
teatro para caníbales en que el mexicano se devore a sí mismo
por la risa, por la pasión o por la angustia, pero que siempre,
como La familia, cene en casa.

—Prólogo a *Un día de éstos* . . .

(What . . . I have sought to create throughout all my career . . .
is a theatre for cannibals in which the Mexican may consume
himself with laughter, with passion or with anguish, but always,
like The Family, dine at home.

—Prologue to One of these days . . .

When Usigli invented the metaphor of cannibalism for Mexican
theatre audiences he was displaying his usual ambivalence toward
them. At the back of his mind was the image of New World savages
created centuries ago by visitors and conquerors from the "civilized" Old World. His patriotic mockery of that stereotype is ac-
companied, however, by a sardonic allusion to early twentieth-
century Mexico, which infuriated him with its sense of cultural
backwardness and inferiority. The conviction among theatre audiences and impresarios that all good drama originated abroad gave
him particular cause for metaphorical abuse. All this, however,
misses the essential warmth underlying his idea that the feast
should be a family occasion. In his play *La familia cena en casa*
(The family dines at home) he shows that the family may undergo
changes as a result of external and internal pressures, but its honor,
its integrity, and its ultimate strength are enhanced. The special
meal becomes a ritual confirmation of its existence. Similarly, by
attending the theatre, Usigli's audiences would be strengthening the
bonds that existed among their members. And this leads to the
metaphor of cannibalism: nourishment by self-awareness. What
Usigli saw as his vocation was the provision of a national theatre, in
which audiences would have the opportunity to devour images of
themselves on stage.

The first chapter of this book investigates the general features of

his quest. Most of the remaining chapters focus on individual plays
in which various facets of his picture of Mexico are displayed. The
final chapter adopts a less detailed approach in order to cast some
light on the more universal dimensions of his production. The point
of departure for the book was an enjoyment of Usigli's plays and a
curiosity about the Mexico that they depict. In other words, it is a
work prompted by a spirit of inquiry rather than the exposition of a
thesis or the testing of a literary theory. It has been written in the
age of deconstruction by one whose literary studies began in the
era of structuralism, but its author—like Usigli—has always preferred to obey his instincts rather than any particular canon. The
critical emphasis chosen in each chapter responded to the nature of
the plays themselves, though two other considerations have had a
vital overall influence. One was the fact that a play, being essentially
different from a literary text, should be contemplated (or imagined)
not merely in its intermediate form as a script but in its full existence as a live performance. The other was a desire to find the
special interrelationship between theatre and society and, by exploring their mutual influences, to reach a fuller understanding of
national traits.

It would not be possible to study all thirty-nine of Usigli's plays in
one volume without excessive superficiality, and to attempt even a
dozen is to run the same risk. But the idea is to reach some
understanding of his theatre as a whole through a selection of the
most representative and most interesting pieces. They are grouped
in categories that enhance the new perspective that this book
attempts to give them. One or two of those studied are admittedly
not among his very best, but neither is any major play omitted. All
contribute in one way or another to our awareness of his purpose,
our evaluation of his success, and our view of Mexican society.

I am indebted to many people, critical studies, and institutions
for the completion of this work. The idea of conducting research on
Usigli began after a seminal paper on the neglect of Spanish-
American theatre in Great Britain's universities, delivered by D. L.
Shaw to an annual conference of the Association of Hispanists in
the 1970s. My ideas were stimulated by student seminars and
essays in Sheffield, and by scholarship in the field of drama promoted by the *Latin American Theatre Review*. Grants from the
British Academy and the University of Sheffield supported research visits to Mexico. In Mexico, Tony and Silvia Stanton provided invaluable help with materials, contacts, advice, and
hospitality. In Sheffield, Audrey Stapley gave indispensable as-
sistance in preparing the book for publication. My wife has encour-

aged and supported the project at every stage, both in Sheffield and in Mexico. Access to the text of Usigli's plays was facilitated by the Fondo de Cultura Económica's edition of his *Teatro completo,* and I am grateful to the publishers for permission to quote from these three volumes. All in-text translations are my own. Finally, I am grateful for permission to use, in chapters 2 and 7, material originally published in different form in *Latin American Theatre Review* (vol. 10, no. 1, 1976): 5–14; *Hispanic Studies in Honour of Frank Pierce,* edited by J. P. England (Sheffield: University of Sheffield, 1980), 1–15; *Anales de Literatura Hispanoamericana* núm. 12 (1983): 13–27; and *Bulletin of Hispanic Studies* 66 (1989): 251–61.

A Theatre for Cannibals

1
Building a Theatre

El vendedor de dulces. Dicen que la obra es mexicana, aunque
con ese apellido del autor . . .
La acomodadora. Si es mexicana, no la verá nadie.
                    —*La crítica de "La mujer no hace milagros"*

(*Confectioner.* They say it's a Mexican play, though with that
author's surname . . .
Usherette. If it's Mexican nobody will see it.)
                    —The Review of "A woman can't perform miracles")

Usigli and the Mexican Theatre

The Revolution did not revolutionize Mexican theatre. During
Usigli's youth, in the years immediately following the violent up-
heaval of 1910 to 1920, changes in the theatre were limited and
gradual. Although the state played a part in institutionalizing certain developments, it was not until Usigli himself matured as a
dramatist that any major breakthrough occurred. Severely critical
of the nation's drama production, Usigli undertook personally (and
without any risk of false modesty) to build a theatre for Mexico.[1]
The modern theatre does not, of course, owe its existence to him
alone, but the general view acknowledges that his contribution was
both unique and—in a crucial period—paramount.[2]
    Usigli's criticisms first became public in newspaper articles of
1931 and, more particularly, in his book *México en el teatro (Mexico in the Theater)* of 1932.[3] In the latter, after making a sensitive
and idiosyncratic survey of drama since pre-Conquest times, he
turned his attention to the twentieth century. The first two decades,
he complained, were dominated by froth, stucco, and cardboard.
There was none of the passion that theatre required, no criticism of
national customs, psychology, or philosophy. Although the decade
since 1923 was important for Mexican theatre, the developments

lacked cohesion and failed to produce a national expression. Budding dramatists were faced with a dearth of good directors and actors, Spanish modes still dominated performances, and audiences were sparse. Usigli's tone became more scathing a few years later in his *Anatomía del teatro* (Anatomy of the theatre) (1939). Mexican audiences wanted dream, melodrama, and sentimentality rather than life. Dramatists lacked technique, actors were inconsistent and unprofessional, set construction was of poor quality, directors had insufficient resources, and drama critics were, in effect, a mindless secretion.[4] Naturally these opinions did little to enhance Usigli's popularity in the drama profession at the time (and led to a brief industrial dispute with the cast of *El gesticulador* [*The Impostor*] in 1947), but it is remarkable how much they are vindicated by histories of Mexican theatre written half a century later.

Recent opinion holds that when the Mexican theatre resumed its natural life after the years of the Revolution, the major nineteenth-century traditions were not quickly eradicated. There was still an emphasis on the supposedly poetic qualities of drama (such as the beauty of acting and the beauty of poetic moments), and the popularity of melodrama held firm. With Spanish actors dominating the stage, Mexican actors imitated both their methods and their accents.[5] (Usigli was particularly merciless in his ridicule of the false prestige attached to pronouncing *c, z* and *ll* in the Spanish way.) It is worth adding, however, that the popularity of reviews and sketches featuring current political and social personalities was an auspicious early development after the Revolution. Commentators tend toward the view that these mainly one-act comic pieces (known as *género chico*) were essentially frivolous material, but the vogue had the undoubted benefit of introducing more criticism, freer expression, and cruder elements of life to the stage.

The origins of the modern Mexican theatre are commonly found in the 1920s.[6] We may attribute this in part to the general attitude adopted by the secretary of education, José Vasconcelos. In 1921 he reinstalled the Secretaría de Educación Pública (SEP) and planned the regeneration of Mexico by means of culture. Education was to involve not only a campaign against illiteracy but the promotion and diffusion of the arts. Founding the Departamento de Bellas Artes in support of the program, Vasconcelos encouraged cultural nationalism. Usigli's analysis of the 1920s clearly demonstrates an affinity with these principles. (Indeed, he admitted to being a *vasconcelista*).[7] For Usigli 1923 is the key year: a Municipal Theatre was created, the Unión de Autores Dramáticos was formed, and a

subsidy was provided to fund a season of works at the famous
Teatro Virginia Fábregas. Five Mexican plays were included in this
season. Another national event that some consider to have been the
key to the future was the Pro Arte Nacional season created by the
so-called Grupo de los Siete in 1925.[8] Within two years more
Mexican plays were performed than in the previous quarter of a
century, and by 1929 the first Mexican work had achieved one
hundred performances.[9] The Teatro de Ahora, formed in 1932, gave
a great boost to the use of sociopolitical themes based on the
Revolution, with campesinos as the main characters. But not everyone agrees that the results of this nationalist impulse were bene-
ficial. According to some, it led to a theatre that was empty and
artificial, that relied on mere local color, melodrama, or propaganda.[10] In effect, it is clear that the issue was often simplified as a
dichotomy between nationalism and universalism. For many, the
healthy way to improve the nation's theatre was to put the best
modern plays from around the world on the Mexican stage. Writers
known as the "Contemporáneos," famous for introducing international authors and trends into the Mexican literary scene, were
among those who founded the Teatro de Ulises in 1928 to provide
this stimulus.[11] It was an experimental theatre, with nonprofes-
sional actors, which performed plays by dramatists such as Eugene
O'Neill in translations made by the founders themselves. Usigli,
always on the fringe of the Contemporáneos despite his friendship
with some of them, clearly recognized the merits of the Teatro de
Ulises while protesting that it was not strictly nationalistic because
it did not perform national works. He was not—as we shall con-
tinually be reminded—one of those who saw universalism and
nationalism as equally valid alternative approaches to a Mexican
theatre.

The state's rather sporadic sponsorship of the theatre, meanwhile, ostensibly encouraged new authors. In 1931 public funds
helped to create the Escolares del Teatro, which became the first
experimental group to stage a national author's work with Francisco Monterde's *Proteo*. This was followed in the same year by the
founding of the Teatro de Orientación,[12] whose approach made it a
successor to the Teatro de Ulises. One of the most significant
events was the completion of the Palacio de Bellas Artes in 1931
(construction work had begun in 1904). This led to the creation of
the Teatro de Bellas Artes, officially inaugurated on 29 September
1934. Programs announcing a season of plays declared that the SEP
had invited the most distinguished Mexican artists to take part in
the drama company and that the repertory would consist of both

Mexican and foreign works. The Secretaría de Educación Pública apparently felt the need to explain the duties of a state theatre company: "La SEP cree que es un deber llevar a la escena las mejores obras mexicanas" ("The SEP believes it to be a duty to stage the best Mexican plays").[13] In the course of time, however, the Teatro de Bellas Artes tended to be run more or less as though it were a private enterprise, hired out (often at minimal cost) to interested parties.[14] In other words, natural forces tended to counteract the nationalist rhetoric of these state interventions. With the public relatively unenthusiastic about Mexican plays, the commercial theatre continued to oppose them. Meanwhile, as Usigli himself pointed out, since the first Mexican film in 1917, a general movement toward filmmaking had been discernible. A short-lived Comité Pro-Teatro was set up in 1940 to promote theatre and improve its quality, and three seasons of national plays were presented in 1943 under the title El Teatro de México, but such efforts were not enough to prevent Mexican drama from undergoing the worst crisis in its existence during the first half of that decade.

A key year in its recovery proved to be 1947. The state made a clear commitment to fostering the arts by creating the Instituto Nacional de Bellas Artes (INBA), with a section devoted to the theatre. (Strictly, the INBA was founded on 31 December 1946.) Its first season of Mexican dramatists included works by Xavier Villaurrutia, Agustín Lazo, Francisco Monterde, and—from 17 May—Usigli's El gesticulador. The political controversy that Usigli's play provoked was one measure of its impact. Here was a national dramatist not merely illustrating features of Mexican life but vigorously questioning the official image of the Revolution and flagrantly censuring the political contradictions of the contemporary establishment. Reaction by the establishment was bound to be sharpened by the fact that the play belonged to a program sponsored by a state institution. But quite apart from this political impact, the play was well received by audiences—rapturously applauded on its first night, in fact. Although the seats were not all filled and the performances were limited to a fortnight (for reasons discussed in chapter 3), this new Mexican play did by any standards mark a new development. Subsequently, of course, it has been incorporated into the INBA's top repertory, as is evident from the program notes for the 1983 performances at the Teatro Jiménez Rueda by the Compañía Nacional de Teatro del INBA: "Público y crítico . . . consideran que El gesticulador es la pieza que representa el punto culminante de . . . la dramática mexicana" ("Public and critic . . . consider The Impostor to be the play that represents the high point in . . . Mexican dramatic art").[15] Within a few years of this event, Usigli set new standards for public performances of Mexican works. He achieved a strikingly long run with *El niño y la niebla* (The boy and the fog) in 1951, and broke box-office records with *Jano es una muchacha* (Janus is a girl) in 1952 (at the Teatro Colón).

There were other signs that the theatre was gaining in strength and health. Experimental groups were formed like La Linterna Mágica (1946), Teatro de Arte Moderno (1947), and Teatro Estudiantil Autónomo (1947; it featured comic sketches and farces on Mexican themes). The Escuela de Arte Teatral began its annual seasons of plays in 1948. The Teatro de Caracol was inaugurated in 1949 by young dramatists who were to become the base of the PROA GRUPO. From 1955 the movement known as Poesía en Voz Alta (Poetry Aloud), (supported by the Universidad Nacional Autónoma), boosted the theatre's development. A vogue for experiment swept through the country. Thriving university theatre groups played an increasingly important role, which climaxed in 1964, when the Compañía de Teatro Universitario won the first prize in an international competition for university groups held in Nancy, France. The 1960s was a period sometimes referred to as the golden age of Mexican theatre.[16] In 1962 the INBA provided the stimulus for a more general public awareness of national drama with a program of the most successful Mexican plays of the past fifteen years, plus a series of new Mexican works. Within thirty-three months, as many as twenty-five national plays were staged by the INBA.

A simplistic impression of success for Usigli and of well-being for the theatre in general should be avoided. In the 1960s and 1970s Usigli experienced bitter failures, particularly with *Corona de fuego* (Crown of Fire) at the Teatro Xola in 1961 and with his state-sponsored Teatro Popular project just over a decade later. The commercial theatre did not overcome its fundamental reluctance to stage serious Mexican works, and most box-office successes continued to be melodramas or shows imported from Broadway.[17] The state's apparent advocacy of a stronger nationalist theatre was undermined by continuing contradictions. An official report on the INBA's policy in 1950 contained all the seeds of ambiguity. Reminding the public that the INBA, though decentralized, was expected to follow general guidelines formed by the state, it continued, "La iniciativa oficial . . . debe dirigirse a la creación de un arte nacional. La iniciativa privada puede—y estrictamente debe—hacer lo mismo, pero puede también dar gran apoyo al arte venido de fuera" ("Official iniative . . . must be directed toward the creation of a national art. Private initiative may—and strictly speaking must—do the same, but it may also lend great support to art from abroad").[18] Not surprisingly, the nationalist aims were not fulfilled. The work of building a Mexican theatre remained incomplete. On the other hand, the tradition of dramatizing national issues was now well established, and this is where Usigli left his mark. The young dramatists who were writing in the 1950s had attended Usigli's courses in dramatic composition at the university. Some turned against him later, but they all came onto a scene in which he had proved the potential of Mexican material. One of the new generation, Luisa Josefina Hernández, was asked whether in the 1980s it was possible to speak of a tradition of Mexican drama. "Sí, a partir de Usigli" ("Yes, from Usigli onwards"), she replied. "La diferencia que hace la presencia de Usigli es la de popularizar un teatro avocado hacia la problemática de México" ("The difference that Usigli's presence made was to popularize a theatre orientated toward Mexican issues").[19]

Theatre as Vocation

It was through a combination of talent, dedication, and industry that Usigli made his career in the theatre. Born on 17 November 1905, he grew up in an impoverished middle-class household in Mexico City during the unstable and economically difficult years of the Revolution. On the death of his father, Alberto Usigli (who was of Italian origin), his mother, Carlota Wainer (of Polish extraction), struggled to raise four children. Conditions in the street caused the young Rodolfo to lead a childhood of frustrating confinement. At the age of twelve or thirteen, however, he began work as an office boy. Later he earned a little money from journalism, but instead of regarding this as a reliable source of income, he took up typing (in both Spanish and English). Once he began working, Usigli received no formal education, yet through sheer effort and enthusiasm he acquired a good range of knowledge and made himself an authority on the theatre.

Usigli's career took several twists and turns. On occasion he experienced severe poverty, which was relieved by part-time employment and free-lance journalism, while at other times he obtained reasonably comfortable appointments. From 1931 he held a post in the summer school of the faculty of Filosofía y Letras at the Universidad Nacional Autónoma de México, lecturing on the history and technique of the theatre. For a number of years he worked with the Radio Department of the Secretaría de Educación Pública. In the late 1930s he was made head of the press office under Lázaro Cárdenas's government. He entered the diplomatic corps in 1944 and was posted to Paris as second secretary at the Mexican Embassy (1944–46). After a few years back in his own country he began a long period of service overseas. As Ministro Plenipotenciario in Beirut (1957–60) and ambassador in Oslo (1960–72), he was in a cultural exile that he referred to as "beirutitis" and "osledad." On his retirement from the diplomatic service in 1972, he returned permanently to Mexico, where he resumed his activities with the national theatre.

This reliance on administrative, journalistic, teaching, and diplomatic activities—common enough among Latin American literary figures—tends to give the impression that his work with the theatre remained a mere sideline. But until his extended posting overseas, the theatre *was* his career (and even abroad he did not cease to write). It was as a young boy that he developed a passion for drama. In one of his prologues he recalled how, at the age of seven or eight, he learned the whole of *Don Juan Tenorio* by heart, including the stage directions (TC 3:282). Throughout his childhood he used to play with puppets, but around 1916 he had his debut as an actor with a group of children in a production of Gregorio Martínez Sierra's *El reino de Dios* (The Kingdom of God) at the Teatro Colón in Mexico City. In 1922, at the Escuela Popular Nocturna de Música y Declamación, he was learning to recite poems and to perform short plays, and the following year he was given the second male part in Pepe Escandón Noriega's *Maldita Revolución* (Damned Revolution). But his interest was not mainly in the performing side of drama. As a teenager, he used to invent dialogues between pencils or fingers. At the age of twenty, he was a theatre correspondent for the magazine *El Sábado* (later known as *El Martes*). After trying his hand at novels (and burning the product), he began writing sketches, attempting in vain to put on a review at the Teatro Regis. Between 1925 and 1931 he read an average of four plays per day, many in French (Molière in particular). Eventually he was to write one play of his own in that language—*4 Chemins 4* (4 Ways 4) (1932)—thus liberating himself from things French (TC 3:293–94). But his first play—in Spanish—was *El apóstol*, published in 1931 in a supplement of the magazine *Resumen,* though not performed. By this time his name as a theatre critic, theoretician, historian, and writer was becoming known. Although he was always resentful of the aloofness and exclusiveness of the Contemporáneos (TC

3:291–92), he began to appear—self-consciously dandified—in their social gatherings. Appointments as a director fell to him, first with the SEP's radio drama and, in 1933, with the Teatro Hidalgo. Then came one of the most formative events of his career. From 1935 to 1936 he was in the United States (with Xavier Villaurrutia) on a grant from the Rockefeller Foundation to study the techniques of dramatic composition and production at Yale University. Soon after his return he founded the Escuela de Teatro de la Universidad (which lasted one year), then he became head of the theatre section in the Departamento de Bellas Artes,[20] and in 1938 he participated in the last season of the Teatro de Orientación as translator and director. He was now in the busiest period of creative writing in his career. Between 1935 and 1940 he wrote some fifteen dramatic pieces, including five of his major full-length works in 1937 and 1938. But his progress was by no means smooth. *Medio tono* (Medium tone), his first play performed in Mexico City, aroused the antipathy of the Church. The Teatro de Medianoche (his two-month project involving mainly national dramatists) collapsed in April 1940 amid hostile criticism. His next four plays received chiefly negative or lukewarm reviews. And in 1947 *Corona de sombra (Crown of Shadows)* was taken off after only one night (11 April), and *El gesticulador* caused a storm of controversy a month later.[21] Some of his works had to wait several years before any theatre was prepared to stage them. Many, of course, are still waiting. Of the thirty-one pieces written by 1963, fifteen have never been performed commercially in Mexico City, and all eight of those written after that year have suffered the same fate. However, he certainly enjoyed one period of good progress. Between 1945 and 1954, ten plays received their first performance in as many years. The early 1950s were clearly the height of his success in terms of his plays' direct impact on theatre audiences. *El niño y la niebla,* produced in the Teatro del Caracol in 1951 after fifteen years of neglect, proved to be a turning point for him. Much to his surprise, critics were suddenly praising his ability, and the theatre was more than satisfied with the box-office receipts. A year later, *Jano es una muchacha* became an outstanding commercial success.[22] However, Usigli had no time to bask in critical acclaim, for once more he was deep in controversy, not only with the Church but with theatre critics and young dramatists who regarded this work as a deliberate potboiler and a betrayal of his integrity. Within two years he was in political trouble again with *Un día de éstos* . . . (One of these days . . .) (1954). Then followed the long personal absence from Mexico. During this period he turned some of his attention to the matter of self-appraisal and public image by adding to his prologues and epilogues, which now occupy some 565 pages in the third volume of his *Teatro completo*. But the performances of *Corona de fuego* in 1961 and *Corona de luz* (Crown of light) in 1969 tended to confirm the impression that his extended exile contributed substantially to the decline of his dramatic skills.

By this time, however, Usigli was being regarded from a different perspective: a figure belonging to the previous generation but acknowledged for his contribution to the growth of the Mexican theatre. *Corona de sombra* had returned to the stage with acclaim. *El gesticulador* had begun to be treated as a kind of classic, and he had received critical attention from abroad. Scholars in the United States had written theses about his theatre. The state publishing house, Fondo de Cultura Económica, had published two volumes of his *Teatro completo* in 1963 and 1966 (the third was to follow in 1979). And in 1972 his achievement was marked by the award of the Premio Nacional de Letras.

Usiglian Theory

"El teatro no es . . . un arte, sino . . . una necesidad, una respiración" ("Theatre is not . . . an art, but . . . a necessity, a form of breathing").[23] This distinction is a first step in understanding Usigli's ideas on the theatre. He was not denying the need for theatre to be artistic, but he was separating it from genres like the novel and poetry to stress its social function. It does not matter that the separation was not wholly valid, for the important point is one of emphasis: drama's fulfillment of human necessity, its capacity to perform roles essential to the communal body. More precisely, theatre opens people's eyes and ventilates their conscience (TC 3:748). Usigli was aware of the essential idealism of this concept. In one of his essays on the subject, he referred to the theatre as a place where the *people* unite.[24] But in a more pragmatic essay, he recognized that this state of affairs certainly did not pertain in his own country. It was the middle class that was the potential audience for a Mexican theatre, and for that reason, a middle-class drama was required (TC 3:445). In his *México en el teatro*, Usigli put forward the view that dramatists were not merely public servants but leaders of the masses in a particularly direct way. Taking his theory to heart, he set himself an ambitious program: to write what he later called "El gran teatro del Nuevo Mundo" (The great theatre of the New World) (TC 3:651–83).[25] Originally his idea was based on the comparison between Mexico (representing the whole of the New World) and a community, or the cast of a play. Instead of putting everything that he wanted to say into one work, he would write a different play around each character (TC 3:654). By 1950 he was therefore referring to most of his previous production as scattered constituent parts of a potentially organic whole. Although "El gran teatro del Nuevo Mundo" remained incomplete, and Usigli made very little future use of the term (as though he had in fact dropped the grandiose project), he persisted with the essential idea, which was to depict Mexico in its everyday life and to explore its psychological, political, and historical character. A critical attitude to his subject matter would be inevitable. "Toda mi obra está escrita bajo el signo de la indignación" ("All my work bears the hallmark of indignation") (TC 3:669), he admitted. But he was not referring to his personal indignation at the state of society or to the indignation that his outspoken criticism caused among members of the establishment. He was alluding to his condition as a Mexican, and to the national tradition of feeling indignant.

In portraying Mexican society on stage, he argued, the central issue was for the dramatist to allow audiences to watch their own activities while retaining a certain distance from the spectacle—to spy on life through a keyhole. The question of realism was therefore one that he treated with considerable caution. While calling for plays dealing with Mexican reality and acknowledging the validity of the term "realist," he did not believe in a documentary-type approach. Theatre, he insisted, was not literal reality but a concentrated, poetic version of the truth (TC 3:297).[26] This attitude not only determined the presence of varying degrees of exaggeration and fantasy in his own plays but entailed a corresponding use of imagination in set design. Though always opposing the tendency toward nonrepresentational, experimental, and "absurd" theatre, he nevertheless emphasized that the stage was not to be presented as a direct imitation of reality. Several of his scripts begin with careful descriptions of the set (furniture, carpets, pictures, curtains), as though he were in fact attempting to create an exact replica of a Mexican scene. But the purpose is more limited: to guide the audience toward the appropriate period, location, and social class. At that point the imagination takes over.

In this context, it is worth mentioning Usigli's views on the realtionship between theatre and cinema.[27] While aware of the inroads that the cinema industry had made into the domain traditionally ascribed to the theatre, he never shared the opinion that the theatre was in permanent decline. To his mind, there were fundamental differences that assured a separate future for both. A first distinction consisted in the fact that motion pictures created a record of a specific period in time and bore the permanent imprint of their date. In due course, therefore, films would be historical pieces fit for a museum. Theatre, on the other hand, retained an enduring relevance. If cinema was best suited to capturing historic moments or showing present life in its external characteristics, theatre excelled in the anecdote disclosing intimate experience and the inner man. Cinema had now assumed the novel's role as escape and entertainment, but theatre was essentially the exploration of situations in which human beings were submitted to tests. If we bear in mind that Usigli's preoccupation with the cinema belonged mainly to the 1930s, then we understand why one or two of his observations seem inexact. (For example, he did not foresee the ability of film to explore the human psyche through close-ups, dream sequences, montage, and the like). But essentially he was making a valid affirmation of the distinctive role of theatre and asserting that the techniques appropriate to each were different: "El buen teatro is siempre mal cinematógrafo" ("Good theatre is always bad cinema").[28]

Usigli enjoyed an unshakable confidence in his own dramatic technique. Whether as an innate ability or a quickly assimilated skill, the actual writing of plays came easily to him as a young dramatist. The only difficulty was in obtaining the original inspiration or idea. (*Medio tono* took him only four days to write [TC 3:444].) By the 1950s he admitted that composition posed increasingly complex problems for him (TC 3:711), but he did not cease to offer opinions and advice, and to convert theory into practice. Without anticipating details that are best reserved for appropriate chapters below, two fundamental and complementary criteria determining his dramatic technique may be noted. One was a matter of aesthetic integrity: the choice of a form that corresponded both to the idea and the anecdote (TC 3:607). However fine the dialogue, the scenes, or the characters, these elements were of no use without a coherent overall structure. The other was a careful attention to the relationship between the events on stage and the attitude of those who were watching. Audience participation of some kind was a crucial aim for the dramatist.

For his early works he chose comedy and farce, believing that laughter and a sense of ridicule were the best responses to evoke in people as they contemplated Mexican political events and personalities (TC 3:304). In the years 1934–38 he developed an interest in bringing melodrama onto the Mexican stage as a method of providing light entertainment and of filling the auditorium (TC 3:448). Although he retained a fruitful interest in comedy and melodrama, the most important development in his attitude to dramatic technique was the decision to introduce a more serious and profound tone into certain plays on Mexican themes (TC 3:492). The possibility of writing a genuine tragedy became a lasting ambition. In his "Primer ensavo hacia una tragedia mexicana" (First essay toward a Mexican tragedy), he outlined his strict personal definition of the genre (virtually denying the term's validity for any drama since the ancient Greeks).[29] From the claim that *El gesticulador* was Mexico's first serious attempt at a contemporary tragedy (TC 3:492), through his debate on historical tragedy as it affected *Corona de sombra* (TC 3:636–37), to the materialization of his theories in *Corona de fuego* (fully discussed in his *Notas*, TC 3:791–815), Usigli demonstrated his conviction that Mexican themes could be well served by tragic drama and that the national theatre tradition would be enhanced by Mexican tragedians.

Though almost obsessed with the ambition to raise the status of Mexican theatre, he never attempted to disguise his debt to internationally famous dramatists. His prologues offer a useful preliminary guide to these names. Ben Johnson, Oscar Wilde, and Eugene O'Neill are mentioned; Shakespeare, Aristophanes, and the Greek classics all came under his scrutiny. Lope de Vega and Ruiz de Alarcón were included. But French works prevailed, and in particular, those of Molière. By Usigli's early twenties, Molière "estaba ya en mi sangre" ("was already in my blood") (TC 3:285). It is possible to draw parallels between *Le Misanthrope* and *Alcestes* (which Usigli called a "transposition" of the French play), demonstrating the function of this early piece as a kind of experiment under expert tutelage. But the full value of Molière's teaching is more diffusely noticed in subsequent comedies, where the Mexican playwright developed a facility for striking caricature, succinct characterization, mordant satire, humorous situations, sustained tension, and even pure slapstick. Plays of the 1930s were especially indebted to the French master.

Eventually, however, Bernard Shaw became Usigli's greatest inspiration. It was an influence that he took pride in advertising. His *Conversaciones y encuentros* (Conversations and encounters) begins with two interviews with Shaw in his house near Saint Albans (England) in 1945.[30] *Corona de luz* is dedicated to him. He possibly acquired the habit of writing lengthy prologues from Shaw, and several of the prologues contain pages discussing Shaw's plays and ideas or use "G.B.S." as a yardstick and a justification.[31] Shaw's influence took many forms. Sometimes it was in the theme or even the action of a play. *La familia cena en casa,* for example, clearly echoes *Pygmalion* in its attention to the social retraining of a young woman. *Jano es una muchacha* is indebted to *Mrs. Warren's Profession* and *The Philanderer* for its frank treatment of prostitution and libidinal behavior. *Corona de luz* takes up the idea in *Saint Joan* that a miracle is "an event which creates faith," whether or not it appears fraudulent. Often the overall framework of Usigli's domestic and romantic dramas is reminiscent of Shaw. The action may concern a family (predominantly middle- or upper-class) whose values are reassessed, particularly as it comes under pressures from the outside world. A son's or daughter's choice of partner frequently becomes a central dilemma. Many of the characters (especially women) eventually come to terms with their situation or discover themselves. Comic situations capture the attention, in particular those where the audience knows that a secret is under threat or a pretense is being put to the test. Usigli admired Shaw's technical expertise (which he described as "classical") and certainly learned a great deal from it. Most of all, however, he owed to Shaw—even more than to Molière or Shakespeare—his understanding of what theatre was, despite differences in their temperament and vision.[32] As he told the Irish playwright face-to-face, the principal aspect of his influence was as a political critic.[33] An inveterate campaigner (of socialist or Fabian persuasion), Shaw unashamedly treated the theatre as a platform for the propagation of ideas and for philosophical, moralistic, and political comment. In his preface to *Mrs. Warren's Profession,* for example, he stressed his overriding didactic purpose. The play was written "to draw attention to the truth that prostitution is caused, not by female depravity and male licentiousness, but simply by underpaying, undervaluing, and overworking women so shamefully that the poorest of them are forced to resort to prostitution to keep body and soul together."[34] Usigli was to write many a prologue explaining equally didactic purposes. For example, his *Tres comedias impolíticas* (Three impolitic comedies) were written to "suscitar la cólera del pueblo mexicano hacia los vicios característicos de pasados regímenes políticos" ("arouse the Mexican people's anger against the vices characteristic of previous political regimes") (TC 3:424). His three historical *Coronas* were intended to teach people about the myths of spiritual, material, and political sovereignty.[35] Even while the prologue to *Jano es una muchacha* claims at first that there is no thesis in the play (TC 3:711), the "Addenda después del estreno" (Addenda after the first night) reveals his intention to "denunciar la doble vida sexual del mexicano" ("denounce the Mexican's double sexual life") (TC 3:730). The most important evidence of Shaw's influence, therefore, is in a political comedy such as *Noche de estío,* which he unashamedly described as a "comedia shaviana" (TC 3:303–5). Political comment apart, this comedy is Shavian for the nature of its central situation. It is a play in which an improbable or apparently unreal event—an essentially theatrical situation like the lady's bedchamber scene in *Arms and the Man*—serves as a concrete representation of an abstract, abstruse, fundamentally real problem. Shaw reinforced Usigli's belief that events on stage should be larger than life. Although faithful to the spirit of social observation, both were inveterate conjurors with reality rather than slavish reporters.[36]

In the light of this evidence, it must be recognized that Usigli formulated nationalist ambitions with his mind fully receptive to foreign influences. To build a Mexican theatre meant to raise his own country to the level of others that were culturally more mature. He was not interested in introducing the latest dramatic techniques and experiments to prove that Mexican playwrights were as competent as any others. With its vital function as a form of public expression and communication, the theatre needed to make Mexico itself a theme. Controversial though he proved to be, both as a dramatist and as a theoretician, Usigli became a key figure, particularly during the late 1940s and early 1950s, helping the Mexican theatre to achieve some measure of maturity. He may not have created a climate in which contemporary national plays could expect a regular commercial success, but he did much to stimulate the self-awareness and sense of identity on which a theatre dealing with Mexican social and political issues could be founded.

2

The Legacy of the Revolution

Usigli's Political Evolution

Criticism of Mexico's social and political scene earned Usigli, from time to time, the hostility of journalists, senior politicians, drama critics, the actor's union, the Church and the "League of Decency." On the other hand, the sponsorship that he received from certain regimes also exposed him to accusations of being a dramatist too eager to win favors, even of being a virtual spokesman for the establishment. Public familiarity with *El gesticulador* and a general awareness of the difficulties surrounding its first performance have led to the common view that the nub of the problem is a misunderstanding of Usigli's attitude to the Mexican Revolution. Without wishing in this chapter to refute or substantiate his claim that it is "una obra revolucionaria" ("a revolutionary work") (TC 3:532), I think it is important to prevent any mistaken idea that he was a "revolutionary author" in any but the loosest of senses. In fact, after undergoing formative experiences during the years when the Revolution was having its most tumultuous effects in Mexico City, Usigli began his adult life with a strongly negative attitude to it: "Los jóvenes de mi generación [en 1923] éramos, en mayoría, antirrevolucionarios como románticos' ("In my generation, the majority of us youngsters were as antirevolutionary as we were romantic") (TC 3:283). Nor was it simply a matter of emotional opposition, for there are indications in a prologue of 1933–35 that he was ideologically antagonistic to a rapid and thorough transformation of society.[1] He showed little sympathy with or understanding of industrial working class or campesino corporate action, believing that the growth of trade unions threatened the stability of government. Moreover, his views on land redistribution were far from progressive. In his opinion, the agrarian content of the Revolution was peripheral (or, to be more precise, "exclusivamente circunstancial y metafísico" ["esclusively circumstantial and metaphysical"]) (TC 3:395), and the campesino needed to be taught

27

that the Revolution was dead so that violent agrarian activity could come to an end. His emphasis was on peaceful coexistence and a readiness to serve the country. Rather than seeking "un socialismo cojo" ("a lame socialism") (TC 3:400), Mexico needed to aim at an integrated society in which each social class retained its essential characteristics. And rather than clamoring for soviet measures or for the dictatorship of the proletariat, "un proletariado sin letras, sin fe, sin respeto por la cultura establecida" ("a proletariat without education, without faith, without respect for established culture") (TC 3:400), the country needed to concentrate on industrial development.

These views look conspiciously conservative or—in the context of a postrevolutionary society—reactionary. As we shall see, they are represented in some of Usigli's early plays. What complicates the issue, however, is the nature of Mexican governments during the 1920s and early 1930s; on the one hand they claimed to be based on the spirit of the Revolution of 1910–20 (and the constitution of 1917), while on the other hand, they manifestly contradicted that spirit in some of their policies. In reality, Usigli's relatively conservative outlook in 1933 had much in common with that of the ruling establishment, but it ran counter to the prevailing rhetoric. Moreover, Usigli's drama of that period was already devastatingly critical of national attitudes, government policies, and leading political figures, with the result that, paradoxically, he soon appeared highly subversive. Although he managed to have *Estado de secreto* performed in Guadalajara in 1936, no theatre in Mexico City was prepared to stage any of his *Tres comedias impolíticas* for well over a decade.[2]

It was the Calles administration (1924–28) and the six years with Calles as Jefe Máximo overseeing the nation's affairs (1928–34) that received the brunt of Usigli's hostility. During Lázaro Cárdenas's term in office, his antagonism toward post-Revolutionary trends began to attenuate. In fact, as we saw in the previous chapter, he became a government employee as head of the regime's press office.[3] By 1938, in an essay supporting his then-unfinished play *El gesticulador,* he was no longer expressing blatantly reactionary views. In place of a concern that Mexico might move too far to the Left, the focus of his criticism became the history of government hypocrisy and demagogy (TC 3:452–77). The problem, he claimed, was not in the nature of the Revolution itself but in the distortions suffered by the Revolution during subsequent years and the corruption of individuals who had led the country (TC 3:532–33). Within a few years, this modification of his views was looking like a radical change. In an essay of 1947 he spelled out his distinction between "la sana y pura idea revolucionaria" ("the sound and pure revolutionary idea") (TC 3:502) and the practical realities that had corrupted the ideal. (He made a similar reference to the pure communist idea [TC 3:515].) Openly debating his relation to the political right and left, conscious of faults in each, he now emphatically stated his allegiance to the left (TC 3:507). This did not smooth the way, however, for the public performance of his political drama. Only his social and psychological plays appeared on stage until 1947, when *El gesticulador* eventually overcame the tactical opposition and achieved its short-lived success. President Miguel Alemán's direction that the play's run should be limited to two weeks, and other difficulties discussed in chapter 3, aroused Usigli's profound hostility. Fifteen years earlier he might well have supported the kind of political program introduced during the Alemán government, but now he became highly critical of the vast expenditure on surface appearances and of the increasing Mexican economic dependence on the United States. He summed it up as "la flor devoradora de los hombres del alemanismo" ("the man-eating flower of Alemanism") (TC 3:750).

After the critical success of *El niño y la niebla* in 1951 and the box-office success of *Jano es una muchacha* in 1952, Usigli could have expected a good reception for his next political play, *Un día de éstos . . .* , two years later. In fact, it provoked a hail of criticism and was withdrawn after thirteen performances. There were conflicting reactions among its critics. While some accused Usigli of idolizing President Adolfo Ruiz Cortines (who had been in office since 1952), others accused him of mocking both the Ruiz Cortines and Alemán administrations. The problem was that in his "aspiración hacia el equilibrio" ("striving for evenhandedness") (TC 3:757), he had left too many ambiguities. Besides, although the play strongly suggests that his political position was evolving toward compromise and even, perhaps, reconciliation with the establishment (though not with Alemán), a residual censure of Mexican leaders and their policies was all too apparent.

Usigli's diplomatic career had an important bearing on the evolution of his political thought. Like other Latin American writer-diplomats, he was influenced by a combination of motives in the choice of this branch of his career: the need to make a living, the prospect of travel, the need to find inspiration for his writing, the desire to serve his country. As in other cases, however, he was not in control of his movements, and his postings could be interpreted either as the honorable recognition of his prestige and talents or as a convenient exile to prevent him from causing trouble at home. His appointment to Paris in the midforties may be seen as a welcome opportunity for him, but the posts in Beirut and Oslo during the sixties must inevitably strike us as a decade of virtual banishment. In effect, Usigli's political dissent ended once he had committed himself to diplomatic service abroad. And then, following the election of his former pupil Luis Echeverría to the presidency in 1970 and his own retirement a year later, he reached the last phase of his political development. *¡Buenos días, Señor Presidente!* written in 1972, offered a clear sign of the author's alignment with the current regime in its dedication to the president: "Al señor licenciado Luis Echeverría Álvarez, Presidente Constitucional de los Estados Unidos Mexicanos, por razones que el corazón y la razón conocen. Con respetuoso afecto." ("To Mr. Luis Echeverría Álvarez, constitutional president of the United States of Mexico, for reasons that both the heart and reason acknowledge. With warm respect") (TC 3:226). This moral support for the president was by no means free from controversy. Four years previously, as minister of *gobernación,* Echeverría had been ultimately responsible for the authorities' handling of student unrest—a situation that led to worldwide notoriety, in particular through the bloodbath in the Plaza de las Tres Culturas in the Capital's Tlatelolco district. Unlike Octavio Paz, Usigli had not resigned his diplomatic post in protest. Subsequently, in the pages of *Plural,* he and Paz had engaged in a polemic concerning his support for Echeverría. Almost alone among prominent writers, Usigli had publicly accepted the official explanation of events at Tlatelolco. After his return to Mexico in 1971, the new regime had given him financial backing for a series of national drama productions.[4] Usigli's act of publicly associating himself with the country's leadership in 1972 is therefore fully consistent with these events. For the present purpose, however, the greatest significance lies in the fact that Usigli was willing to be identified with Echeverría's policies near the beginning of his *sexenio.* There are two ways of interpreting this. At the time, the president looked set to reduce corruption, authoritarianism, violent repression, inefficiency, and economic dependence. Even now, some historians still see him as a president belonging to the left of the political spectrum,[5] despite his subsequent compromises with the Right. On the other hand, according to a leftist point of view, "Echeverría was not embarking on a new 'Mexican road to socialism.' Rather, he was trying to modernize and rationalize Mexican capitalism."[6]

In perspective, we may see how Usigli evolved from opposition to the Revolution in the 1920s to accommodation with the Partido

Revolucionario Institucional in the 1970s. Of course, his political progress can no more be described as a general drift to the left than the PRI can be regarded as a party of the left. The official party was founded in 1929 to unite a Revolutionary group that seemed capable of tearing itself apart and to ensure a civilized framework for the inevitable power struggle. At the same time, the party would give national expression to the targets of the Revolution.[7] However, if Lázaro Cárdenas took it toward the left with his land reform and nationalization policies of the late 1930s, Miguel Alemán steered it to the right a decade later by shifting the emphasis from social objectives to the expansion of the economic infrastructure. Fluctuations—mostly between less extreme poles—characterized the party's evolution over the next half-century. In the face of political and economic pressures, the PRI modified aspects of the electoral process and the system of government to increase the voice of opposition and the representation of opposition parties in the Chamber of Deputies. Echeverría himself was responsible for some of the reforms. In the 1970s, therefore, the relatively mild criticism of a dramtist like Usigli was easily absorbed by the system because, in effect, it had become an integral part of official policy in the regime's attempts to democratize without radical change. Not that the government was even then willing to tolerate all types of adverse comment on stage. Although President Echeverría spoke publicly about the need for greater freedom of expression, a form of censorship still operated for performances in the commercial theatre (as opposed to the experimental theatre at university centers or the Fine Arts Institute). Producers were required to submit scripts for authorization by the Jefatura de Espectáculos, and according to one writer who experienced censorship during the 1970s, "there are endless cases of plays prohibited by this office."[8]

It is in this context that we must place Usigli's own faltering, though conscious, political development. From youthful antirevolutionary iconoclasm, he progressed to a period of admiration for the pure revolutionary idea (during the Cárdenas era), and eventually to a virtual acceptance of the Revolution in its institutionalized form. If one lasting feature was his hatred of humbug, another was his distrust of radical developments. Moreover, despite his poor relationship with some regimes, he often had friends in high government positions and held a number of administrative and diplomatic posts. He was never wholly alienated. Indeed, in certain respects he appeared eventually to have undergone that notorious process sometimes known as co-optation: "the process by which individuals or groups independent enough to threaten the ongoing domination of a single group or party (in this case, the PRI) are traded small concessions or favors in exchange for moderating their demands and reducing their challenge to the dominant group's control over the system."[9] I am not suggesting that Usigli consciously set out to buy "small concessions or favors," but that like most of Mexico's intellectuals, he found it impossible to retain complete independence of thought while still seeking openings for his work. As we shall see in chapter 3, the case of *El gesticulador* demonstrates the particular difficulty of dramatists with this control by the dominant group.

Tres comedias impolíticas and the *Farsa impolítica*

Usigli saw politics as an integral part of daily life in Mexico rather than as an optional or specialized area of activity. As one of his characters observes, "La política es una especie de filología de la vida que lo concatena todo" ("Politics is a kind of philology of life that links everything together").[10] Naturally enough, few of his plays are void of political content. Seven, however, could be described as political drama in the sense that affairs of state are at the core. The earliest were grouped together as *Tres comedias impolíticas* (Three impolitic comedies):

> *Noche de estío* (Summer night) (written 1933–35, first performed 1950)
> *El Presidente y el ideal* (The President and the ideal) (1935, not performed)
> *Estado de secreto* (State of Secrecy) (1935, first performed 1936)

From virtually the same period was his *farsa impolítica* (impolitic farce):

> *La última puerta* (The last door) (1934–36, not performed)

Shortly afterward he wrote his *pieza para demagogos* (play for demagogues):

> *El gesticulador (The Impostor)* (1938, first performed 1947)

The next, begun in this early period but completed two decades later, was his *fantasía impolítica* (impolitic fantasy):

Un día de éstos . . . (One of these days . . .) (1935–53, first
  performed 1954)

And at the end of his career came his *moralidad* (morality):

¡Buenos días, señor Presidente! (Good morning, Mr. President!)
  (1972, not performed)

The term *impolítica,* ironically describing five of these plays, takes
advantage of a double meaning: "unpolitical," and "imprudent" or
"impolite". The negative prefix pretends to deny the plays' literal
relevance to Mexican politics while it actually draws attention to it.
Simultaneously, there is a hint of the tactless and undiplomatic
quality derived from the political attitudes displayed in the drama.[11]
To these seven may be added six plays with a notable political
content at a subsidiary level, although they do not concern us in this
chapter: *El niño y la niebla* (The boy and the fog) (1936, first
performed 1951); *Medio tono* (Medium tone) (1937, first performed
1937); *Otra primavera (Another Springtime)* (1937–38, first performed 1945); *La familia cena en casa* (The family dines at home)
(1942, first performed 1942); *Los fugitivos* (The fugitives) (1950,
first performed 1950); and *Las madres* (The mothers) (1949–60, not
performed). A glance at the dates of composition of these thirteen
plays shows clearly how prolific the mid-1930s were for Usigli's
political ideas. Some of the output may be attributed to his attendance at the course on theatre composition and direction in the
United States. But the full explanation lies in the orientation of his
artistic inspiration and purpose as he began his career. Heavily
satirical, these works of the 1930s seem designed to compel the
audience to think about two types of problem: in the first place, the
burning issues of the day; and in the second place, the underlying
and persistent problems of Mexico. As the dates of public performances demonstrate, the early and more overtly political works
encountered production problems. After the first cluster of plays,
he turned away from current affairs to emphasize the more permanent issues, eventually abandoning comedy and farce as dramatic
forms appropriate to political subjects. In the early 1930s, however,
he was convinced that tragedy was wrong for "una materia de
chatos perfiles trágicos, como la política de nuestros países de
América" ("a material of blunted tragic features, like the politics of
our countries of America") (TC 3:304). Comedy in the style of
Aristophanes, Molière, or Shaw and farce in the manner of Jules
Romains were the forms that commended themselves to him.

In chapters 3 and 4 I shall examine the political plays corresponding to Usigli's mature and later periods, but what concerns us here
is the early period, in which he grouped the comedies on the
dominance of Calles and the transition to Cárdenas under the
heading *Tres comedias impolíticas.* It makes good sense to add the
farce, *La última puerta,* in order to capture a full impression of the
period. Instead of treating all four works equally, I shall make only
brief comments on three, singling out the best, *Noche de estío,* for
individual analysis, particularly with a view to showing the effects
of comedy and farce on the political themes.

The "Nota importante" inserted at the beginning of *Noche de
estío*'s script advises us, with amusing irony, that any similarity to
Mexican political or social life is "puramente casual y absoluta-
mente desaconsejable" ("purely accidental and absolutely inadvis-
able"). Usigli's prologue to the play, however, frankly indicates the
factual basis of numerous features (TC 3:412–13). The play was
inspired, he admitted, by the burning issue of the time: the presidential succession. Moreover, although the characters were all fictitious, some of them contained allusions to notable political figures
of the day. He does not name them, but the General is easily
recognized as Plutarco Elías Calles, while the minister of finance's
name, Paniagua, stridently echoes that of the real-life Alberto J.
Pani. According to Usigli's prologue, the idea of a temporary sei-
zure of a radio station by a group of communists was based on an
actual event of 1932. In the aftermath of that episode, a secretary of
state appointed one of the assailants as assistant director of an
official educational broadcasting station (roughly as in the play).
The threat of direct action by a workers' organization had its source
in a real situation of 1935. Even the unscheduled ringing of cathe-
dral bells (act 1) actually occurred on 10 May 1933 at the first
showing of a certain Mexican film.

Usigli acknowledged the unlikelihood of the play's events taking
place literally as he had organized them, but he felt justified as a
dramatist in stretching the limits of probability. The result is a taut
and entertaining situation comedy, with sharply satirical effects.[12]
One summer's night in the Minister of Finance's house a series of
accidents has brought together a number of people, including two
cabinet ministers and a *caudillo* figure known as El señor General.
The comic situation arises from the characters' misinterpretation of
events (for example, the failure of lights and telephones because of
heavy rain), which seem to isolate them in the building in the midst
of a communist takeover of the country. In the atmosphere of crisis,
and with the old regime apparently overthrown, the characters

begin to direct recriminations against each other. It proves to be a perfect situation for unmasking the truth: under stress and with nothing to lose—or so they believe—the characters end their customary pretense and role-playing, and speak their minds. The outcome is a powerful impression of underlying dissatisfaction among all sectors of society. One of the specific issues is the widespread lack of integrity throughout the country, which is expressed both in the dishonorable treatment of women and in the corrupt appointments system among government officials. But there is an underlying complaint that the General has failed to fulfill his promises, exposing himself to the hostility not only of Catholics and landowners but also of revolutionary idealists. Unemployment and poverty are said to be rife, class differences persist, one set of tyrants has been replaced by another. "¡Y todavía dicen que son revolucionarios!" ("And they still say they are revolutionaries!"), exclaims the typist in her exasperation (TC 1:205). Even the Minister of Finance lowers his mask of obsequiousness, rounding on the General with the accusation that by clinging to power he has become the kind of *caudillo* that he claimed to have eradicated from Mexican politics. When the General himself eventually loses his temper and reveals his awareness of the hidden truth, his speech becomes a model of self-ridicule.

"Nosotros, por lo menos, suspendimos la revolución. Y si todo ha sido obra nuestra—obra mía, digamos la verdad—y si he recogido frutos, es porque no tengo el miedo de unos, ni la mediocridad de otros, ni la estupidez de los demás." (TC 1:209)

("We, at least, suspended the revolution. And if everything has been our own work—my own work, let's be frank—and if I have reaped benefits, it's because I haven't some people's fear, others' mediocrity, or the stupidity of the rest.")

In other words, the comic situation serves as a pretext for allowing Usigli to express some home truths from behind a transparent shield. He uses it to even greater advantage, however, at the moment of anticlimax, when the communist coup proves to be pure imagination. This sudden reversal shows Usigli at his best in handling comic situations. Six workers in overalls enter the house to repair the telephones. Their purpose, however, is completely misunderstood. The General takes a courageous stance at what he believes to be the imminent arrest or execution of those present. With great humor deriving from the sharp contrast between imagined high melodrama and real humdrum events, the critical moment arrives. As the workmen leave one of them draws not a gun but a bill for them to sign. From this amusing spectacle Usigli immediately leads on to the nub of his satire.

> El Señor General. Un momento. (Los obreros se vuelven.) ¿Son ustedes comunistas?
> Obrero Cuarto. (Sonriendo.) Por supuesto, señor general.
> Obrero Segundo. Naturalmente, señor. Estamos sindicalizados. (Salen majestuosamente.) (TC 1:212)

> (The General. Just a minute. (The workers turn.) Are you Communists?
> Fourth Worker. (Smiling.) Of course, General.
> Second Worker. Naturally, sir. We're unionized. (They go off majestically.)

Of course, the workmen have recognized the General and interpret his question as a test of their allegiance to him. The true position of Mexico's communism is exposed. Far from representing a threat to the established order, it is safely diluted and integrated into the system created and controlled by Calles. Although the courtesy and dignity of the workmen serve to ridicule the bemused General for an instant, he soon resumes control of himself and others. (He even decides to find posts in the establishment for the three communist activists who seized the radio station.) In the remaining scene the comic situation is completed with renewed satire of each character as he resumes his mask. With the *caudillo* once more in command, the other characters are ridiciously obsequious. In this play, as in *El gesticulador,* people's hypocrisy is exposed; here, however, it is converted into an amusing spectacle, by contrast with its more somber treatment in the later play.

Although this situation is the central comic element in *Noche de estío,* its success depends upon the creation of an appropriately frivolous atmosphere. To this end, Usigli resorts to a number of comic devices. From the raising of the curtain, a moment of slapstick sets the audience laughing (in the darkness, the Minister of Finance smashes a priceless vase). Comic mannerisms are used (as when the Minister displays his indecision and anxiety by uttering a pensive "Sí. Ummm" six times during the beginning of act 3). The dramatist is not averse to using the simplest forms of humor. The name Paniagua is an allusion not only to Alberto J. Pani but, of course, to the supply of bread and water by an unpopular minister of finance. There is even a variation on a joke known in music halls throughout the world.

El Señor General. Sea sincero y no mire el reloj. ¿O espera usted a alguna mujer?
El Ministro Paniagua. A ninguna, señor; a quien espero es a mi esposa.
El Señor General. ¿Ya ha llegado usted a eso?
El Ministro Paniagua. Señor General, el día que eso pase, habré acabado y presentaré mi renuncia. (TC 1:172)

The General. Be sincere and don't look at the clock. Or are you expecting some woman?
Paniagua. None, sir; it's my wife I'm expecting.
The General. Has it come to that now?
Paniagua. General, the day that happens I'll have finished and I'll hand in my resignation.

Such utterances usually have an indirect relevance to the satirical theme of the play (in this case, of course, the misdirected machismo of the country's leaders). But their greater function is to surround and heighten the effect of jokes that directly attack political issues, such as the following allusion to the public secret concerning Calles's political influence from behind the scenes and the hegemony of the "Northern Dynasty":

El Ministro Paniagua. Se dice que así como en los pueblos, para ir a cualquier parte, hay que pasar por casa de la novia, en la política mexicana, para hacer algo, hay que pasar por Baja . . .
El Señor General. ¡Chist! Puede oír alguien. (TC, 1:173)

Paniagua. They say that just as in small towns, to get anywhere, you have to go via your girlfriend's house, in Mexican politics, to do something, you have to go via Baja . . .
The General. Shsh! Somebody might hear.

Noche de estío deserves to be regarded as distinctly more successful as a dramatic piece than the other plays with which it is grouped. Two fundamental criticisms have been leveled against the *comedias impolíticas:* "Fallan por el carácter casi periodístico de su enfoque. . . . Pero su verdadero fracaso artístico obedece a razones de concepción y diseño. . . . Pretenden dar una visión ironizada de la realidad contingente sin lograrlo ni al nivel más elemental" ("They fail because of the almost journalistic character of their approach. . . . But their true artistic failure derives from questions of conception and design. . . . They claim to give an ironized vision of contingent reality without achieving it at even the most elemental level").[13] In the case of *Noche de estío,* the first of these judgments is only partially justified. Despite the specific references to political issues of the mid-1930s, the play makes a number of telling points with an enduring relevance to Mexican political life, and Usigli's later plays return to them. If the problem of Calles's dominance was to end within a year of the play's composition, the question of undemocratic processes was to persist over half a century later. Complaints of poverty and social divisions within a supposedly revolutionary society were to continue unabated. Above all, however, this play makes use of a contrived situation in order to lower people's masks and expose their underlying hypocrisy. The situation itself may be dated, but the national trait thus revealed is one that Usigli regarded as perennial. As for the artistic conception of *Noche de estío,* the negative appraisal is by no means valid. The satirical treatment of real issues and living personalities is successful despite their inevitably transient relevance. But the great achievement is the creation of a dramatic situation that is both ridiculous and fascinating. Imprisoned within a house by their own unfounded suspicions, the characters are forced into an entertaining interplay of personalities and ideologies. Like them, the audience has to await the denouement before being sure that the whole affair has been founded on false interpretations. They are taken gradually out of reality into an imaginary world before being thrown abruptly back into reality with a fresh understanding of it. The concentration of the whole play's action into this single situation creates an aesthetically pleasing structure, almost classical in its neatness.

El Presidente y el ideal is far more vulnerable to adverse criticism. This is partly because it is the play that offers the most specific satirical comment on a current political issue. The transitional period between the era dominated by Calles and the consolidation of political power by the new president, Lázaro Cárdenas, provides the scenario. Calles, we should remember, had been president of the republic from 1924 to 1928, had controlled the country from behind the scenes as Jefe Máximo de la Revolución from 1928 to 1934 (the *maximato*), had selected Cárdenas as president, and had failed to control the new man. He represented a severe threat to the new government until Cárdenas eventually expelled him to the provinces in 1935 and deported him the following year. The main action of *El Presidente y el ideal* closely follows this pattern. A shadowy figure named as El Jefe announces (in semidarkness) that he has decided on a new president. As the play progresses, we notice the growing independence of this president and the threat of countermeasures. At the end of act 2, cabinet ministers are hinting at the likelihood of intervention by El Jefe, and by the end of act 3 it is common knowledge that he is maneuvering to overthrow the president. The reflection of political reality is completed in the epilogue, where newspapers announce the expulsion of El Jefe Máximo de la Revolución. Perhaps the most memorable aspect of this ending is the way Usigli associates political survival and defeat with sheer chance. A man selling lottery tickets shouts: "¡Cincuenta mil pesos para perder la vergüenza! ¡Cincuenta mil pesos para ser Jefe Máximo de la Revolución! ¡Cincuenta mil para ser Presidente de la República! ¡Aquí está la suerte! ¡Aquí!" ("Fifty thousand pesos to lose your shame! Fifty thousand pesos to be Supreme Leader of the Revolution! Fifty thousand to be President of the Republic! Here is where you get lucky! Here!") (TC 1 : 350). To the country at large, these political events are therefore made to appear as mysterious and unpredictable as a lottery. Mexico's supreme executive position, the presidency itself, is reduced to a ridiculous spectacle.

Besides creating a parallel between the main action and the major political events peculiar to the years 1934 and 1935, Usigli devoted a vast array of individual scenes to the ridicule of attitudes and political trends during the first two years of Cárdenas's term in office. Those particularly worth mentioning are the visit by a youthful communist schools inspector to a dilapidated school, the meeting of industrialists worried by financial losses and pay demands, the meeting of the textile workers' confederation to call for another strike, the banquet where top generals discuss loyalties and end up drunk, and the violent occupation of an estate by abused and impatient campesinos. The land redistribution program receives severe criticism for the loopholes that allow cynical landowners to retain their property, the administrative errors and delays, and the violent abuse of the situation by extreme revolutionary elements. The industrial scene comes under heavy fire: Usigli's complaints range from plaintive industrial magnates to militant trade unions. Specifically, he makes frequent allusion to the high number of strikes by Mexican workers and ridicules the pretexts used by union leaders when calling for a stoppage.[14] Education reforms provoke severe mockery, with schoolteachers and university professors faring badly. But this is seen as part of the more general problem created by the spread of communism, which Usigli satirizes viciously for its doctrinaire attitude and for its the use of empty rhetoric.

El Presidente y el ideal has an entirely different form from *Noche de estío*. Instead of a taut, single plot and situation, it consists of a mainly unconnected series of situations (sixteen *cuadros*, a *pró-*

logo, and an *epílogo*) and a great number of characters. It is documentary drama, based on the idea that the audience should be offered glimpses, one-by-one, of a wide variety of scenes from Mexican life. This kind of drama, akin to the "epic theatre" that developed in Germany during the 1920s, obeys principles that were alien to Usigli, in particular, the ascendancy of content over form, and of veracity over illusion. After *El Presidente y el ideal* he did not return to it—fortunately, because the excessive length of this play (half of the cuadros could be omitted) exaggerates the effect of a piecemeal approach and enhances the lack of cohesion and dramatic tension.

These technical defects might, in their own right, explain the play's failure to appear on stage. But in any case, no theatre manager was prepared to risk a work that heavily satirized several features of Cárdenas's own regime. *Estado de secreto*—a different proposition since it referred fairly obviously to the influence of a now discredited Calles—had the marginally greater success of a production in Guadalajara in 1936. The preliminary note to *Estado de secreto* pessimistically states, "La acción en México; ayer, hoy, mañana y siempre" ("The action in Mexico; yesterday, today, tomorrow and always") (TC 1:351)—pessimistically, because the play shows the triumph of political corruption, the survival of the gangsterism associated with Calles, and the threat to the elected president from a more powerful figure operating behind the scenes. The protagonist, Ildefonso "Poncho" Suárez N., a cabinet minister who runs casinos and contraband operations, faces a crisis when one of his men shoots a political enemy. In a telephone call, the president demands Poncho's resignation. However, Poncho defiantly refuses to resign and impudently points out that El Jefe, who gave him his post, will help him to retain it. In act 3 we watch this prophecy being fulfilled. Poncho has made a deal with both El Jefe and the Director of the Party; the Director instructs his demonstrators at the Party headquarters to change their main chant from "Abajo Suárez eNe" ("Down with Suárez N.") to "Arriba Suárez eNe" ("Up with Suárez N.") (TC 1:396); the president himself is being compelled to resign; Poncho begins to prepare for his own likely succession to the presidency; and the play ends with him and his men counting their profits from gambling and prostitution. It is clearly an outspoken indictment of Mexico's recent political history, particularly in its satirical attack on the notorious gangsterism of the period. (Historians inform us of "gambling casinos and brothels owned by important *callistas*" and report that "troublesome persons were executed or 'suicided.' ")[15] But as a play, it ranks as the weakest of the *comedias impolíticas,* badly marred as it is by melodramatic action and superficial characterization.

In these three plays political comment and laughter exist together. Affairs of state and politicians are converted into amusing and ridiculous spectacles. Essentially the same result is produced by the *farsa impolítica.* For Usigli, farce rarely meant sheer slapstick or buffoonery. It was, he explained, a means of concentrating on essentials and drawing out the suggestive qualities of his subject matter.[16] In *La última puerta* the farce consists in the exaggeration of a situation to the point of absurdity. People waiting in an anteroom for an audience with the Minister age visibly as the time passes. One of the exasperated characters is a deputy sent on a "secret" mission by the Cámara de Diputados to ascertain whether the Minister exists. A number of Trade Unions have asked the Senate and the President for the same information. Eventually the waiting people run out of patience, open doors, and begin to break things. They are on the point of opening the last door when it opens with a loud click and the Minister's voice is heard. Precisely at that moment, his private secretary announces that the Minister has resigned. The main purpose of this farce is to ridicule the *antesala* system, whereby citizens queue in anterooms to seek a personal interview with a minister, bypassing the formal procedures, usually in the hope of obtaining some personal favor. (Usigli himself had personal experience of the long periods of waiting that were involved.) The nature of state bureaucracy is at issue. Government ministers are displayed as inactive and faceless, failing to account publicly for their behavior. But in a more general sense, the questions raised are why the citizens should need to resort to unofficial interviews and how they have been led to accept them as legitimate practice. Implicitly, moreover, the people seeking audience with the minister are guilty of participating in a ridiculous system.

It is important for us to notice that the *antesala* system provides a context for a thorough ridiculing of Mexico's political scene. Each character represents a particular social phenomenon, and each is satirized in turn: the journalist for offering bribes in exchange for information; the secretaries for attending to their personal appearance and amorous relationships instead of working; the students for holding demonstrations so frequently that they forget the cause of their latest protest; the *diputado* for his affectation, pride, stupidity, and ineffectiveness. The list could be extended to include twenty-one other cases, from the Minister's private secretary to a tramp, who are lightly and briefly ridiculed for traits not inherently concerned with the main theme of waiting and wondering.

What gives *La última puerta* a more enduring quality than the *Tres comedias* is its capacity to be interpreted as a universal allegory. If we distance ourselves from the local setting and the political context, we recognize a reflection of the human condition. Life is presented as an absurd, pointless state of being, in which we seek in vain the answers to our inquiries while we wait interminably for access to a Supreme Being and are mocked by the final void and frustration. The play has been shown to anticipate Samuel Beckett's *Waiting for Godot*.[17] These existential implications are secondary, however, to Usigli's actual intentions. Strictly, *La última puerta* shares the same source of inspiration as the *Tres comedias* and takes a similar approach to the problem of dramatizing Mexico's political scene in the 1930s. With *El gesticulador*, Usigli was to change his methods.

3
The Revolution, Politics, and Hypocrisy:
El gesticulador

In his analysis of *El gesticulador,* D. L. Shaw maintains that "the predominant aspect of the work is the expression of political protest and criticism."[1] According to the slightly more recent study by J. W. Kronik, on the other hand, "the historical reality of the play is a metaphor for the nature of fiction and the nature of language."[2] It is important for us to recognize that this more universal interpretation—however legitimate and intelligent—stems from critical rather than authorial intention. There can be no doubt that Usigli wrote the play as a critique of Mexican political life ("la revolución es la causa, la atmósfera y el efecto de esta pequeña pieza" ["the revolution is the cause, the atmosphere and the effect of this little play"], he declared at the time of its composition).[3] As for Mexican audiences, moreover, if they have taken its references to historical reality as a metaphor for anything at all, it is as a metaphor for the perennial reality of their country. But it is undeniable that Usigli consciously introduced into this play what Kronik calls a "self-referentiality as dramatic creation,"[4] or a constant reminder to the audience that the spectacle is fiction and that the very reality that it pretends to depict contains theatrical or fictive elements. As we shall see later, this choice of metatheatre serves to underline the essentially theatrical quality of Mexican political life as a spectacle.[5] A further dimension of the play, however, is the image of human aspiration checked by the bonds of mediocrity and environmental circumstances. Metatheatre is vital to this theme, too, since it shows the tendency for alternative levels of reality to become substitutes for the mundane and the commonplace.

The Role of the American Professor

The Rubio family are still tidying up after moving into their new home when the audience first sees them. The domestic scene is broken by the arrival of a stranger hoping to use a telephone. Oliver Bolton, a young professor from Harvard University, has a role of fundamental importance in act 1. As a historian specializing in the Mexican Revolution, like César Rubio, he makes possible the discussion in which events of 1914 (real and fictitious) are brought to the audience's attention. These events give an early historical perspective to the play's action and ensure that the contemporary situation is seen thereafter in relation to the Revolution's period of armed conflict. Secondly, as an individual endeavoring to advance his own career, Bolton may be compared with Rubio. The subsequent plot of *El gesticulador* is created by both professors' imposition of their wills on reality and by their respective betrayals of truth. Rubio deceives his American colleague (and later the rest of Mexico) with a deliberate distortion of identity and historical accuracy. Bolton (whose gullibility is tantamount to voluntary self-deception) breaks his word not to divulge the source of his (false) information. Thirdly, Bolton's fortuitous breakdown near Rubio's house introduces a sense of the power of chance in people's lives and in Mexican politics. And lastly, he has a role as a United States citizen in a Mexican play, with inevitable and carefully planned dramatic effects. Most of these effects are ultimately of political significance.

In the presentation of Bolton, Usigli displays a profoundly ambiguous attitude toward Americans. Several features seem chosen to create a favorable reaction from the audience. His physical appearance is described in stage directions as pleasant (TC 1:732), his dress and courtesy lead to César Rubio's remark that he appears a decent person (TC 1:733), and his spoken Spanish is marred only by a slight accent and a minor idiomatic stiffness. Rubio's willingness to offer hospitality is based on the desire to give the foreigner a favorable impression of Mexico. In other words, there is no strident anti-Yankee feeling here. To a large extent, his salient characteristics are designed to form a sharp contrast with Rubio's. His fair complexion, smart attire, youthful vigor and cheerful optimism all contrast with the appearance, age, and demeanor of the Mexican professor. In status, too, there is a significant difference: the American is a car-owning tourist employed by a prestigious foreign university (whereas Rubio, without telephone or employment, is a virtual exile inside his own country). Naturally, the American's relative affluence and his university's ability and willingness to advance generous funds in support of historical research reflect negatively on the impecunious position in which Mexican society places its professors. It is in these respects that the ambiguities in the presentation become important. From time to time we notice how Bolton is gently satirized. He pronounces Spanish as though he had learned it in Spain, not in Mexico; he readily offers money as the solution to any problem. Above all, he is the object of a unified Mexican attitude. Elena is the first to express the typical group hostility toward an outsider, with a joke inverting traditional white racist attitudes: "Con los americanos nunca sabe uno: todos visten bien, todos visten igual, todos tienen autos. Para mí son como chinos; todos iguales" ("With Americans you never know: they all dress well, they all dress the same, they all have cars. For me they're like Chinese; all the same") (TC 1:733). (In actual fact the joke is double-edged, for those who are mocking him—Elena, the audience, and the dramatist—know that the wealth that they are ridiculing is something that fundamentally they all envy.) A few minutes later César Rubio himself briefly introduces the national prejudice against Americans. He stops using the relatively respectful expression "este americano" when his envy interferes: "si ganara [yo] lo que este gringo" ("if I earned what this gringo earns") (TC 1:736–37). And Usigli maintains the gentle Mexican satire when Rubio complains to Bolton that Americans buy everything: "Los códices, los manuscritos, los incunables, las joyas arqueológicas de México; comprarían a Taxco, si pudieran llevárselo a su casa" ("Codices, manuscripts, incunabula, archeological jewels from Mexico; you would buy Taxco, if you could get it home") (TC 1:742). The intention is clear enough: the dramatist is forming an empathy between the Rubio family and the Mexican audience. What happens on stage must be accepted as a reality in which the audience can see itself. Finally, there is an important political point overlooked by most commentators on this play. After his return to the United States, Bolton publishes material that attracts the attention of the Mexican press and the Mexican president. As a consequence, an investigation into Rubio's credentials is undertaken, and his candidature for election to the governorship is organized. In other words, political events in Mexico are directly determined from within the United States. The dialogue includes a brief and lighthearted allusion to the problem.

> *Cesar.* Ya sabes cuánto se interesan los americanos por las cosas de México . . .
> *Elena.* Si no se interesaran tanto sería mucho mejor. (TC, 1:737)

> (*Cesar.* You know how interested the Americans are in Mexican things . . .
> *Elena.* If they weren't so interested it would be a lot better.)

Usigli does not give the issue prominence, of course, but it provides one more instance of his nationalist attitude, besides offering an indictment of a notorious political reality.

Historical Reality and Artistic Invention: 1914

Acts 2 and 3 of *El gesticulador* depend not only on the previous intervention of Oliver Bolton in Rubio's life but on the elaborate creation of a historical background. In order for Professor Rubio to adopt the identity of General Rubio, Usigli invented a hero of the Revolution killed in action. It is necessary for the audience—while being aware of this hero's fictive nature—to accept his verisimilitude. Usigli therefore had to choose an appropriate historical context and connect his fictitious creation with well-known figures and events. It is interesting to notice what political activities he decided to invent for his hero. Firstly, the general took up arms following the Creelman-Díaz interview of 5 September 1908 (TC 1:740). In other words, he perceived the hypocrisy in the dictator's declaration to an American journalist that he would not object to political opposition and foresaw a weakening in Díaz's position. Secondly, the general met Francisco Madero and convinced him of the need for revolution, thus prompting him to publish his book *La sucesión presidencial en 1910*. This means that besides being one of the first leaders to take military action, Rubio was an inspiration for the more peaceful tactics of the Club Central Anti-Reeleccionista. He was allied to both the proletariat and bourgeois rebellions. The fictitious general's image as an ideal man of action, leader, and organizer is enhanced by further description of his involvement in the first battles, his travel throughout the whole of the country to whip Madero and various politicians into action, and his preparation of the November expeditions. He is presented as more radical and more positive than the historical figure Madero, whose government he is said to have criticized. Like other Revolutionary generals, he rose against Huerta, but Usigli keeps him at odds with Carranza, Villa, and Zapata in order that his image should not be tarnished by the diverse faults attributed to those leaders by the historians.

Equally revealing is Usigli's choice of the date and circumstances of General Rubio's death. According to the conversation between professors Rubio and Bolton, the general disappeared on the night of 17 November 1914. A few months earlier, it will be recalled, Huerta had resigned. (His regime surrendered unconditionally on

14 August.) A confused and chaotic phase of the Revolution en-
sued, characterized above all by a power struggle between the rival
leaders. In October, a convention (first in Mexico City, then in
Aguascalientes) had failed to reconcile the different factions, who
now tended to be grouped as *constitucionalistas* (Carranza,
Obregón, and others) and *convencionistas* (Villa, Zapata, and
others). Mexico City, the scene of frequent disorder and violence,
was occupied by the *convencionistas,* who had elected Eulalio
Gutiérrez their president. Carranza had abandoned the capital at
the beginning of November and was to establish his government in
Vera Cruz on the twenty-sixth of that month. These details help us
to understand the context of General Rubio's fictitious "disappearance," on the night of 17 November, while he was travelling
with his assistant and two adjutants. According to César, the general was crossing the mountains of Nuevo León to make his way to
Monterrey and then to Mexico City, where he had an appointment
with Carranza in December (TC 1:742, 744). But clearly his journey could not have led him to such a meeting. This political confusion and instability is an important aspect of the background.
Another vital issue is the fact that Carranza had indeed called upon
generals to support him against the *convención.* Among those who
responded positively were Obregón, Antonio I. Villarreal, Lucio
Blanco, Pablo González, and Eduardo Hay.[6] Are we perhaps to
imagine that Rubio was about to be included in their number? From
the dialogue in act 3 between César and Navarro we learn that
General Rubio was assassinated by his adjutant (Navarro), and that
the latter was rewarded by promotion to the rank of colonel (TC
1:784). When Bolton is told of the general's murder he asks
"¿Quién ordenó este crimen?" ("Who ordered this crime?") This is
where Usigli introduces his greatest indictment of the period, in
César's explanation: "Todo . . . las circunstancias, los caudillos
que se odiaban y procuraban exterminarse entre sí . . . y se
asociaron contra él" ("Everything . . . circumstances, the leaders
who hated each other and were trying to exterminate each other
. . . and joined forces against him") (TC 1:743). If the other generals conspired against Rubio, they must have seen him as a threat of
a very special kind. Their reasons must be found in the characterization of Rubio offered by Bolton: he was the one man with a
total concept of the Revolution. He was participating in order to
achieve the Revolution's overall aim, not to benefit one region in
particular, not to make personal gains, and not to satisfy an urge to
destroy. He was, in fact, a pacifist. In short, we may infer that the
other generals wished to eliminate any reminder of the true ideals

of the Revolution. Through this piece of fiction, therefore, Usigli was implying that those ideals were in effect quite cynically suppressed in or around 1914.

For the full impact of his criticism, however, we need to look a little further. In order for Bolton to jump to the conclusion that Professor Rubio and the general are one and the same, Usigli had to invent a plausible explanation for the general's survival. This much was simple enough, but the trickier problem was to argue how it would be possible for the general to survive an assassination attempt and yet disappear entirely from the public eye for twenty-four years. The invention that Usigli chose—because it was believable—was fundamental disillusionment. Here, too, we find an important indication of Usigli's attitude to the Revolution. We are told that the general was convalescing when news arrived of Carranza's Law of 6 January 1915 and appointment as first chief of the Revolution. But his morale was destroyed "cuando supo que la revolución había caído por completo en las manos de gente menos pura que él" ("when he learned that the revolution had fallen completely into the hands of people less pure than himself") (TC 1:745). Clearly, it is not merely the degeneration of the Revolution into a power struggle but also the emergence of Carranza as the dominant force that Usigli saw as the problem.

The law referred to here was ostensibly the materialization of Carranza's promises to the common people that there would be agrarian reform: it provided for expropriation of land from the large estates and its return to Indian villages, and it led to the creation of the Comisión Nacional Agraria.[7] Why, it might be asked, should General Rubio react negatively to an event that seemed to promote one of the original causes of the Revolution? Usigli did not intend to suggest his character's pique or envy when César explains that by that time the name Rubio and the general's deeds had been virtually forgotten. What he meant to imply was that the general now recognized the inevitable corruption of the ideals. Carranza was assuming the mantle of champion of the underdog, but Rubio could perceive the underlying falseness of this position. A former senator from the days of the *porfiriato,* with a background in a family of landowners, Carranza had campaigned strictly for moderate reforms based on a return to the 1857 constitution. It is argued by many historians that his overtures to the proletariat were largely tactical, and of course it is an established fact that his agrarian law led to relatively few changes during his term in power (and for more than a decade beyond). In other words, Usigli was showing how, like his fictitious hero General Rubio, the ideals of the Revolution faded into the background around 1914 and 1915.

Contemporary Reality and Artistic Invention: 1938

Despite the importance of references to 1914, the emphasis of the play is on the present rather than on the past. The dramatist indicates on his script, "Epoca: hoy" ("Time: the present"), guiding us firstly to the year of composition, 1938, and secondly to the date of the first performance, 1947 (a "present" that will be considered below). A stage direction in act 2 describes one of the characters as president of the town council of Allende, while various references throughout the play clearly locate the action in the north of Mexico. Once critic has deduced that the Rubio family has moved to the Monterrey district, and perhaps to the town of Allende, fifty kilometers north of that city.[8] Whether this makes the place too specific does not matter greatly. The important point is that the approximate temporal and geographical location should be readily identified by a Mexican audience to give an unmistakably national (and provincial) context to the critical material enacted on stage. Usigli's mainly negative criticism is conveyed, in fact, simultaneously in two ways: via the words of his characters and via the dramatic situation as it develops.

Let us consider the most obvious and outspoken comments: those made by Professor Rubio in act 3, when he has fully assumed the identity of a reformer and confidently senses the relation between political action and integrity. His overriding criticism is that Mexico is riddled with hypocrisy: "Dondequiera encuentras impostores, impersonadores, simuladores; asesinos disfrazados de héroes, burgueses disfrazados de líderes; ladrones disfrazados de diputados, ministros disfrazados de sabios, caciques disfrazados de demócratas, charlatanes disfrazados de licenciados, demagogos disfrazados de hombres" ("Everywhere you find impostors, impersonators, simulators; murderers disguised as heroes, bourgeois disguised as leaders; thieves disguised as deputies, ministers disguised as wise men, political bosses disguised as democrats, charlatans disguised as graduates, demagogues disguised as men") (TC 1:782). The listing of different types of culprit helps to give this speech the impact of an emotional tirade. But it is also worth noticing that it has the effect of suggesting that people in all walks of life are guilty of putting on false appearances. From the political point of view, the boldest and most controversial accusations are those leveled against political figures, heroes of the nation, leaders of the people, deputies, and ministers. Their status covers up their crimes and stupidity, their revolutionary rhetoric disguises their bourgeois, undemocratic, demogogic, or even tyrannical nature.[9]

Navarro's successful career may be considered a perfect illustration of Rubio's accusations. It has been built on rewards for services rendered to men in power: theft, pimping, executions, and murders (TC 1:782). All Mexican leaders, according to Rubio, have resorted to using people like Navarro instead of suppressing them. Usigli clearly saw the criminal element in Mexican politics as a serious cause for concern. In his earlier comedy, *Estado de secreto,* the principal character, Poncho Suárez N., is both a cabinet minister and a gang leader. The paradox could hardly be greater: in act 1 he receives reports on contraband operations and casino profits, and in act 2 he dictates a letter praising the Mexican Revolution. One of his men kills a political enemy, but Suárez resists calls for his own resignation, bribes the party's director, and with the support of El Jefe, looks forward to his own eventual rise to the presidency. *El gesticulador* offers the impression that little has changed since the days of Calles, in this respect at least. Handguns carried by Rubio's political allies testify to the danger of violent behavior at the plebiscite. The gangster-politician Navarro attempts to achieve his ends by intimidation, blackmail, and bribery, and when they fail, he resorts to assassination. He is successful not only in disguising his complicity in the crime but in winning the people's support for his candidacy and thus ensuring for himself the governorship. The future governor will be a man combining hypocrisy, demagogy, conservatism, self-interest, gangsterism, and homicide. The plays' action therefore suggests that political success contradicts truthfulness and moral scruples. An additional indictment of the system stems from the ease with which Navarro blames the assassination on an act of religious fanaticism. Álvaro Obregón's shooting only a decade before, officially attributed to religious fanaticism, was thought by many to have been a political assassination, possibly even with the complicity of President Calles himself. Usigli was surely ridiculing such use of a religious pretext.

Comparedwith Rubio, Navarro is—as Usigli remarked in one of his epilogues—the more common type in Mexican history (TC 3:475). But Rubio's leading role in the play makes him the more complex and more striking *gesticulador.* As his son is only too ready to remind him, César's pretense dates back to the years in Mexico City, when the family disguised their relative poverty (and the professor's inability to earn an acceptable salary) by borrowing furniture and cutlery whenever guests were expected. In this respect, Rubio is presented as a typical Mexican head of family, stretched to maintain his desired social standing. We have insufficient evidence to be sure whether or not to believe the professor's protestations that he sacrificed himself in those years for the sake of his family's survival, his son's career, and his belief in the university as an ideal (TC 1 : 729). It is Miguel again who accuses him of acting dishonestly in moving north to his hometown in order to blackmail local politicians into helping his career. This other aspect of Rubio's pretense may be interpreted as a symptom of the nationwide predisposition toward nepotism and blackmail in political life. It then becomes only a short step to the instinct of extracting financial advantage from a visitor who apparently has cash to spare. And one further short step takes Rubio to the state of mind required to deceive Bolton. Even in the nature of this act of deception may be noted a degree of ambiguity. As César always maintains (for example, when defending himself against his son's accusations in act 3), he does not actually lie to Bolton in act 1. And in act 2, when the professor assumes the general's identity, he makes no false affirmation to the investigating delegation. During the performance we—as audience—tend to retain a greater capacity to respect the man because he does not resort to outright mendacity. In perspective, however, we may quite easily recognize that this is merely the enactment of another kind of hypocrisy. Rubio is creating a false situation while simultaneously deceiving himself (and perhaps us) that he is still within the bounds of honorable behaviour.

One of the most effective aspects of the portrayal of Rubio as *gesticulador* is the presence of characteristics with which we can sympathize or which we can even like and admire. From the earliest scene in the play, we sympathize with the father/husband who seems genuinely affectionate toward his daughter and wife (affectionate, too, toward his son as the action develops), shows signs of distress with the failure of his career, and appears to be embarking on a new venture to transform the course of his life. His words of comfort to Julia, his sense of hospitality toward the visitor—these are manifestations of a generous disposition. His extensive knowledge of Mexican history reveals an admirable professional expertise. As the second act develops, there are signs that Rubio possesses enviable tactical skill, the ability to handle delicate situations, and a self-confidence in his relations with other people. One of the most important points in his favor, however, is the guilt that he experiences after deceiving Bolton and the reluctance to spend the earnings from that deception. His conscience is cleared only later, when he believes good will come out of the lie. In other words, we realize not only that this man has moral scruples but that his aspirations lie beyond financial gain. It is something that helps us to see his performance as the general as an act of fulfillment, converting a life of failure into one of purpose and achievement. Usigli is very careful throughout the second act to counterbalance Rubio's silence about his real identity with a number of extenuating circumstances. These are: *(a)* fear of the punishment to which his duplicity threatens to expose him; *(b)* hope that once the deception is complete, nobody else will be affected by it; *(c)* awareness that Bolton himself would find his career damaged by a public admission of the truth; *(d)* vacillation by Elena between rejection of the falsehood and acquiescence (which in the end amounts to collaboration); *(e)* the excessive willingness of some members of the local delegation to believe the change of identity; and *(f)* coincidence and chance, leading to fortuitous interruptions at critical moments and eventually to Emeterio Rocha's positive identification of César as the one whom he had known as Rubio in childhood.

Not only this, but we are also strongly influenced by the evident virtues of Rubio as a people's candidate for the state governorship. Estrella, Guzmán, and Salinas praise him strongly in the opening scene of act 3 for the popular support that he has won, the ability to listen to others and limit his words to the absolutely essential, and the ability to win over the president and others in powerful positions. Significantly, it is Salinas—previously the most difficult member of the delegation to convince—who now proves the staunchest supporter. Usigli takes care to offer visible evidence of Rubio's desire to represent the poor people: the unkempt appearance of his room, the unostentatious personal attire in which a general's badge is his only luxury. Rubio's new role has transformed his facial expression to serene nobility, self-assurance, and dignity (as the stage directions inform us [TC 1:775]). His bearing and demeanor are now those of a man convinced of the value and justness of his actions. He speaks of his political function as though it were a newly discovered sense of mission. The notion of politics as a career that puts a person in contact with the roots of things (TC 1:775) contains a naive optimism that we feel to be a welcome contrast to the cynicism manifest elsewhere in the play. The declaration that "el gran político viene a ser el latido, el corazón de las cosas" ("the great politican comes to be the heartbeat, the heart of things") (TC 1:776) suggests that Rubio has acquired an ideally altruistic sense of the politican's social purpose. We can see a

degree of justification in his protest to Navarro: "Empecé min-
tiendo, pero me he vuelto verdadero" ("I began by lying, but I have
become true") (TC 1:783).

And yet it is precisely these aspects of his performance that
convert him into a more serious indictment of Mexican political and
social reality than the overwhelmingly despicable character
Navarro. Whatever the extenuating circumstances, the promising
signs, and the likeable behavior, Rubio is guilty of the very hypocrisy that he condemns in the nation as a whole. And of course his
self-awareness (the justification of his act by claiming it to be
commonplace) reveals how deeply ingrained the problem is. How
many people in the audience, we wonder, excuse him on the
grounds that he is turning a defect to good use? If Usigli attenuates
any antipathy we may have for Rubio, it is surely in order to show
us that the tendency to be a *gesticulador* is not confined to others
(whom we contemplate from a distance) but belongs to us, too, as
we watch and tacitly accept the virtue of the professor's impersonation.

Usigli treats Rubio's impersonation as a metaphor for certain
practices that were frequent in Mexican politics. As a candidate for
the state governorship, the university professor falsely assumes the
identity of a hero of the Revolution. Vast popular support therefore
accrues to him. The phenomenon that the dramatist is satirizing
here is the device, frequently employed by Mexican politicians, of
disguising the true nature of their policies with superficial revolutionary credentials. According to Usigli's essay "Epílogo sobre la
hipocresía del mexicano" (contemporaneous with *El gesticulador*),
"la demagogia . . . , para fines de publicidad, ha calificado de
revolucionarios a muchos gobiernos que, aunque encabezados por
caudillos de la revolución, eran negras equivalencias de atrasadas
tiranías que, en vez de objetivarse sinceramente como tales, se
cubrían con la piel de la revolución" ("demagogy . . . , for the
purpose of publicity, has described as revolutionary many governments which, though headed by leaders of the revolution, were
black equivalents of out-of-date tyrannies which, instead of honestly recognizing themselves as such, disguised themselves with
the skin of the revolution") (TC 3:461–62).[10] The constitution of
1917 is cited as an example: it offers the impression that what is
written will become a reality, allowing no perception of the problems that will arise later; it creates "una apariencia de lo que no es"
("an appearance of what is not so") (TC 3:461). By the same
process whereby a man who bows and scrapes in public acquires
respectability, even though he may beat his wife indoors, Mexican

governments have gained reputations based only on external images: "la dictadura porfiriana hace de México un país aparentemente democrático; el gobierno actual, un país aparentemente izquierdista, etcétera" ("the dictatorship of Porfirio Díaz made Mexico an apparently prosperous and civilized country; the government of Madero, an apparently democratic country; the present government, an apparently left-wing country, etc.") (TC 3:462).

It is striking that the contemporary government should have borne some of his criticism in this essay and—presumably—in the play itself. Lázaro Cárdenas usually has been considered, both inside and outside Mexico, as an exception to the tendency to pay lip service to the Revolution's ideals. Before Usigli's play and essay were written, Cárdenas had nationalized the railways and the oil industry, begun large-scale land reform, sent Calles into exile, and adopted a benevolent attitude to the labor movement. The United States historian John Edwin Fagg captures the man's popular image when he writes that Cárdenas's election "signified a massive renewal of the Revolution" and that he "came as near as was humanly possible to fulfilling its promise—or threat." According to Fagg, Cárdenas "established himself as a living myth among leftists and the poor."[11] Those historians who examine the detail of the Cárdenas administration, however, tend to be less content to apply a "left-wing," "revolutionary," or "radical" label to him. On the economic policies, for example, the writer in *Historia general de Mexico,* Lorenzo Meyer, summarizes as follows: "Puede decirse que al finalizar el gobierno del presidente Cárdenas, las corrientes radicales que pretendían modificar sustancialmente la estrategia del desarrollo alejándose del modelo capitalista, habían sido neutralizados" ("It may be said that when President Cárdenas finished his term in office, the radical currents that were seeking a substantial modification of development strategy by moving away from the capitalist mode, had been neutralized").[12] Another historian, Judith Adler Hellman, supports Usigli's contention about the use of empty rhetoric: "Cárdenas's speeches and those of his top ministers were full of talk of 'state ownership of the means of production', 'worker cooperatives', and 'worker's democracy as the first step towards socialism.'" Yet he would make "rhetorical turnabouts." For instance, "In February 1936, Cárdenas went on to reassure capitalists that, 'The government desires the further development of industries within the nation since it depends upon their prosperity for its income through taxation.' In retrospect it is clear that the policies he had in mind were inspired by the doctrines of socialism, but were in fact piecemeal reforms rather than revolutionary transformations."[13]

Less prominent than the criticism made via the roles of Rubio and Navarro are secondary issues relating to the political establishment. It is in act 2 of the play that they are raised. As we have seen above, one point of concern for Usigli is the expectation harbored by Mexicans like Rubio that to know influential people, or to possess information about them, is a promising way of advancing one's own career. According to the five officials sent to investigate Rubio's identity, the state has been run on undemocratic lines by the outgoing governor, and there is a danger that the choice of Navarro as candidate would imply *continuismo*—that is, the new administration would continue to employ the same people, follow the same policies, and protect the same interests (TC 1:765–67). Apparently, the present governor has been guilty of intrigues, excluding talented persons from the power process. There is some mockery in the fact that the five who make this complaint have themselves suffered such exclusion, but the overriding concern is that sharp divisions have caused a potentially volatile situation. Another criticism made in passing is of the corruption among the men in power. In the case mentioned in the play, the state budget has been expended and salaries have not been paid, but the governor and his employees have been able to purchase valuable properties. Not that the five officials are themselves impeccably incorruptible. For César Rubio to become a candidate, it will be necessary for them to bend or change the legal requirement for a minimum of twelve months' residence. But the prospect does not perturb them, and besides, they refer to precedents such as the bypassing of the constitution in Mexico City (TC 1:768). A further issue obliquely introduced is the question of regional supremacy. Guzmán entices Rubio with the prospect of political progress based on support from the north: "Gobernador . . . . ¡y quién sabe qué más después! Todo el Norte estaría con él" ("Governor . . . and who knows what next! The whole of the North would be with him") (TC 1:766). With this hint that the national presidency itself could be Rubio's with such a power base, we are reminded of the so-called Northern Dynasty. A disproportionately large number of presidents of Mexico between 1910 and 1940 originated in northern states (nine) as opposed to the west (one), the core (four), the south (two), and the federal district (one).[14] Usigli's views on this are reflected in those of General Rubio: "Nunca creyó César Rubio que la revolución debiera hacerse para el Norte o para el Sur, sino para todo el país" ("César

Rubio never believed that the revolution should be made for the North or for the South, but for the whole country") (TC 1:767).

The party itself receives some mockery and implied criticism. When the five officials visit Rubio's house, there is clear rivalry between the party's local representative, *el licenciado* Estrella, and the municipal president, Epigmenio Guzmán. Estrella's insistence that his function as delegate of the party makes him the natural leader and spokesman eventually earns him the honor, but not before we have been able to glimpse a hint or two of the confusion (and possibly resentment) that his domineering behavior creates. Usigli caricatures Estrella's pompous and affected manner, and in naming the party "El Partido Revolucionario de la Nación" directs his mockery unmistakably at the Partido Nacional Revolucionario, or rather the Partido de la Revolución Mexicana, as it had recently been renamed in its new form. (In 1947, on the play's first performance, the satirical effect of juggling with the words had lost none of its mordancy, for the party had just been dissolved again and reborn as the Partido Revolucionario Institucional.) Meanwhile, we notice in passing that the party never doubts the success of its candidate in the plebiscite—and with good reason, since even in the 1960s it was still possible for Pablo González Casanova to write that since 1929, when the government party was founded, it had never lost a presidential election, an election for governor, or an election for senator.[15] Usigli satirizes the party's false advocacy of genuinely democratic elections through the ostentatious words of Estrella: "El Partido, como el instituto político encargado de velar por la inviolabilidad de los comicios, ve en la reaparación de usted una oportunidad para que surja en el Estado una noble competencia política por la gubernatura. Sin desconocer las cualidades del precandidato General Navarro, prefiere que el pueblo elija entre dos o más candidatos, para mayor esplendor del ejercicio democrático" ("The Party, as the political institution charged with watching over the inviolability of the voting, sees in your reappearance an opportunity for the birth in the State of a noble political competition for the governorship. Without ignoring the qualities of General Navarro as precandidate, it prefers the public to choose between two or more candidates, for the greater splendor of the democratic process") (TC 1:765). The control exerted by the party (indeed, by the president himself) over the selection of candidates is one of the play's subsidiary criticisms. Incidentally, it is the party's insistence and the party's mistake that lead to Rubio's conversion into a hero and subsequently into a martyr. Navarro explains the national need for heroic sacrificial victims: "Y México necesita de sus héroes para vivir" ("Mexico needs her heroes in order to live") (TC 1:798). Usigli's description of *El gesticulador* as "Pieza para demagogos" probably does not refer to Rubio. The professor is a false hero, a deceiver, a gesticulator, but he is not actually seen behaving like a demagogue. On the contrary, he is more concerned with responding to the will of the people than with imposing his own ideas on them. Navarro, however, emerges as a striking example of a demagogue in a scene at the end of act 3. After Rubio's assassination, a large crowd gathers outside his house. Navarro leaves the room and faces the crowd. By stages, his speech changes their hostile murmuring to a hostile-but-indefinite murmuring, then to a murmur of approval, and eventually to a clamor of approval (TC 1:796). The audience has witnessed the process of distortion, fully aware of Navarro's responsibility for the murder. His voice becomes simultaneously a vehicle for untruth and a means of persuasion, his words a mixture of lies and rhetoric. It is an instance of stark hypocrisy and powerful demagogy in which we can perceive all the tricks. Navarro's tactics are all the more evident because of the barrier between him and us: the fact that he is outside the room that we see on stage, and that we hear words separated from the dynamic effect of a personality. First he pretends to deal openly with the accusations against him, denying any guilt, promising to help any inquiry, and reinforcing the false story about a religious fanatic. He avoids an argument with his principal accuser and simply continues to rely on emotional impact. He appeals to the crowd's susceptibility to revolutionary jargon ("en defensa de los ideales revolucionarios . . . mártir de la revolución . . . . víctima de los fanáticos y los reaccionarios") ("in defense of revolutionary ideals . . . martyr of the revolution . . . victim of fanatics and reactionaries"). (TC 1:796) The key to his success is the way he turns Rubio's death to advantage: he admired Rubio, he will construct memorials to his name, he will honor Rubio's family. In short, his supreme tactic is to transform his enemy's cause into his own. Perhaps the ploy works too perfectly for us to believe it literally possible, but like other features of *El gesticulador*, this operates at a heightened level of reality. In his "Epílogo sobre la hipocresía del mexicano" Usigli explains that "La demagogia no es otra cosa que la hipocresía mexicana sistematizada en la política" ("Demagogy is no more than Mexican hypocrisy systematized in politics") (TC 3:461). It is the demagogues who, arguing among themselves, convert their individual points of view into generalized "truths." It is the demagogues who have been responsible for the propaganda that deceptively persuades people of a party's revolutionary quality.

The Political Impact of the First Performance: 1947

Overviews of Mexican history tend to see the 1940s as the beginning of a new era. From one point of view, the end of the Cárdenas regime meant the end of the Revolution (or at least the interruption of its progress), while from another it marked an appropriate time to shift the emphasis away from social reform to economic prosperity.[16] Some of the specific comment delivered in *El gesticulador* began to look less relevant. In this new era the role of the military declined sharply. Manuel Avila Camacho, the last general to occupy the presidency, ended his term in office the year before the play's first performance. Time had seen many of the old military heroes laid to rest. And in any case, in the age of the technocrats, a candidate for governorship did not need to be an officer with a reputation dating back to his active service during the Revolution. From the point of view of a playwright dedicated to the frank revelation of national characteristics, two developments in particular were auspicious. One was the creation of the Instituto Nacional de Bellas Artes at the end of 1946.[17] Surveys of Mexican theatre highlight this event as an indicator of government sponsorship of the arts, while pointing out President Miguel Alemán Valdés's intention that the INBA should serve to strengthen national culture and foster a wider awareness of it.[18] The other promising event, manifesting an apparently liberal attitude toward the arts, was a speech delivered by Secretario de Gobernación Héctor Pérez Martínez, in which he addressed the issue of freedom of expression in Mexico. Usigli was to remark bitterly some years later that the new government had thus tricked many people—including himself—into believing its promises before it became apparent that the hopes were being offered merely for political advantage (TC 3:541).

El gesticulador certainly tested the regime's sincerity over freedom of expression. It was the absence of such freedom that had prevented any staging of the play in 1940. The local authorities had rejected it on the grounds that it had an unacceptable bias against the Revolution that was not counterbalanced by criticism of "los cochinos burgueses" ("the bourgeois pigs") and "los repugnantes capitalistas" ("the repulsive capitalists") (TC 3:493). Since then, the play had been restricted to private readings until its publication in a magazine (1943) and in book form (1944).[19] Under the new régime the director of the INBA's theatre department, Alfredo Gómez de la Vega, seized the opportunity (which he had been seeking for three years) to give the play its first performance (TC 3:541). Opposition, however, began even when rehearsals were underway. The INBA's director, Carlos Chávez, and some of the Comité de Lecturas tardily attempted to have the play withdrawn when they became aware of its contents. This move failed, only to be followed by disruptive maneuvers from within the Asociación Nacional de Actores. Rumors about the content of Usigli's essay *Anatomía del teatro* (written in the 1930s, but republished in the Sunday supplement of *El Nacional* in 1947) led hostile actors to claim that the dramatist had published defamatory remarks about members of the acting profession. A meeting held to read the offensive passages ended with the decision that objections had been exaggerated, and the actors chose not to suspend the production of *El gesticulador*. But the episode is an indication of the hostility already fermenting among many of those who knew of the play's content or had read Usigli's outspoken (and rather simplistic) comments in essays like "Epílogo sobre la hipocresía del mexicano" and "Doce notas." Some felt themselves alluded to, while others regarded Usigli as an enemy of the Revolution.[20]

During the fortnight of the play's run audiences packed the theatre. On the first night public enthusiasm was so great that Usigli left his seat in the stalls to acknowledge the applause on stage. *El gesticulador* became a talking point among theatregoers. As for the critics, however, there was a sharp contrast between the mainly favorable reaction of those concerning themselves with the work as theatre and those commentating on its political content. Various charges were leveled against it.[21] One was a complaint that it was written by an employee of the present regime, giving the impression that Usigli was being sponsored to attack previous regimes (an error compounded by the critic's unawareness that the government was busy finding an appropriate way of shortening the play's life). Another type of complaint was that the play was excessively fault-finding and dealt only with the negative side of the situation. It belonged to a genre inferior to serious theatre. Although there is some justification for the view that Usigli had focused predominantly on negative character traits and on social and political shortcomings, there is, of course, no logical conclusion that the work was unworthy of the theatre. In reality, what disturbed such critics was not the question of aesthetic standards but the uncompromising censure to which the nation and its values were subjected.

Above all, it might be added, it was the adverse comment on the nation's political system that proved offensive. This leads naturally to the most serious charge. Given that the present political system was the one that had grown out of a revolution, and bearing in mind that it was fostered by a political party that called itself revolutionary (the Partido Revolucionario Institucional), the Revolution itself was deemed to be under attack. *El gesticulador* was declared to be antirevolutionary and to serve the interests of the reactionary opposition to the government. Whatever the case for claiming the play to be antirevolutionary (and I shall discuss it below), there is no doubt that reactionaries did indeed welcome it as publicity for their cause. As Usigli admitted, he was applauded by the Partido de Acción Nacional (which in those days included fascist ingredients in its right-wing policies), while the Liga de la Decencia (which had condemned his previous production) recommended people to attend performances.

Once President Alemán became aware of the controversy aroused by performances of *El gesticulador,* he ordered members of his cabinet to see the play and called a meeting to consider what action should be taken. At least one cabinet minister (Alfonso Caso) defended Usigli, but a majority were hostile. Resisting the temptation to cancel the production (and rejecting a call for Usigli to be relieved of his post in the diplomatic service), Alemán chose a course of action that would avoid any public outcry while at the same time denying the play some of the extra attention that it might have claimed. He sent instructions to the director of the INBA, via the secretary of education, to shorten the play's run from three weeks (which had been promised) to two weeks (which was the norm established by previous plays in the season). As far as the government was concerned, the crisis was over; but from Usigli's point of view, the administration's hostility was to continue for some time.

An inquiry as to whether the play might be permitted in the commercial theatre was made to the minister of *gobernación,* Pérez Martínez. The latter declared that he had no personal objections, but since putting on *El gesticulador* alone could be inconvenient and troublesome to the government, he suggested that it be included among a number of plays to be performed alternately. On that occasion, therefore, the matter was dropped. Usigli found a perfect example of *gesticulación* in the response of the minister and was later to comment on the capacity of politicians to act: "La política es grande escuela de teatro" ("Politics are a great theatre school") (TC 3:555). When the play was staged for two weeks in

October of the same year at the Teatro Virginia Fábregas, the reception was mysteriously quiet, and instead of a packed auditorium it had only a sparse attendance. The explanation may lie partially in the loss of impetus caused by the delay between the two performances. But there is also every likelihood that political interference played a part. According to Usigli, a high union official had thought himself alluded to in the play.[22] Several groups of workers asked for an official suspension of the dress rehearsal, and when that failed, the Federación Teatral arranged for sabotage of a different kind: at one ticket office the public were told that tickets were sold out. In the months that followed, productions of *El gesticulador* in Chihuahua and Oaxaca also created consternation among local officials.

It is worth noticing in passing that Usigli's misjudgment of the nature of the Alemán regime persisted even during the days in which his play was being brought to an early closure. On 30 May he declared that nobody in the present government could have any reason to feel unfavorably alluded to in the play (TC 3:532). Two weeks later he wrote still more fulsomely in praise of the president and his administration.

La sobriedad con que el presidente Alemán denogó todas las peticiones de suspensión es digna de consignarse. Implica el más celoso cumplimiento de su deber y el más cabal respeto a sus funciones como gobernante. Marca el principio de una nueva conducta política y ética, y representa la mayor derrota que haya sufrido la podrida demagogia oficial. (TC 3:530)

(The sobriety with which President Alemán rejected all requests for the play's suspension is worth recording. It implies the most zealous fulfillment of his duty and the most proper respect for his task as a ruler. It marks the beginning of a new political and ethical conduct, and represents the greatest defeat that corrupt official demagogy has suffered.)

Were it not for Usigli's habitual frankness, the inclination might be to interpret this attitude as *gesticulación* on the part of a dramatist worried about the future of his other plays or a government employee anxious to preserve his post. It is difficult to imagine that he was not already entertaining doubts about some of the individuals in the cabinet, such as Pérez Martínez, whom he was later (1962) to describe as an "actor" (TC 3:555). Before long, of course, he was to become extremely bitter whenever he referred to the Alemán *sexenio*. Whether because he was disillusioned or because he was frustrated, he found signs of hostility toward him in possibly insignificant episodes, such as the rejection of his proposal for a *teatro histórico mexicano* and the refusal to sponsor a study visit to England. There are hints of exaggerated indignation in his belief that a photograph of President Alemán attending a funeral was not published because Usigli by chance was standing at his side, and perhaps a sense of persecution in his claim that on several occasions he was followed home by suspicious vehicles (TC 3:559).

During the 1950s foreign interest in the play grew steadily. (This was particularly true of the United States, where a television version was shown in 1953). A Mexican film version appeared in 1957, but it was not until the 1960s that theatres in Mexico City again produced the play. By now its controversial nature caused less reaction, and the public reception was favorable. It was beginning to occupy its place as one of the landmarks in Mexican drama, and its severe criticism of Mexico marked it as part of a growing trend among literary and dramatic works. In the novel *La muerte de Artemio Cruz,* for example, Carlos Fuentes's eponymous protagonist reduces César Rubio's diatribe against Mexico to the level of moderate criticism with his vigorous denunication of the country's "conciencia adormecida por los discursos falsos de hombres mediocres . . . sus líderes ladrones, sus sindicatos sometidos, sus nuevos latifundios, sus inversiones americanas, sus obreros encarcelados, sus acaparadores y su gran prensa, sus braceros, sus granaderos y agentes secretos, sus depósitos en el extranjero, sus agiotistas engominados, sus diputados serviles, sus ministros lambiscones" ("conscience numbed by the false speeches of mediocre men . . . its thieving leaders, its submissive unions, its new large estates, its American investments, its jailed workers, its profiteers and its great press, its laborers, its armed police and secret agents, its foreign deposits, its greasy-haired speculators, its servile deputies, its greedy ministers").[23]

Usigli himself wrote ruefully in 1961 about the continued validity of his play's message (TC 3:565–66). But probably the best indicator of his cynicism is the plan for a sequel to *El gesticulador,* which was to be entitled *Los herederos (The heirs).* Although the play was never completed, we know from Usigli's prologues what kind of theme and characters he had in mind. It was to be set in the age of the technocrats, with Navarro still governor, Julia now married to him, and Miguel Rubio a senator and candidate for the governorship. Miguel was to fall inevitably into the gesticulation that he had previously condemned (TC 3:566). It is worth adding that even in the 1980s audiences at the state-sponsored performances of *El gesticulador* still saw some relevance in the allusions to false appearances and revolutionary rhetoric, and in the satirical treatment of the monolithic ruling party.

This is a suitable point to discuss the matter of *El gesticulador*'s disposition toward the Mexican Revolution. In Usigli's own words, the essence of his case is the following:

> Es una obra revolucionaria. . . . En *El gesticulador* está implícita y evidente la lucha entre la verdad de la Revolución original y la mentira en que la ha ensombrecido aquellos que, sin pureza ni capacidad creadora, se han valido de ella para fines personalistas y malvados, no reparando siquiera en el daño que causaban así al hombre y al espíritu de la Revolución. (TC 3:532–33)

> (It is a revolutionary work. . . . In *The Impostor* there is an implicit and evident struggle between the truth of the original Revolution and the lie that has darkened it, thanks to those who, without purity or creative capacity, have made use of it for personalist and villainous ends, not even noticing the harm that they were thus causing to the man and spirit of the Revolution.)

There can be no doubt that the role of Navarro is precisely that of the negative side of this struggle. Up to a point, the lies may also be found projected into the figure of César Rubio (as I have argued above). Equally clear is the existence of a struggle in the play between this betrayal of the Revolution and the alternative values that Miguel names as "truth." As if it were taking revolutionary action, moreover, the play violently rebels against its milieu and exposes itself to danger for the sake of a set of ideas. In these negative respects, therefore, Usigli's case may certainly be admitted. But the other part of his argument is more difficult to accept in its entirety. To what extent, it may be asked, does this play actually present the Revolution or the Revolution's aims as admirable? As noted above, the play reflects Usigli's view that the Revolution was corrupted before it was complete. In the person of General Rubio he gives us an embodiment of the Revolution in its purest form during the years 1908 to 1914. But the man is drawn in the vaguest of terms: "un hombre extraordinario," "el más grande revolucionario," "el hombre que explica la revolución mexicana, que tiene un concepto total de la revolución," "el único caudillo que no es político, ni un simple militarista, ni una fuerza ciega de la naturaleza," "un gran militar . . . pacifista," "el caudillo total," "el hombre elegido" ("an extraordinary man," "the greatest revolutionary," "the man who explains the Mexican revolution, who has a total concept of the revolution," "the only chieftain who was not a politician, nor a simple militarist, nor a blind force of nature," "a great military . . . pacifist") (TC 1:739–44). His early rebellion against the dictatorship of Porfirio Díaz is made clear, as is his criticism of the Madero government, his rebellion against Huerta, and his differences of opinion with Carranza, Villa, and Zapata. But to tell us what he rejected is not the same as informing us of his aims or ideals. In other words, this portrayal of General Rubio indicates no more than sympathy for some elusive revolutionary ideal.

Usigli also argues—in his essay "El caso de *El gesticulador*"— that Professor Rubio expresses some of the positive side of this struggle: "redimido de su mentira, transfigurado por la fe en la vitalidad de la Revolución, y que muere por ella" ("redeemed from his lie, transfigured by faith in the vitality of the Revolution, and dying for it") (TC 3:534). Here, too, however, there is a problem over the absence of specific revolutionary ideology. We recognize traits compatible with revolutionary zeal, such as the desire to be in contact with the people, to retain some of the trappings of a humble life-style, to prevent power falling into the hands of thieves and assassins, to do good for his country (TC 1:773–83), but in detail this looks no more revolutionary than philanthropic, patriotic, and democratic. The play is therefore not fully compatible with the description "una obra revolucionaria." Instead of voicing the ideals of the Revolution, it expresses negative criticism of the corrupt system. Like General Rubio, the ideals are shown to have faded by 1914, and Usigli shows no determination to revive them.

In the light of this conclusion, it can readily be understood why critics of the revolutionary Left did not find their own political position represented in *El gesticulador,* and why the Right could welcome the play. It attacks the existing system, which had been formed under the auspices of the Revolutionary Party. To the extent that the work is both void of revolutionary ideology and capable of being used to the advantage of conservative interests, it is vulnerable to the accusation of being antirevolutionary or reactionary. In perspective, some kind of parallel can be drawn between César Rubio (history professor and pseudorevolutionary) and Rodolfo Usigli (dramatist and idealist). Like his character, Usigli was—for expediency—claiming revolutionary credentials on the basis of rebellion against the establishment and the advocacy of certain abstract notions. In reality the work, like Usigli at the time (and like his character, Rubio), belongs to the broad Left, the political position that he claimed for himself in the following terms: "Las izquierdas . . . constituyen para mí la única atmósfera política tolerable, amplia y sana" ("The left wing . . . constitutes for me the only political atmosphere that is tolerable, broad, and healthy") (TC 3:507).

The Mexican Family

Although *El gesticulador* is primarily political drama, the focus of attention is actually a single Mexican family. In the first scene of the play, before Professor Bolton's arrival introduces a change of emphasis, it is the family tensions that draw our interest: the discontent caused by their move to the north, the general frustration, the antagonism between two generations, the mutual criticisms, and so forth. It is a family scene that occupies the opening of act 2 (preceded only very briefly by the appearance of Navarro as El Desconocido) with matters such as guilt, personal integrity, money, and the future of the children under discussion. And it is again family scenes that dominate the second half of the final act (until the triumphant emergence of Navarro), and even the last moment of the play returns us to the son's relationship to, and memory of, his father. Throughout the whole play, whatever political material may come to the foreground, family matters remain present in the background. While Rubio and Bolton discuss the Revolution, Elena enters and leaves the room several times (and Julia once)—an activity that has a marked visual impact on stage, serving as a reminder of the whole family's involvement in any issues affecting César. During the committee's interrogation of Rubio, all the family are present, exerting a constant pressure while simultaneously playing their own part in the falsification. (Incidentally, Estrella—the party's representative—insists that the women should not be excluded during the political investigation because they represent the Mexican family [TC 1:759].) Even Rubio's argument with Navarro is not isolated from involving the rest of the family; on the contrary, Miguel surreptitiously listens, his physical reactions (an anguished expression, his head held in his hands [TC 1:783]) a clear representation to the audience that this scene too has wider repercussions.

The essence of the predicament illustrated by this Mexican family is the constant conflict between aspirations and limitations, ambitions and mediocrity, dreams and problems, success and failure, fantasy and reality. As the curtain rises on the first act, Julia, standing on a chair, is the focal point of the audience's attention. Her sense of isolation is the first problem to be raised, her preoccupation with money the second, and her desire to be more attractive the third. Without delay, Usigli has taken us straight to the heart of her discontent. In the course of the play he encourages sympathy for her natural need for love, admiration, comfort, and security while suggesting that her attitude is excessively simplistic and self-centred. Julia fails to see beyond the domestic situation, accepts the social and moral values handed down from the older generation, and in a single-minded search for self-aggrandizement is perfectly willing to benefit from deception and falsehood. Even her father's death is converted into social advantage, so that her grief is counterbalanced by satisfaction: "¿No comprendes, mamá? Él será mi belleza" ("Don't you understand, Mother? He will be my beauty") (TC 1:797).

To some extent, Miguel shares this desire to escape from the family's mediocrity: "He hecho todos los esfuerzos . . . primero contra la mediocridad, contra la mentira mediocre de nuestra vida" ("I have made every effort . . . first against mediocrity, against the mediocre lie of our life") (TC 1:789). But essentially his aspirations are of a different kind: above all, "vivir la verdad" ("to live the truth"). Specifically, this means escaping from the pretense implicit in the two environments he has known: the home and the university. It means avoiding the influence of his father, perpetrator of those lies in his capacity as head of the household and university professor. Miguel suffers the worst irony of all the characters, for the play ends by indicating his destiny to remain frustrated in his search and haunted by his father's untruthful image. He discovers truth in a limited form: the true identity of César Rubio, the true character of General Navarro, the true cause of his father's death, and the true nature of his fellow citizens. But it is useless to him. His frustrated needs are represented also in the conflicting feelings he holds for César. As a son, he shows the desire for affection, leadership, and understanding, but his uncompromising distaste for hypocrisy proves stronger (as we observe when he fails to warn his father in time about Navarro's assassination plot). Naive and anguished, he lacks the capacity for positive action. (Usigli referred to him elsewhere as " 'el pequeño Hamlet' de la verdad" [" 'the little Hamlet' of truth"] TC 3:566].) Together with his sister, he creates a rather unfavorable image of the younger generation. (Usigli's pessimistic view of student behavior is the subject of further attention in the next chapter.) The dramatist does, however, encourage our compassion toward him, and that in turn helps us to share the despair as we see Mexican youth, with its innocent aspirations toward ideals, which are inevitably either corrupted or embittered.

The only member of the family who does not immediately appear to be ruled by dissatisfaction is Elena. Her philosophy is summed up by the words "Se es pobre como se es morena" ("One is poor just as one is dark-skinned") (TC 1:736). Male-dominated (like Julia), utterly faithful to her husband, uncomfortable about the pretense but indecisive and reluctantly acquiescent, she acts as a conscience, a protector, and a pacifier. Even she, however, unintentionally betrays anger over the level of her husband's income, and even she aspires toward better living conditions (as is indicated in her idea of emigrating to the United States and opening a shop or restaurant). Her overriding ambition, though, is not materialistic. She needs a husband who can live at peace with his conscience, and a contented and harmonious family. Of course, her aspirations, too, are frustrated. In particular we notice that at the time of the plebiscite she desperately hopes that César will fail so that she may keep him for herself. Here, too, is a cause of frustration, for even his dead body becomes the property of the people.

If César Rubio is considered not in a political context but in his role as an individual and as head of the family, the imposture that he commits may be seen as an attempt to achieve the fulfillment that has previously escaped him. From the opening scene of the play he manifests a sense of failure: "Yo perdí todos esos años . . ." "Tú misma me crees un fracasado, ¿verdad?" "Mira la cara de tus hijos: ellos están enteramente de acuerdo con mi fracaso" ("I lost all those years. . . ." "You yourself think I am a failure, don't you?" "Look at the faces of your children: they entirely agree about my failure") (TC 1:729–30). A close examination of the causes of this psychological state reveals two different kinds of aspiration. The first is to improve the material quality of the life of his family. The second is to attain some kind of ideal or give a transcendental value to his life (TC 1:729, 789). César, therefore, completes the picture of a Mexican family in which each member desires or dreams of something that is beyond his grasp. But in two ironical ways Usigli allows him to achieve his ambitions. As Elena implies in words to Miguel, when an individual cannot reach a target in his own life, he can seek to reach it vicariously through his children (TC 1:788). César's death will convert this ambition into a reality, at least to the extent that it refers to economic and social status. And with equal irony, Usigli arranges for César to enjoy (all too briefly) the sensation that his dreams of greatness have materialized: "Estoy viviendo como había soñado siempre" ("I am living as I had always dreamed of living") (TC 1:787). Much of the play's tension in the central act depends upon the audience's partial sympathy with

César's dreams and upon our fascination with the idea of fiction becoming reality. The audience is surely encouraged to recognize this imposture as—among other things—the possibility of fulfilling our aspirations against all the odds. This theme is certainly Mexican, but it is by no means exclusively so. It is one of the universal features of *El gesticulador*.

The Universal Dimensions

Usigli's interest in the dichotomy between truth and falsehood is another theme that transcends the Mexican sociopolitical context. In one aspect, the question is presented as a psychological issue. As was noted above, Miguel's disquiet derives principally from his family's constant pretense. But in the course of the play, we notice that his complaint about falsehood overflows from the domestic context into the environment at large. More significantly, Miguel's desire is converted from a specific, concrete reality into the abstract noun that always seems to be on his lips.

César. Qué derecho tienes a juzgarme?
Miguel. El de la verdad. (TC 1:731)

(*César.* What right do you have to judge me?
Miguel. That of truth.)

"Quiero vivir la verdad." (TC 1:731)

("I want to live truth.")

Elena. ¿Qué es lo que has oído, Miguel?
Miguel. La verdad. (TC 1:788)

(*Elena.* What is it that you've heard, Miguel?
Miguel. The truth.)

"Quiero la verdad para vivir . . . . Tengo hambre y sed de verdad." (TC 1:790)

("I want the truth in order to live. . . . I am hungry and thirsty for truth.")

"Si yo tuviera un hijo le daría la verdad como leche, como aire." (TC 1:790)

("If I had a son I would give him truth like milk, like air.")

"Nada es más grande que la verdad." (TC 1:790)

("Nothing is greater than truth.")

"Yo seguiré buscando la verdad." (TC 1:792)

("I shall continue seeking truth.")

"Diré la verdad ahora mismo." (TC 1:798)

("I shall tell the truth this very minute.")

"No es eso lo que me importa. . . . Es la verdad." (TC 1:798)

("That is not what matters to me. . . . It's truth that matters."

"¡La verdad! . . ." (Telón) (TC 1:799)

("Truth! . . ." [Curtain])

In most of these cases the abstract noun signifies an elusive ideal. Julia's incomprehension and antipathy for her brother correspond to her own character, but we recognize some validity in her complaint that Miguel is mad, searching fanatically for truth as though it did not exist (TC 1:793). And at the end of the play it is not only Miguel's final use of the abstract noun that draws the audience's attention to the transcendental nature of his predicament but also the use of sunlight as he steps out of the room in which the image of his father's lie casts its shadow (darkness). This visual effect depends partly on Christian imagery combined with European literary traditions, where light symbolizes truth, knowledge, and understanding, in addition to virtue. But I think it is worth adding that Usigli is using it in the land of the Aztecs, whose tradition sees the sun as the god of war (Huitzilopochtli) needing to be fed with human blood to stay alive. In other words, if the sun is both life giving and life taking, its brilliance is both benevolent and noxious, and its abstract significance is both of knowledge and of ignorance (blindness). Usigli's stage directions emphasize the negative impact of the sunlight: "El sol es cegador" ("The sun is blinding") (TC 1:799). Miguel must face a world in which an ignorance of his father's true identity (with consequent harmful effects on him) has become the norm; the "truth" in that world at large is the falsehood that he has always desired to avoid.

This broader aspect of the play's meaning is enhanced by the way in which the dramatist shakes our trust in supposed facts and events. In making Rubio a historian, Usigli ensured that we could watch the process whereby a distortion of "real" events becomes historical "fact." This historian, who has always presented a false public image, now impersonates a national hero. Moreover, by uniting his identity with that of General Rubio, the history professor actually changes the previous records. According to the official version of events, the general's death has been ascribed to 1914, but the result of this act of deception is to create a new official version of his career and a new date of death: 1938. If a historian is seen to fabricate such untruth before our very eyes, we in the audience are encouraged to feel a degree of suspicion about the accuracy of all official versions. Written history becomes subject to doubt. The American lecturer in history, Bolton, does nothing to enhance our confidence in historians. Although protesting that history is not a novel and that his students require the facts (TC 1:746), he possesses such an amazingly melodramatic imagination that he cannot accept as true anything that fails to meet his expectations. On the death of Ambrose Bierce he admits, "Mi tesis es más romántica, quizás" ("My thesis is more romantic, perhaps") (TC 1:739). On the question of Professor Rubio's failure to publish his specialist information, he rejects the probable explanations (inertia, the idiosyncratic idea that there are already too many books around, or simple infertility) because he cannot conceive of personal or national circumstances different from his own: "No es posible. . . . No es lógico un historiador que no escribe lo que sabe" ("It's not possible. . . . A historian who doesn't write up what he knows is not logical") (TC 1:744). As for the matter of a historian's objectivity, Bolton falls lamentably short of acceptable standards. He is excessively gullible, seems intent on using history to advance his own career, breaks his word, and leaps into print with indecent haste to publicize his (false) information. Between them, therefore, the two historians give us very little confidence in the reliability of published accounts of the past, and even the accepted versions of the Revolution are thrown open to doubt. We become susceptible to Rubio's cynical view of history as illusion, evasion, and self-deception: "La historia no es más que un sueño. Los que la hicieron soñaron con cosas que no se realizaron; los que la estudian sueñan con cosas pasadas; los que la enseñan sueñan que poseen la verdad y que la entregan" ("History is no more than a dream. Those who made it dreamed of things that did not materialize; those who study it dream of things past; those who teach it dream that they possess the truth and that they are handing it on") (TC 1:746).

In other respects, too, the play's action evokes our sense of a hazy border between fact and fiction. It purports to represent people in a real social, historical, and geographical context, yet its plot depends almost entirely on two astounding—should I say incredible?—coincidences: the car breakdown bringing together two experts on the same phase of Mexican history, and the common name *and* birthplace of Professor and General Rubio. A third coincidence—the role of Navarro as murderer of both Rubios—is less crucial to the plot, but its very existence further suggests that Usigli had something special in mind. Of course, coincidence is a traditional dramatic technique for creating unusual or critical situations. It creates the possibility for César Rubio's impersonation to take place, as it also prepares the way for his status of heroic candidate in state elections and for his assassination and substitution by a notorious demagogue. Thanks to the coincidences, Usigli was able to create an imaginary situation that—if the audience was willing to suspend its disbelief in the traditional way—could serve as a critique and a distorting mirror of contemporary Mexican reality. Moreover, it is worth remembering the sheer entertainment value of watching events that are lifelike and yet larger than life. The coincidences are not, however, mere dramatic devices in this play. Usigli gave some indication of this face in a response to the particular criticism that there is an apparent lack of cause in the encounter between Rubio and Bolton: "Probablemente no se ha querido aceptar, no digamos tanto la ley aristotélica de la probabilidad imposible, como el azar que preside la vida y la muerte del mexicano" ("Probably there has been an unwillingness to accept, let us say not so much the Aristotelian law of impossible probability, as the chance that presides over the Mexican's life and death") (TC 3:493). As these words demonstrate, he was not denying that he saw the use of chance as an artistic technique made perfectly reputable by Aristotelian principles, but he was more intent on emphasizing the important role of chance in Mexican history.

Recuérdese aquel grupo de *dorados* villistas que dejaba al azar de una pistola giratoria la muerte de cada uno. Y hay mil ejemplos más. Si César Rubio tuviera una conciencia de sus límites—si el mexicano tuviera una conciencia de sus límites—, sería un ser lleno y completo en sí mismo, consciente, satisfecho y aun orgulloso de su destino. Pero César Rubio es, en el principio, un hombre vacío que deja escapar su poder por todas sus puertas y ventanas abiertas, a quien un azar hace cerrarlas y llenarse hasta un punto de explosión.

(Let us not forget that group of Villa *dorados* who left each member's death to the luck of Russian roulette. And there are a thousand more examples. If César Rubio were aware of his limitations—if the Mexican were aware of his limitations—he would be a full being, complete in himself, aware of his destiny and satisfied with it—proud of it even. But César Rubio is, at the beginning, an empty man who lets his power escape through all his open doors and windows, a man whom chance causes to shut them and fill himself to the point of exploding.

Chance, therefore, has been seen to operate in well-known national situations. It is an essential factor in creating the possibility for the Mexican people to transcend their sense of limitation and to achieve their full potential. And then, to clinch his argument, Usigli proceeded to remind his readers of the importance of the national lottery: "Es difícil concebir a México sin la casualidad—la mitad por lo menos del mexicano es azar puro" ("It is difficult to imagine Mexico without coincidence—at least half of the Mexican is pure chance") (TC 3:493). (His final point, incidentally, was that coincidence had played a significant part in major events throughout the world.)

Coincidence therefore serves to illustrate the role of chance and the need for chance in Mexican reality. In the opinion of one critic, "As a directly political drama, the piece [El gesticulador] can be considered defective or unconvincing for its series of contrivances,"[24] while another more bluntly declares that "one such coincidence in each act is rather hard to swallow."[25] There is no denying that our sense of watching images of real life enacted on stage is interrupted or impaired by the combination of these highly improbable events. But the question then arises whether this is not all a part of Usigli's intention. If we are constantly reminded of the theatrical quality of the scenes unfolding before our eyes, is it not because the dramatist wishes—by exaggeration—to make us aware of the theatrical quality of Mexican life? This is the persuasive opinion of critics like John W. Kronik, for whom "the image reflected back to us is double: the Mexican scene and the play itself,"[26] and David William Foster, who inclines toward the more specific conclusion that for Usigli, Mexican life is a theatrical spectacle because of the dominant concept of public life and political activity that it imposes on its citizens.[27] In fact, it could be said that the cases of gesticulación outlined earlier in this chapter are instances of theatrical behavior: the family's pretense, the false claims to be revolutionary, and above all the imposture of César Rubio. El gesticulador is therefore justifiably considered to be metatheatre in the sense of a work that is not only a mimetic representation of life but the formal image of human existence's theatrical and dramatic qualities.[28] As Kronik puts it, the play "recognizes itself as an imposture that condemns posturing."[29] The audience watches the play on two levels simultaneously. The first level is that of the protagonist's career: Rubio seeks a way out of his mediocrity, takes advantage of circumstances, campaigns for election to a governorship, achieves fame, and is assassinated. On a secondary level there is an intricate interplay of truth and falsehood: Rubio changes his identity, behaves as though he were the other, and fulfills the destiny of the other. To be more precise and explicit, we might say that in May 1947 Alfredo Gómez de la Vega played the part of a professor playing the part of a general. The audience in the Palacio de Bellas Artes could watch the stage image of life being converted into a subsidiary theatrical situation. In every performance of *El gesticulador* the same phenomenon recurs. Indeed, to take things one step further, some of the characters within the play can observe a theatrical performance in which they can see others deceived into accepting fiction as truth. Miguel's role in particular becomes technically important here, for he more than any character watches his fellows from a detached position. When he peers out from his hiding place during the conversation between Navarro and Rubio (act 3) he is helping to create a metaphor for the differences of standpoint between father and son, role player and searcher for the truth.

Dramatic Technique

This last point is a clear indication of the close link between dramatic intention and dramatic technique in *El gesticulador*. By examining briefly a few other technical features of the play, it will be possible to reach a more complete understanding of the impact on an audience. Let us picture the stage as the curtain rises at the beginning of the first act: a few modest pieces of furniture, the walls and ceiling of a wooden house in poor condition, and four actors (at least one of whom is of Indian or mestizo blood) visibly showing the effects of the heat. The stage is intended to suggest an environment recognizable to a Mexican audience as a northern province. And this set remains throughout the play (though it undergoes superficial changes for act 3). The audience is encouraged to become involved in the plight of a family whose home is that stage. Into their home a new set of outsiders arrives in each act: in act 1, the American professor; in act 2, Navarro (unidentified) and the group of local politicians; in act 3, Navarro and his men. Visually, therefore, the audience receives the impression that the outside world is forcing an entry into the Rubio's home, that events are breaking into the family's lives. By act 3 the home's physical appearance has been transformed into that of an office. The first people on stage are politicians, and members of the family enter from the outside—all of which serves to emphasize visually the transformation of the private individual into a public figure (and an individual family into figureheads).

The structure of *El gesticulador,* based on the perception that the three acts are separated from each other by intervals of a month, allows Usigli to create great suspense. Each act is a single continuous unit, with an action complete in itself, yet each one either raises questions or is expected to answer them. In the interval between acts 1 and 2 we are confronted with several uncertainties: whether Rubio will maintain the deception, what the consequences will be for him, what his family will do about it, how he will escape from the situation if the need arises. All of these questions (except the last) are partially answered in the course of act 2. But by the end of the second act our doubts are far more acute, because the risks are now far graver. In addition we are now particularly curious to know why César—who has expressed guilt about the acquisition of money by this deception—is maintaining the imposture. Dramatic tension is a complement of these structural features. In act 1 a tension is created between the truth as we perceive it and the story created out of Rubio's imagination. As members of the audience, we are intrigued to follow the ingenious course of this deception, particularly because we are aware of César's reluctance to tell an outright lie. It is in act 2 that the greatest use is made of this tension, however. The fabric of the lie is so brittle that the slightest jolt would destroy it completely. When a team of five officials comes to investigate the matter of Rubio's identity, our standpoint allows us to trace the situation through its series of crises with a mixture of fear for the safety of César, hope that truth will be victorious, and (perhaps unwillingly) hope that the imposture will survive intact. A dozen times the scene is on the point of collapse, but recovers (saved by noncommittal replies, silence, interruptions, deviations, and misunderstandings).

Usigli was a master of simple dramatic devices to command and sustain the audience's attention. It is worth recalling that as the curtain lifts at the beginning of act 1, Julia, standing on a chair, draws the eyes to her attractive form. The same eye-catching effect is achieved at the opening of act 2, where her figure is enhanced by the lightness of her dress. Although Julia's provocative vulnerability is a minor aspect of the play's theme, it is not subtle character revelation that Usigli had in mind here. In the course of the play humor is introduced from time to time as a means of maintaining interest or sharpening the senses—the kind of humor, for example, with which Julia denigrates herself three times in the opening moments of act 1, trivializing her anguish at the same time as she helps the audience to feel a sense of harmony with the actors. Humor also serves, however, to ridicule a particular group of characters in the play: the local politicians. When the five investigators arrive on stage, they cause amusement in a variety of ways. Firstly, Guzmán and Estrella display an exaggerated sense of self-importance. Secondly, other members of the group rush clumsily to intervene with their question. Thirdly, there is petty rivalry over the leadership. All of this combines to create a series of false starts to their interrogation and a general atmosphere of disorderliness. Two of the characters, Treviño and Garza, speak simultaneously and at times almost in unison, giving an impression of unintelligent and herdlike behavior. There are, in fact, touches of farce in the early part of the scene. Having established a lightly satirical tone, Usigli then allows the farce to be transferred from the speech and actions of the five officials to the mission that has brought them to Rubio and the process by which they are deceived. We are left in no doubt that the importance attached to digging out a buried hero is farcical, and naturally the improbability that five people would be so gullible as to be convinced by Rubio's imposture is farcical, too. As a dramatic device the use of farce in this scene therefore becomes crucial. (When the play is performed, the effect is more emphatic than when it is merely read.) The audience could never believe in the verisimilitude of such action if it were presented naturalistically. But Usigli overcomes the problem by turning it into a mixture of joke and fantasy. Instead of looking like real life, the scene looks thoroughly theatrical, with the consequent advantage that it allows Usigli to satirize the theatricality of political behavior. In the third act a similar—though not identical—effect is achieved when the local politicians again act in a farcical manner, this time at the prospect of confronting Navarro. Their fear, cowardice, bravado, and caution (emphasized by the joking repetition of the expression "por las dudas" ["just in case"]) all help to prevent the audience from taking the scene too seriously and reacting with disbelief. It is thoroughly melodramatic material, and Usigli ingeniously exaggerates it rather than toning it down. Once again, the theatrical nature of the events is what he emphasizes, with good satirical effect.

One of the principal aims of Usigli's plays, once the audience's attention has been claimed, is to achieve our emotional involvement in events and characters on stage. In the final scenes of El ges-

ticulador, we experience several different emotions, sometimes in harmony with the characters and sometimes not. I should like to consider the range of emotions covered in the second half of act 3, and the ways in which they are aroused, with a view to assessing the final impact of the play. The central scene in this act is the long-awaited confrontation between Rubio and Navarro, with its powerful invective and its moral triumph for César. It is the high point in Rubio's career, and we are stirred to feelings of admiration and approval, which override (though never dispel) those of doubt and discomfort. But we are not allowed to draw any confidence from César's bold and impressive behavior because we have already seen Navarro making secret plans with his henchmen. Throughout the scene, therefore, we sense an undercurrent of menace. Usigli then creates a last, brief dialogue between César and his wife, in which Elena repeatedly urges him not to go to the plebiscite (a clear echo of Shakespeare, whose Calpurnia makes vain pleas to *her* Caesar).[30] The intention is all too clear, and we are filled with a sense of impending danger, which endures throughout the following scenes. Miguel's indecision irritates and frustrates us; Julia's confidence offers us a slight glimmer of hope; but Elena's desperate need for her husband is the emotion that influences us most. I think that in these scenes in which Usigli is preparing his characters—and us— for the news of Rubio's death there are several intentional incongruities. Instead of being dominated solely by the feelings that the audience most expects—anxiety for César's safety and a determination to protect him—each character harbors a self-centered urge. Miguel inflexibly agonizes over his search for integrity; Julia basks in reflected glory; and even Elena, who admittedly shows great fear for her husband's plight, is partly swayed by the desire to keep him for herself. This means that instead of focusing our attention on César's impending death, Usigli diverts it temporarily to the problems of other members of the family, until Elena eventually banishes her selfish feelings and, after a moment of confusion, turns her thoughts (and ours) to the question of his survival. Her words "Que viva" ("May he live") (TC 1:794), followed by silence and then the sound of an approaching car, briefly instill in us appropriate feelings of impending disaster. But the point that I wish to make is that until this moment we have been distracted from our feelings about César Rubio, and when we return to them, the impact of his death is not as great as it could have been. Perhaps in an attempt to remedy this problem, some performances of *El gesticulador* have disregarded the dramatist's text here and shown Rubio's death on stage (in the background).[31] But the sound of a shot being fired and the ensuing spectacle create feelings of shock and perhaps excitement or outrage rather than pathos. The melodramatic quality of the action becomes dominant.

It is important to note that the family's grief is not by any means overwhelming: Elena retains a dignified self-control; Julia "llora sin extremos" ("cries with restraint") (TC 1:795), and soon expresses her sense of consolation in the prestige (or "beauty") that César's death has given her; Miguel seems dominated by frustration and despair at the hold that his father's imposture will exert on his life. Usigli has not attempted to transfer a powerful feeling of sorrow from the stage to the auditorium. Moreover, a different matter rapidly supersedes our reaction to Rubio's death: the demagogy of Navarro. The villain's return to the house creates the strong impression of an intrusion into the family's affairs. From our point of view, his arrival on stage diverts our feelings and creates effects such as indignation, anger, and even hatred. For a few minutes Navarro becomes the center of attention, as he addresses the crowd of people, and the emotional impact of César's death is further reduced. A mixture of feelings is caused by this skillful and utterly hypocritical performance, and by its success: grudging admiration, bitter amusement, outrage, and incredulity. Finally attention turns to Miguel, with the result that it is his plight that controls the emotions of the audience as the curtain falls. Helpless in the face of the demagogue's triumph and the people's belief in Rubio's heroism, Miguel faces the total collapse of his aspirations. In spite of his irritating weakness, we feel pity for him now. And the negative outcome of his own search for integrity, eleveated to a quest for Truth, fills us, too, with despair as in the closing moments our minds are turned to future generations.[32] If this impression of the audience's emotional involvement in the second half of the final act is even partially accurate, then it has an important bearing on any decision that we make about the nature of El gesticulador as drama.

It might not seem important to wonder whether the play is a tragedy were it not for Usigli's now famous claim: "Creo poder afirmar que, hasta ahora, El gesticulador constituye el primer intento serio de una tragedia contemporánea realizado en el teatro mexicano" ("I believe that I can affirm that, until now, El gesticulador constitutes the first serious attempt at a contemporary tragedy undertaken in Mexican theatre") (TC 3:492) As we shall see when examining Corona de fuego (Crown of fire), Usigli's ambition to write in the tragic mode derived from a mixture of personal and nationalistic interest. From the 1940s onward he adopted the kind of attitude that Clifford Leech referred to in 1969: "In universities everywhere there is earnest discussion on whether 'tragedy' can now be written. It would not be so earnest if there were not a feeling that a civilization without tragedy is dangerously lacking something."[33] The question that arises, therefore, is whether Usigli's pretensions are justified. When he uses the term "tragedia contemporánea," I assume that he means not only a tragedy about contemporary events (which is the emphasis that he gives in the essay "Doce notas" [TC 3:478–94]) but also one based on contemporary dramatic standards (rather than on the Aristotelian and neoclassical precepts that control *Corona de fuego*). *El gesticulador* unquestionably conforms to the loose, popular definition of the word *tragedy* given in the *Concise Oxford Dictionary* as a "sad event" or a "calamity." Without too many reservations, we could also grant that it possesses a number of features that could be called "tragic" in the context of the theatre. It has a theme of great seriousness or—to use Aristotle's word—magnitude. The protagonist aspires toward (and reaches) great heights before his downfall and death. He needs to make great moral decisions. He comes to grief as the result of an error of judgment or inner failing. He and other leading characters are seen to be pitted against forces too powerful for them. They are endowed with the capacity to express profound thoughts at appropriate moments. Sharp reversals in the situation and discoveries of previously undisclosed information help to create a plot founded on cause and effect. The audience experiences emotions that include pity and fear. In the final analysis, however, the term "tragedy" does not seem appropriate. One of the main problems is the weak and hypocritical background of the protagonist and his rise to importance through dishonesty. This is his flaw (his hamartia), it is true, but we must question whether it is sufficiently compensated by virtues and whether he ever attains the stature of a tragic hero. For Donald Shaw the problem is rather different: "The dramatic forces in play are not in any kind of balance. . . . It is not two irreconcilable but equally justified views of Mexican political behaviour which finally confront each other in the play. . . . From such a clash, in which the audience's support is all engaged on one side, tragic pathos is inevitably absent."[34] Although I would not emphasize the need to balance the dramatic forces in this way, I certainly agree that the fundamental question is the extent and type of audience involvement, as analyzed above. Too little strength is given to our sense of pity (toward César or the family as a whole.) There is pathos, but there is no feeling of the transcendence or uplift that comes when the suffering opens up some kind of promise. There are tragic ingredients, but too many extraneous elements intrude. In the end, *El gesticulador* proves to be a serious political satire rather than a tragedy.

4

Politics and Fantasy

The underlying idea of El gran teatro del Nuevo Mundo was to provide a series of plays mirroring Mexican life over an extensive period of time. The *Tres comedias impolíticas, La última puerta,* and *El gesticulador* would therefore fall into place as pictures of the 1930s. Around 1949, with this grandiose project in mind, Usigli launched himself into a retrospective survey. With *Los fugitivos* (The Fugitives) (1950) he illustrated the ethical degeneracy of the leading social class on the brink of the Revolution. Set in the wealthy home of a family of *porfiristas* in 1908, this melodrama uses the unwanted pregnancy of a businessman's daughter as the means of drawing out the family's evasion of truth. The action occurs against a background of industrial disputes that are closing factories and causing violent clashes with troops. In the foregound Usigli shows a family torn by conflicting interests and ideologies. Business deals convey the sense that Mexico is selling itself out to foreign interests. Meanwhile, the daughter sacrifices herself in a marriage of convenience (thus clinching a business transaction), one of the sons (symbolically named Porfirio) confirms himself as a staunch supporter of the regime, and a second is cast out for his sympathies with Madero. The daughter's spurned fiancé also leaves to join the *maderistas* with a parting accusation that the family erroneously believe themselves to be immortal and that their condition as fugitives from reality will end once there is a revolution. Not without good reason, this play has been seen as an oblique criticism of Miguel Alemán's regime, and of the plans to have him reelected.[1] But Usigli presented it as the first stone in the edifice that would eventually be his Gran teatro (TC 3:665). The second stone was *Las madres* (begun in 1949, though not actually completed until 1960). This play takes us into the period of conflict, with its three acts set, respectively, in 1915, 1916, and 1917. A street in the heart of Mexico City forms the scene for a series of episodes illustrating life among the citizens of a capital occupied now by Zapata's men, now by Carranza's. At the center of the piece is a mother, dedicated to her son, struggling to make ends meet. (The autobiographical element is clear.) In its political attitude, *Las madres* confirms Usigli's antipathy for the confused and violent power struggle during the Revolution and reasserts his view that the original ideals were lost. One of the characters—a journalist—puts forth what appears to be the authorial point of view: "Creo en la Revolución, pero creo que los partidos lo corromperán" ("I believe in the Revolution, but I think the parties will corrupt it") (TC 2:648).

There is therefore some continuity between these two plays and those discussed in the previous chapters. Irrespective of the fact that they were written specifically for the Gran teatro project and that the political dimension is secondary rather than predominant, they aim to give the audience an impression and a critique of Mexican life. In the next chapter I shall link this trend with Usigli's development of a realist theatre. But for the present, what concerns me is a contrasting evolution in his political theatre. His last two political plays were to be set not in Mexico itself but in ostensibly fictitious countries. At the same time, one of the qualities of the previous works was to be developed from a subsidiary feature to the very basis of the action. It will be recalled that they all depend quite heavily on the use of theatrical situations, created by the introduction of literal improbability into their plots, that range from the strange circumstances that hold the characters imprisoned in *Noche de estío* to the masquerade in the second and third acts of *El gesticulador*. In other words, even while writing directly satirical commentaries on Mexico, Usigli deliberately shunned a plainly realistic plot, firmly believing in the need for theatre to be larger than life. This inclination toward a literally improbable action led him to outright fantasy.

Un día de éstos . . .

Usigli's "fantasía impolítica en tres actos" ("impolitic fantasy in three acts") was written mainly in 1935, although the third act had to be rewritten twice before the play was completed in 1953 (TC 3:761n). *Un día de éstos . . .* therefore belongs partly to the era of the three political comedies and partly to a much later period. There is some affinity with the political material of the early plays, but the broader vision clearly conforms to the more ambitious designs of the dramatist in the 1950s.

The action occurs in a fictitious country named Indolandia. An emergency meeting of cabinet ministers is called to discuss the assassination of the president and to choose an interim head of government. For various reasons, the more obvious choices are eliminated: the minister of *gobernación* and his undersecretary have both shared the president's fate; the aging head of the supreme court declares himself medically unfit; the leader of the government party does not wish to be considered because it would disqualify him from eventual election to a full term in office. To avoid delays and the danger of instability, the cabinet appoints the senior official of the undersecretary of *gobernación,* an unknown and unqualified member of the public. This surprise appointment has sensational consequences. The man appointed as interim president, José Gómez Urbina, expels the ambassador of a major world power, the Estados Unidos de Demolandia, for interfering with internal political affairs. Demolandia threatens invasion unless Indolandia immediately repays its foreign debt. To raise the money, Gómez Urbina demands that former presidents contribute sums proportionate to their vast wealth. Then, with the debt paid and the international crisis settled, Gómez Urbina turns to domestic issues: bringing to justice the conspirators responsible for his predecessor's death and calling for new presidential elections. The former issue is close to a resolution, with evidence pointing to one of the former presidents. But this is not the only potential source of danger. Gómez Urbina has become so popular in the country at large (75 percent declare in his favor) that he yields to persuasion to defer elections and hold on to the almost dictatorial power that he is enjoying. A shot fired at him from a crowd of people misses its target, but the ensuing crisis causes an abrupt deterioration in his health. He dies, leaving a clamor of voices as each minister stakes his own claim to the presidency.

This plot summary demonstrates that it is not only the name of the country that gives *Un día de éstos . . .* its fantastic quality. Among numerous incredible events, three stand out as being particularly farfetched: the selection of a relatively minor civil servant with no political training to act as interim president; the extraction of huge sums of money from former presidents; and the settlement of the foreign debt problem at a single stroke. Usigli admitted that in this play, by contrast with *El gesticulador,* the verisimilitude of events was less important to him than the flight of the imagination (TC 2:750). Before examining the use of fantasy more closely, however, I should make it clear that Usigli's inspiration manifestly derived from earthbound realities: Indolandia's national flag has Mexico's green and red (but in two horizontal rather than vertical stripes); The Partido Único is reminiscent of the monolithic Partido

Nacional Revolucionario/Partido de la Revolución Mexicana/Partido Revolucionario Institucional; the Congregación General de Trabajadores del País transparently represents the Confederación de Trabajadores de México; and the former presidents enjoy the kind of influence, wealth, and power that they notoriously have in Mexico itself. The constitution of Indolandia bears conspicuous resemblances to that of Mexico, particularly in its stipulation that no president may ever be reelected to that office. And one of the most important similarities to Mexico—though it is not exclusively valid for that country—is the sense of economic dependency on a large and powerful country to which Indolandia is indebted and by which it feels threatened. In fact, in his prologue to the play Usigli once drops the mask completely, writing; "en México—perdón, en Indolandia' ("in Mexico—sorry, in Indolandia") (TC 3:758).

The use of fantasy must therefore signify a careful choice. One obvious purpose of the dramatist is to satirize. Fantasy enables him to exaggerate the situation that he wishes to mock. An almost panic-stricken dread of social unrest and violent agitation is what creates the conditions under which Gomez Urbina is appointed to the interim presidency. For the attempted coup d'état in act 2, burlesque produces the desired mocking effect. The satire directed at specific political figures is perhaps the greatest beneficiary of this fantastic context. There is little doubt that some of the former presidents of Indolandia are caricatures of certain former Mexican presidents. The most conspicuous and entertaining is Miguel Alemán's counterpart in the play, named El Licenciado Germán (for the amusement of linguists), who gives speeches that are often masterpieces of self-irony. In the following, he contrasts the economic policies of Gómez Urbina with his own:

> "Donde yo hacía subir los precios, usted los baja; donde yo hacía bajar la moneda, usted la sube. . . . ¿No sabe usted que el indolandés padece la fiebre de gastar más de lo que tiene, y que hay que mantenerlo en esa ilusión para que no le sobre dinero, porque en cuanto le sobra lo tira en tonterías? Mi política hacia Demolandia fue siempre clara: préstenme ustedes lo que quieran, que no soy yo quien tendré que pagarlo sino mis sucesores." (TC 2:510)

> ("Where I used to raise prices, you lower them; where I used to lower the exchange rate, you raise it. . . . Don't you know that the people of Indolandia suffer the fever of spending more than they have, and that you have to keep them under that illusion so that they don't have money to spare, because as soon as they have it they throw it away on rubbish? My policies as regards Demolandia were always clear: lend me what

you wish, because it will be my successors, not me, who have to pay it back.")

In effect, this amounts to a simplified and exaggerated summary of complaints made against Alemán's presidency by his critics. The humor derives both from the audience's awareness of this comparison and from the character's innocent unawareness that his pride is directed toward a patent folly. Although Usigli avoids the more controversial and dangerous accusations of corruption in the Alemán administration, he satirizes the former president mercilessly through repeated references to El Licenciado Germán's personal wealth and propensity toward spending. Germán's first instinct when a colonel brandishes a weapon and takes the former presidents hostage is to buy himself out of trouble:

> (*El Licenciado Germán, tranquilamente, saca una libreta de cheques y la deposita en la mesa ministro.*)
> Coronel Judas. ¿Qué es eso?
> Licenciado Germán. Mi libreta de cheques. Mi única arma, Coronel. Y no es blanca. Fije usted mismo el calibre del cañonazo que desea. (TC 2:511)

> ([*Germán calmly takes out a checkbook and deposits it on the table.*]
> Colonel Judas. What's that?
> Germán. My checkbook. My only weapon, Colonel. And it's not empty. *You* choose the caliber of ammunition that you wish.)

After *El gesticulador* Usigli had personal reasons for feeling aggressive toward Alemán, and *Un día de éstos* . . . was, of course, appearing within two years of the latter's presidency. But the effect of satirizing him through fantasy was both to create a thin protection and to replace outright vindictiveness with ridicule. In general, the fantasy in this play therefore serves to enhance the satire while reducing the captious criticism.

We cannot rule out the desire to provide sheer entertainment by means of these fantastic variations on the theme of Mexico. The humorous speeches and the scenes of burlesque undoubtedly support this intent, as do dramatic techniques such as the suspension of information and the use of surprise. What seems to me to be the chief function of the fantasy, however, is the provision of a form of entertainment that is more akin to wish fulfillment than to amusement. The dramatist is inviting the audience to ask the question, What if . . . ? In particular, he raises the question, What might an unqualified and inexperienced member of the public do if given the presidency? Referring to the fantasy in this play, Usigli wrote that "el mexicano es un ser para el cual nada es impossible" ("the Mexican is a person for whom nothing is impossible.") (TC 3:751). The dramatist's challenge might be described as that of converting the manifestly impossible into the merely improbable.

Let us consider briefly what this play suggests is important to the common citizen. One clear indicator is the dialogue between President Gómez Urbina and the ambassador of Los Estados Unidos de Demolandia. At first, the ambassador displays a blatantly condescending attitude while he attempts to impose his country's will on arrangements for Indolandia's elections. Gómez Urbina acts with patience and dignity before reversing their relative positions. On a personal level, Gómez Urbina satisfies the audience's desire to witness the humiliation of a dominant figure: "Tenga usted la bondad de ponerse de pie para eschucharme, señor Embajador" ("Kindly stand up to listen to me, Mr. Ambassador") (TC 2:498). On a national level, however, the satisfaction becomes all the greater when the Mexican audience notices clear references to the United States: "Señor Embajador, ante todo, no estamos en una película de las que hacen los norteamericanos en Hollywood, en las que el héroe extranjero salva al país ajeno de la destrucción y la muerte" ("Mr. Ambasador, first and foremost, we are not in one of those films that the Americans make in Hollywood, in which the foreign hero saves someone else's country from destruction and death") (TC 2:498). Strictly, the Americans and the people of Demolandia are presented as quite distinct from one another. (For example, the ambassador's language is not English; it consists of Spanish words with their letters arranged in reverse order.) But the allusion is all too clear, and we can be in no doubt of Usigli's intention to appeal to the nationalistic wish to avoid humiliation. When the questions of political intervention and economic domination are raised, moreover, the intent is highly serious. In the prologue to this play the links with the United States are spelled out for us. Usigli expressed the fear that "un día de éstos . . . podemos convertirnos en República Administrada por Estados Unidos" ("One of these days . . . we can turn into a Republic Administered by the United States") (TC 3:750). The dramatic situation therefore allows him to fantasize about every Mexican's aspiration for his country. It is important for us to notice that here, as elsewhere, the dramatist's ideal course of action depends upon national unity. In his imaginary country the citizens rally to fend off the threat from abroad. Workers flock to the banks to contribute a day's wage, businessmen make voluntary donations, householders give jewelry, shop prices are reduced. The patriotism extends to the armed forces, who are stationed at strategic places throughout the country and are ready to give their lives for Indolandia. Admittedly, the former presidents are reluctant to pay substantial sums, but eventually they, too, are brought into the state of harmony created by this unified effort. Faced with a military threat from a dominant power, Indolandia receives an invitation to form an allegiance with a country named La Cruz del Sur (led by a *caudillo* reminiscent of Juan Domingo Perón, whose first two terms as president of Argentina ran from 1946 to 1955). Here, too, Usigli chose a thoroughly nationalistic course of action for his fictional president: Gómez Urbina rejects the offer. He also rejects a proposal from the trade unions that Indolandia should become affiliated to the Federación Asiática Socialista (obviously representing a major power from the Eastern bloc). In his role as the exponent of national unity, Gómez Urbina carefully steers a fairly central course through the political landscape. Those subjected to criticism belong to the notional extremes, such as generals and communists. All classes of people, Gómez Urbina declares, are equally precious (TC 2:506). In other words, Usigli entertained no prospect of actually eliminating social distinctions, though humanitarian attitudes were an integral part of this government that he magically created. As a final indicator of the nationalist tenor of Gómez Urbina's policies, it should be noted that, according to one of the suspicions entertained by critics of *Un día de éstos* . . . (recalled with amusement in the prologue), Usigli had been commissioned to write the play by President Ruiz Cortines to serve as a warning to the United States on behalf of the Mexican government (TC 3:770). With hindsight it is fairly clear that although the foreign debt was substantial after Alemán's program of economic expansion, political relations with the United States were incomparably better than during the years of crisis caused by Cárdenas's nationalistic measures, and that this part of the play draws its main inspiration from the 1930s, when much of it was first written. But however malicious these critics may have been, they were right in one respect: on one level, *Un día de éstos* . . . operates as patriotic propaganda.

There is no doubt that in his nationalistic approach to political and economic affairs President Gómez Urbina embodied one of the dramatist's ideals. A careful examination of *Un día de éstos* . . . , however, reveals that this representative character emerges as an imperfect figure whose blemishes appear most conspicuously in the third act, shortly before his death. Gómez Urbina's growth in moral stature is phenomenal. From the inconspicuous and rather tentative man named in the text as "El ninguneado" ("Mr. Nobody"), he develops into a champion of Mexican rights and a leader capable of unequivocal decisions, bold actions, and skillful tactics, who is idolized by a majority of the people. But many in the audience would find fault with his authoritarian methods. No consultation (with the cabinet or with advisers) takes place before the ambassador of Demolandia is expelled or before various other substantial political decisions are taken. In order to suppress a military revolt, he summarily executes the officer sent to arrest him (the personal nature of this action being emphasized by the fact that he himself fires the weapon). Thus far, some might excuse his failure to consult, debate, or negotiate on the grounds that he needs to act quickly and decisively to impose morally commendable policies and to circumvent the obstacles that the old guard would put in his way to protect their interests. But in the third act Usigli converts the matter into a major dilemma, hoping to draw his audience's attention to the excesses of which Gómez Urbina is guilty. On the one hand, the president begins act 3 in a favorable light, tired and saddened but triumphant over the international crisis, resolutely pursuing the investigation into his predecessor's assassination even at personal risk. On the other hand, he commits the ultimate error of yielding to the temptation to retain power beyond the stipulated period. The scene that features his appearance on the balcony in front of a huge crowd presents this decision ambiguously, offering the possible idea that he is acting altruistically, obeying the will of the people, and avoiding a riot. He asks the crowd to allow him to call elections; the crowd rejects his request and chants his name; and so he thanks the people and promises to fulfill his duties. Close attention to his speech, however, suggests that his opening words are no more than a tactical posture.

"Pueblo de Indolandia. Acato y respeto vuestra voluntad soberana, pero quiero pediros que me relevéis de un deber superior a mis fuerzas y a mis luces. Os pido permiso para convocar a elecciones. . . . Esa es mi manera de serviros mejor: ceder el sitio al que pueda hacer más por la patria." (TC 2 : 540)

("People of Indolandia. I obey and respect your soverign will, but I wish to ask you to relieve me of a duty superior to my strength and intelligence. I request permission to call elections. . . . That is how I can serve you best: by giving way to one who may do more for our country.")

Knowing in advance that a plebiscite overwhelmingly favors his retention of power, he begins by acknowledging the supreme importance of the popular will. He then introduces a note of manifestly false modesty and blatant paradox, aware that only minutes after the declaration of Indolandia's economic independence nobody could possibly have a stronger claim to patriotic service than he. This key scene must therefore be interpreted not as humble acquiescence to the people's determination but as astute manipulation and skillful oratory. It is, in fact, a moment when Gómez Urbina becomes a demagogue. Though his act of demagogy is less obvious than that of Navarro in *El gesticulador,* the term is no less valid. If there were any doubt about the matter, it would in any case be removed when we recalled the previous scene where, resolved to pursue his policies despite the opposition of the former presidents, Gómez Urbina acknowledges that the only way forward involves (as Licenciado Aguirre puts it) "la dictadura, la violación a la constitución" ("dictatorship, violation of the constitution") and declares, "Podré . . . abolir la constitución y proclamar una nueva. . . . No habrá ya elecciones, y yo haré justicia como sea necesario" ("I shall be able . . . to abolish the constitution and proclaim a new one. . . . There will no longer be any elections, and I shall carry out justice as necessary) (TC 2:536). Mindful that the principle of *la no-reelección* had been crucial to the Revolution, that Obregón had been assassinated when he was due to stand for a second term, and that other presidents had been tempted to tamper with the constitution of 1917 (Alemán included, of course), Usigli was clearly presenting this decision as a negative feature in his protagonist's development. Moreover, there is additional cause for interpreting the play as, ultimately, a pessimistic analysis of Mexico's political character. Not only does the ideal president abuse his power and fail to heed the constitution, but the citizens either willingly or inadvertently encourage his degeneration. As in *El gesticulador,* Usigli shows us how susceptible the masses are to the influence of one individual's personality, thereby suggesting their need for a charismatic leader converted into a kind of mythological hero. Gómez Urbina's dying words express the dramatist's idea: "Los mitos son nuestros mayores enemigos. ¡Realidad, más realidad, como aire! . . . En nuestro pueblo no debe haber ni traidores ni tiranos" ("Myths are our greatest enemies. Reality, more reality, like air! . . . Among our people there must be neither traitors nor tyrants") (TC 2:542). Usigli did not give him a death at the hands of an assassin—which would make him share the fate of César Rubio—but a death produced by natural causes, as though it were decreed by some higher power as the enactment of ultimate justice.

The controversy surrounding the first performance of *El gesticulador* was matched seven years later by the almost unanimously hostile critical reception of *Un día de éstos* . . . after its opening night in January 1954 at the Teatro Iris. The play lasted only thirteen nights before it was withdrawn. In some respects the critics echoed the disquiet voiced about the previous play: the overt mockery of prominent political figures (such as Miguel Alemán).[2] The fairly crude treatment of the trade union leader, moreover, seemed calculated to alienate the sympathy of a further substantial number of critics. By Usigli's own admission, however, the most widespread complaint was that he was attempting to curry favor, fawning over President Ruiz Cortines (TC 3:768). Presumably this criticism was determined by the few superficial resemblances between Mexico's current president and Gómez Urbina. Adolfo Ruiz Cortines, formerly a chief clerk in the department of *gobernación* and later secretary of that ministry, had begun his term in office by moves against the corrupt acquisition of wealth and other excesses of the previous regime and by attending to an economic crisis (punctuated by high inflation and the devaluation of the peso). But as we have seen, the figure of Gómez Urbina was—considered in its entirety—not one with which President Ruiz Cortines would gratefully be identified. (There were indeed some critics who believed that Usigli was mocking Ruiz Cortines.) The problem, therefore, arose from critics misunderstanding Usigli's intentions in the play.

As we shall see in the case of *Corona de luz,* ambiguity is sometimes an exceedingly useful technique in Usigli's theatre. But in *Un día de éstos* . . . the ambiguity lies in the dramatist's uncertainty rather than in the action (on stage or off stage) or in the motives of characters. What happens, and why, are indeed questions that we ask ourselves, but it is because of certain rapid changes of direction in the action and one or two unconvincing character developments. For the sake of brevity, I will reduce the problem to two principal characters: General Ávalos and President Gómez Urbina.

Ávalos plays a crucial role in the investigation of President Matías's assassination and the punishment of all those implicated in the deed. This theme changes direction in several respects. Firstly, in act 2 we learn that evidence points unmistakably to the involvement of a former president in the assassination, and Gómez Urbina is given names and details. In the last act, however, we are told that all this evidence was false, and the name of the real culprit is now handed to the president. This change tends to introduce a lack of confidence in the new evidence, though Usigli does not appear to intend it. Secondly, our attitude to the dead president undergoes an important alteration when we discover that he had been about to sell his country to a foreign power. It means that Usigli introduces the possibility of excusing the assassination as a patriotic act. Thirdly, and most significantly, our attitude to Ávalos is in a constant state of flux. In act 2 he supports Gómez Urbina's policies and helps to suppress an attempted coup. In act 3 an intense dialogue between him and the president creates the suspicion that we must regard Ávalos as the instigator of the assassination. When Gómez Urbina orders him to castigate the guilty person, stage directions indicate that the audience must be left in little doubt: "Los dos se miden con la vista un momento, hasta hacer sentir que Gómez Urbina acaba de dictar la sentencia de muerte de Ávalos" ("They size each other up for a moment, until it may be sensed that Gómez Urbina has just sentenced Ávalos to death") (TC 2:539). Ávalos promises to fullfill his duty and leaves the stage. At this point, our attitude to him is highly complex. We have been thinking of him as a man of loyalty and integrity, but now—suddenly—we realize that we must also think of him as a political assassin. While Ávalos is off stage, a shot fired from the crowd narrowly misses Gómez Urbina and kills Captain Peláez. In the light of Ávalos's ruthless defence of the national interest, his complicity in this deed cannot be ruled out. How then are we meant to react to him when he reappears on stage, repeats his promise to fulfil his previous duty, but also asks to be allowed first to find the latest assassin? He declares this plot to be the work of Matías's friends, and it seems probable that Usigli was trying to exonerate him. But the clumsy arrangement leaves a cloud of suspicion that does not fully disperse. Our view of Ávalos then undergoes one more radical change when the dying Gómez Urbina—with almost his last words—reverses his own attitude to the general. It leaves the audience in a state of uncertainty, for we realize that our final assessment of Ávalos has a strong bearing on our understanding of the play's overall political message.

Before reaching a conclusion about this, however, we need to turn our attention to the other problematic character, Gómez Urbina himself. By the middle of act 3 the interim president has developed from the confident, decisive leader that we saw in the previous act into a figure torn by opposing forces. His ideas of justice, clean government, and national independence undergo severe pressure from the prevailing reality. There is no longer a clear distinction between right and wrong, particularly after the revelations about President Matías. The most important choice that he is compelled to make is between a duty to his conscience and a duty to the people. If he brings Matías's assassin to justice, he throws the country into chaos. If he obeys the constitution and calls elections (in which he is ineligible), he contravenes the will of 75 percent of the population. His decision is a compromise between the two duties: he will pursue the ideal of a just castigation of the assassin while yielding to pragmatism over the question of retaining power. At the last moment, however, with his last breath, he exactly reverses this decision, and this is the point where our attitude to General Ávalos becomes a crucial matter: "General . . . Ávalos . . . Tenía usted razón. La idea . . . salvar la idea. En nuestro pueblo no debe haber ni traidores ni tiranos. Cuídelo usted mientras viva . . . Y viva mucho" ("General . . . Ávalos . . . You were right. The idea . . . save the idea. Among our people there must be neither traitors nor tyrants. You take care of it for as long as you live . . . And may you live long") TC 2 : 542). It amounts to an admission that he was wrong to persist with the investigation and wrong to ignore the constitution. The audience is now left, therefore, with a number of problems. Gómez Urbina could be seen as a man, corrupted by circumstances, who abuses his power. On the other hand, this final speech converts him into the more heroic figure of a man seeking to reconcile two conflicting forces, and dying as a consequence of his failure. The transformation is too abrupt and too short-lived. Moreover, by allowing this character virtually to exonerate General Ávalos, Usigli himself gives the impression of condoning political assassination for a just cause. Is this his intention, or is he pessimistically depicting a country fated to be subjected to cycles of violence, prone to the corruption of ideals, and divided by rivalries?

Usigli was evidently frustrated by the public's failure to understand *Un día de éstos* . . . For the record, I should quote the explanation that he gave to one of the government ministers in 1954.

> Le expliqué . . . que la pieza registra la traición, el asesinato y el azar, elementos históricos de México; que defiende el derecho a la soberanía, la independencia y la autodeterminación de los pequeños países; que señala el único castigo eficaz para los gobernantes prevaricadores, y enseña, además, que en el *desgarriate* y la anarquía está la salud contra las dictaduras. Él, según me dijo, no había captado nada de eso. (TC 3 : 770)

> (I explained to him . . . that the play records treachery, assassination and coincidence, historical elements in Mexico; that it defends the right of small countries to sovereignty, independence and self-determination; that it indicates the only effective punishment for prevaricating rulers, and that it teaches, moreover, that the source of protection against dictatorships is dissent and anarchy. He, according to what he told me, had not captured any of that.)

If I have not followed this explanation point by point in my analysis of the play, it is because the dramatic work does not faithfully reproduce the same emphasis.

It might be added that the play's failure is not by any means simply a failure to communicate the dramatist's intention. Despite the success of individual scenes (such as the meeting of Gómez Urbina with the former presidents in act 2), there is insufficient overall cohesion in the work. Too many issues vie with each other for central importance. Gómez Urbina's psychological problems are sacrificed for greater attention to political comment. Issues related to internal politics are badly combined with the (temporarily supreme) matter of economic independence. And in the final analysis, it must be concluded that the sense of political naiveté suffusing the play is the result of an uneasy combination of caricature and realism. While the humor is not extensive enough to create a comic satire, the fantasy does not take us far enough into the realm of imagination to create a parable.

¡Buenos días, señor Presidente!

Almost two decades later Usigli returned for the last time to overtly political issues with another fantasy, *¡Buenos días, señor Presidente!* Although the attention that this play has attracted owes more to the political content than to its quality (it was not performed in the commercial theatre during the dramatist's lifetime), a brief analysis here is indispensable if we are to reach an accurate overall impression of Usigli's development. The piece is in effect another attempt to answer the question, What might happen if— through amazing circumstances—an entirely new type of leadership came into power? A young political activist, Harmodio, struck unconscious while leading a demonstration, awakens to discover that the government has fallen and parliament has named him president. In his new role, Harmodio shows early signs of pride, impatience, intolerance, authoritarianism, and corruption. He is drugged and imprisoned. Awaking in a dungeon, he reflects on his mistakes. Released and reinstalled in the presidency, he acts with clemency and seeks conciliation with his enemies. But there are schisms within his own party. His rivals cause betrayal and bloody repression. He is killed by the crowd while attempting to restore harmony, and in the ensuing power vacuum, the former president resumes his role in government.

In the first place, it is important to acknowledge the superficial similarity that this plot bears to Calderón's *La vida es sueño:*[3] the sudden acquisition of supreme political power by a young man, his reprehensible behavior, his imprisonment (in Calderón it is a renewed imprisonment), his self-analysis and reform, his release, the restoration of his power, and his enlightened behavior at this second opportunity. Usigli is particularly close to *La vida es sueño* in Harmodio's monologue in the dungeon during the interlude, where a good deal of the meditation is on abstract themes such as liberty, morality, life and death, dream and reality. But Usigli follows Calderón no further than the end of the first *cuadro* of the second act, inventing in the final *cuadro* a denouement of his own. As he explained in his "Análisis, examen y juicio de *¡Buenos días, señor Presidente!*" "El mecanismo que me interesaba sobre todo era sólo el que permite trasladar a Segismundo de la pesadilla de su prisión en la montaña al sueño de su primera etapa en el palacio real de Polonia, de éste a la nueva pesadilla en su caverna, y de ella, en fin, al nuevo sueño de lucha, victoria, perdón y gobierno" ("The mechanism that interested me above all was only the one that allows Segismundo to be transferred from the nightmare of his prison in the mountain to the dream of his first stage in the royal palace of Poland, from the latter to the new nightmare in his cave, and from there, finally, to the new dream of struggle, victory, pardon and government") (TC 3:821). In other words, in his search for the means of converting an essentially fantastic situation into a dramatically possible one, he discovered a safe, proven, and universally respected model in one of the world's classics. His play is not essentially Calderonian in its inspiration, but it takes advantage of the Spanish Golden Age masterpiece in order to elevate its own tone, enhance its quality, and create a more abstract meaning.

¡Buenos días, señor Presidente! is actually described not as a fantasy but as a "moralidad en dos actos y un interludio según *La vida es sueño*" ("morality in two acts and an interlude in accordance with *La vida es sueño*") (TC 3:226). Although it is not a literary exercise to produce a modern version of the Calderón play, Usigli's description loosely implies that it is a didactic work in which moral issues are represented in allegorical form on stage. Anyone familiar with recent Mexican history would notice the play's connection with events that attracted the attention of the world's press in July, August, and September 1968. At that time the government was faced with unrest and demonstrations among students from secondary schools, the National Polytechnic, and the National Autonomous University. At the heart of this movement of protest among the young was a general discontent with Mexico's social and political progress under the regime of President Gustavo

Díaz Ordaz, though specific causes of dissatisfaction could also be found within the relationship of educational establishments to the political hierarchy. Besides violating university autonomy, the government's riot police—and other squads with a less official status—handled the situation with a steadily increasing brutality. Many students were beaten and arrested, and some were killed. This in turn gave the students a sense of united purpose, which they demonstrated in their acts of rebellion (the occupation of buildings, the hijacking of buses, the building of barricades, and the holding of large rallies). It is clear from the evidence of participants that the student movement became a highly organized affair (a national strike council, political brigades, a rotating directorate, and the like.[4] A list of demands was drawn up, concentrating on the repressive nature of the current establishment. As other dissidents joined the student movement, the government was faced with a major crisis. With the country's stability threatened, the sense that the world was assessing its ability to cope, and the start of the Olympic Games scheduled for October, the administration required a prompt and decisive solution. In ¡Buenos días, señor presidente! Usigli invites us to imagine one kind of extreme measure: the government stands down and permits the students' movement to take over the nation's affairs. On 2 October 1968, however, another kind of extreme measure was taken. A gathering of some six thousand people in the Plaza de Tres Culturas, Tlatelolco, was surrounded by approximately ten thousand troops and attacked by rifle and machine-gun fire. Dozens of students were killed, hundreds were wounded, and over a thousand were arrested. The effectiveness of this solution to the threat posed by students and dissidents was undisputed, but the sheer ruthlessness of the government's agents caused an outcry. Octavio Paz resigned from his post as ambasador in Delhi; Usigli did not follow suit. On the contrary, he drew the hostility of Paz and many others by suggesting that there was some justification for the government's action. Usigli's friend and former pupil Luis Echeverría Álvarez, who was minister of *gobernación* at the time, was inevitably associated with the policies adopted by the police and armed forces to handle civil unrest (although responsibility was taken by the secretary of defense and the president).[5] Within two years he had become president, and before long, Usigli had returned to Mexico to undertake government-sponsored work in the theatre. As I mentioned in chapter 2, ¡Buenos días, señor Presidente! bears a warm dedication to President Echeverría.

It is impossible to separate the play from these polemical matters. Since it fantasizes on the theme of an alternative government response to a powerful student movement, we must give careful attention to the implications of Harmodio's development and to the role of other characters. Having mentally adjusted to his discovery that he has been made president, Harmodio publicly confirms that his government will maintain the existing parliamentary system, with periodic popular elections. Its program will involve the expropriation of land from large landowners and a redistribution to the legitimate owners, the people (TC 3:234). There will be no political prisoners. An extensive welfare program is planned. Thus far, therefore, Harmodio behaves in accordance with ideals pursued by the student movement. By the end of act 1, however, he has begun to reveal less idealistic inclinations. He rejects a recommendation by parliament (that his government should include persons with proven experience), orders the arrest and execution without trial of senior figures in the previous administration (a command that is modified after advice from his colleague), and attempts to blackmail a young woman into visiting his private rooms. Usigli appears to be implying that human nature's basic inclinations inevitably find expression when power provides the means for their gratification. A reformed Harmodio in act 2 applies lessons that he has learned about the need to conform to the law, act with generosity and integrity, and create a spirit of harmony. He pardons General Félix—the previous president—from the death sentence and decides to form a coalition government in which a place will be found for members of previous regimes and representatives of opposition parties. In fact, his behavior in this act embodies the Usiglian political ideal of national unity for the common good. It gives the dramatist the opportunity of testing the success of tolerance, compromise, and fraternity as the solutions to a political crisis and, as the denouement of the play reveals, it enables him to suggest that such measures hold little hope of success.

Harmodio's reform is offset by the betrayal of his closest friends and the schisms within the movement that he once led. As in *El gesticulador* and *Un día de éstos* . . . , the final catastrophe is precipitated by an assassination during a mass assembly. Usigli's fear of the outbreak of violence once again determined the pattern of his theatre. There is no more hope at the end of *¡Buenos días, señor Presidente!* than in the cynical finales of the other two plays. General Félix restores order by returning to power, but this does not represent Usigli's simple approval of Mexico's solution in 1968. The authority vested in his dramatic figure offers a severely menacing picture, twice glimpsed in the parenthetical words spoken by President Félix.

"General Asdrúbal . . . Sírvase ver que se restablezca un orden absoluto y sobre todo que no haya un sólo disparo—*por ahora*—" ("General Asdrúbal . . . Kindly see that absolute order is restored, and above all that not a single shot is fired—*for now*—") (TC 3:274; the emphasis is mine)

"Ahora que el pueblo y los jóvenes han despertado del mal sueño que soñaban, entablaremos nuestro diálogo con ellos. *A nuestra manera.*" ("Now that the people and the youngsters have awoken from the bad dream that they were having, we shall enter into our dialogue with them. *In our own way.*") (TC 3:275; the emphasis is mine)

And the implication that further bloodshed may be forthcoming is surely contained in the President's last reference to the young citizens:

Solón. Ahora son todos nuestros hermanos, señor, ¿o no?
Félix. Esto está por ver todavía. ¿No mataron ellos mismos a sus hermanos, tan jóvenes? (TC 3:275)

(*Solón.* Now they are all our brothers and sisters, sir, or aren't they?
Félix. That remains to be seen. Didn't they kill their own brother and sister, young as they were?)

Since these are the final words of the play, their ominous quality is carefully chosen for its impact on the audience as the curtain falls. If this ending is applied to the situation in 1968, it might be inferred that Usigli was not—in the play at least—defending the harsh measures of the regime but indicating his view that the young would themselves be incapable of resisting the corruptive effects of power, while the establishment would always be able to justify its brutality by referring to the dissidents' own resort to violence. Usigli's moralizing use of the theatre in this instance is interesting because it represents an important body of opinion within Mexico. While not advocates of brutal repression, these people hold the view that unruly dissidence only gives the opportunity for ruthless elements in the establishment to retaliate with violent methods.

It would be wrong, however, to assume that Usigli was limiting his thoughts to this specific Mexican context. In his "Análisis, examen y juicio de *¡Buenos días, señor Presidente!*" he refers to the obvious relation between the play's situations and characters and events throughout the whole world in 1968 (TC 3:841). In May of that year France epitomized the political confrontations between the students and the police. Although in some of its aspects the rebellion was a university affair, it quickly spread from academic matters to ideological principles, from students to workers, from Paris to other parts of France. It attracted the support of important intellectuals and the attention of the world's press, and it brought certain tangible (though limited) achievements after the rubble and barricades had been removed. The cases of France and Mexico were especially significant in terms of social disorder and media coverage, but Usigli would be perfectly aware that they were by no means isolated incidents and that they represented a worldwide spirit of protest among the underprivileged and the young. His own diplomatic career ensured that he was able to adopt an international perspective on such matters. This more general meaning is suggested by the limitation of essentially Mexican features in *¡Buenos días, señor Presidente!* Although the setting is given as "la época actual en un país indoamericano" ("the present time in an Indo-American country"), there is no strong hint like the joking similarity to the Mexican flag that we find in *Un día de éstos . . .* , no transparent mockery of real political figures, and no carefully contrived allusions to Mexico's own political system. Indeed, by contrast with Mexico, there is a parliament, and a military officer has been occupying the presidency (Mexico's last military president was in the 1940s). The names of the main characters contain obvious symbolic qualities: "Harmodio" contains the words *harmonía* (harmony) and *odio* (hatred); "Félix" is a blending of *feliz* (happy, successful) and *fénix* (phoenix); while "Diosdado," "Alma," and "Victoria" have simple meanings (God-given, soul, and victory). A few characters have mythological names, such as Casandra (alias Victoria) and Captain Heracles. Political groups are given the abstract titles *deltas* and *gammas,* so that we notice not their actual ideologies but the mere existence of different factions. In all, the method seems designed to create more of a universal allegory than a national satire.

At this point in our analysis it is useful to notice that Usigli's play offers relatively little comment on purely ideological aspects of the rebellion. Two things interest the dramatist: the chances of the idealistic protesters achieving their aims if they were given the opportunity and the confrontation between the young generation and the older people occupying influential posts. Having dealt with the first of these, with its political consequences, let us now consider the second (briefly anticipating a theme that will be of concern in chapter 8). The play is barely under way when the question of age arises. At first it is a passing reference.

Harmodio. El general Félix . . . El viejo Félix.
Félix. Treinta y nueve años cumplidos, señor. (TC 3 : 229)

Harmodio. General Félix . . . Old Félix.
Félix. All of thirty-nine years old, sir.

It is a fairly lighthearted moment, but Harmodio has clearly touched a sensitive nerve, and the audience is immediately aware that an aspect of the struggle is the young generation's tendency to think of those in power as *los viejos*. Harmodio has been leading a demonstration organized by the Partido Fraternal de la Juventud. He assumes that his new government will be formed from its members, but parliament recommends the inclusion of experienced politicians. As he presents this recommendation to Harmodio, the former president, Félix, displays his attitude to the question of age: "El Parlamento *(sonrisa)* recomienda en su decisión que utilice usted también la colaboración de los . . . senectos que tenemos cierta experiencia en la conducta de las riendas del ponder." ("Parliament [*he smiles*] recommends in its decision that you also use the collaboration of us . . . veterans who have a certain experience in holding the reins of power") (TC 3:230). Two things in particular are striking here: Félix's dignified irony and the insistence that age is associated with experience. Usigli does not miss the opportunity a little later to show that even Victoria is surprised by Harmodio's youthful naiveté: "Eres tan niño aún . . . señor Presidente!" ("You're still so childlike . . . Mr. President!") (TC 3:242). In the play's dialogue there is no further discussion of the age difference between the old regime and the new. However, a performance of the play (as opposed to a reading) maintains a visual indication that the series of betrayals, rivalries, schisms, and killings are all perpetrated by the young against the young. When the older generation regains control, General Félix's last words remind the audience of the crimes committed by the young, inspiring a sense of pity as well as of condemnation. The overall impression, however, is less compassionate, being an exposure of the young's inexperience, impatience, and passion, which eventually exact their toll.

By the time he wrote *¡Buenos días, señor Presidente!* Usigli was in his midsixties. Irrespective of the evident diminution of his creative faculties, the play's theme may be connected to his personal circumstances. His greatest success as a dramatist belonged to an earlier decade; his own rebelliousness was a part of his youth. Always concerned with the problematic relationship between parents and their children, he gradually identified himself more closely with the middle-aged and older characters in his plays, until he eventually became preoccupied with the experience of aging. Leaving until chapter 8 a fuller analysis of this theme, it is important to notice here the unfettered intolerance that he developed toward the frivolous nature of the young. In his analytical essay on *¡Buenos días, señor Presidente!* he complained of students "vestidos de carnaval fugándose en pijamas y otros atuendos nunca antes portados en la calle, y que se entregan en las esquinas, en cafés y restaurantes, en el metro, los autobuses y tranvías . . . a ejercicios de deliquio sexual" ("in carnival dress, making off in pajamas and other attire never before worn in the street, indulging, on street corners, in cafés and restaurants, on the metro, the buses and the trams . . . in unrestrained sexual conduct") (TC 3:825). And then, more wistfully, he drew attention to the way old people like himself feel their world to be more real: "Creemos o sentimos que nosotros somos los seres reales y ellos sólo figuras en un rompecabezas onírico del que tendrán que salir para cuajar como seres existentes y venir a lo que nosotros soñamos que es nuestra realidad y que por nuestra parte pensamos que no cambia" ("We think or feel that we are the real beings and they are only figures in a dream-puzzle from which they will have to emerge so as to materialize as existing beings and come into what we dream is our reality and which we for our part believe to be unchanging") (TC 3:825). In the play itself we notice how the aged dramatist has shown the young characters three aspects of their dreamlike quality. He has revealed that the sovereignty of youth is of limited duration. He has demonstrated the insubstantiality of life itself. And he has suggested that their aspirations are fantastic, while the order represented by the older generation is permanent.

¡Buenos días, señor Presidente! does not deserve to be dismissed out of hand as a bad play. The structure, for example, is carefully worked to emphasize the main direction of the theme. Act 1 focuses on the way in which a promising situation is corrupted by Harmodio's negative character development, while act 2 shows his reformed character to be helpless against the remorseless degeneration of the circumstances. The interlude creates a natural pivot between the two. As usual, Usigli shows his natural talent for dramatic situations. At the start of the play he immediately commands the audience's attention with two types of devices: shots and voices in the dark and, soon afterward, the surprise of Félix's greeting, "¡Buenos días, señor Presidente!" The subsequent process of discovery (by Harmodio and the audience simultaneously) is also well handled, Harmodio's early disbelief delaying the emergence of this situation as a real state of affairs. Suspense is quite effectively introduced at the end of act 1 (where will Harmodio's arrangements with Alma, etc., lead?) and at the end of act 2, *cuadro primero* (how are we to take Diosdado's warnings of treach-

ery?). It is worth noting, moreover, that this play is a little more technically advanced than most of his works. Various special effects help to speed the plot along or to evoke a sense of the passage of time: light and dark, unidentified voices off stage, clocks chiming, radio bulletins. One particularly useful device giving a shorthand effect is the rapid moving of spotlights from one face to another during Harmodio's inauguration in act 1. In the same scene the symbolic quality of the four ministers is suggested by their statuesque appearance (they look like wax models). And to create a sense of the semireality of certain scenes, the lighting is adjusted to blur the set—a feature that is particularly noteworthy in the dungeon during the interlude. In the final analysis, however, the play's weaknesses predominante. Too many fundamental changes take place in the two brief acts. None of the characters becomes convincing. The lack of attention to Harmodio's character development is a particularly grave defect, and the excessively long monologue in the interlude fails to resolve the problem. In the final *cuadro* the intrigues between the various parties and individuals occur too abruptly. But most seriously of all, the political and philosophical issues are presented in an excessively facile and superficial manner. It may well be fair to conclude that Usigli's moralizing intent impaired the dramatic qualities of the piece.

As we have seen in these chapters on political drama, Usigli's methods underwent striking changes from the 1930s to the 1970s. The most important aspect of this evolution was the abandonment of comedy and farce as forms appropriate to such subject matter and the adoption of a fundamentally serious mode. Another significant development was the increasing use of fantasy and allegory, with its consequent tendency to shift the emphasis away from purely Mexican political affairs toward more universal dimensions. Certain political preoccupations remained fairly constant, however. *Caudillismo* continued to be one of the principal targets of Usigli's criticism. Even when the Jefe Máximo himself was no longer the direct inspiration, there would still be a powerful leader, with the characteristic virility and charisma (Rubio and Navarro in *El gesticulador;* Gómez Urbina in *Un día de éstos* . . . Felix in *¡Buenos días, señor Presidente!*). He might be wise and circumspect, seeking the public good (Rubio in act 3; Gómez Urbina in acts 2 and 3), or he might be a protector of vested interests, with criminal tendencies (Navarro). But he was always dangerous because of his demagogic qualities, the enormous power vested in him personally, and his propensity to take the law into his own hands. The monolithic nature of the Revolutionary party is another recurring theme (though not in the last play). Political violence emerges as one of Usigli's greatest concerns. The assassination of Rubio in *El gesticulador,* the two assassinations in *Un día de éstos . . . ,* and the two in *¡Buenos días, señor Presidente!* have counterparts, of course, in the political murders punctuating Mexican history. It is significant that in the plays, most of these killings occur during a mass political assembly, demonstrating Usigli's continuing belief that violence was endemic in Mexican society. Finally, the hypocrisy pervading the political system (and society at large) persistently found its way into his drama. There are ample examples from the earliest to the latest plays: the obsequious behavior of characters at the end of *Noche de estío* once the general is back in charge; the lip service paid to communist ideology in *El Presidente y el ideal;* the orchestrated public demonstration by party members in *Estado de secreto;* the routine protest by students in *La última puerta;* the claims to patriotism by acquisitive former presidents in *Un día de éstos . . . ;* the pretense by Diosdado that his resort to force obeyed some altruistic ideal in *¡Buenos días, señor Presidente!* not to mention the notorious cases of Navarro and Rubio in *El gesticulador.* Perhaps the most disturbing aspect of Usigli's vision is the extension of corruption into the younger generation, as illustrated by the planned sequel to *El gesticulador* and by the conclusion of *¡Buenos días, señor Presidente!*

Considered as a whole, these plays are thoroughly antagonistic toward Mexican politics. In different ways they all adopt an essentially satirical approach, in that they unmask and attack the world that Usigli knew. It is important to note that the last three political dramas represent a slight shift of emphasis, since they are not wholly negative and mocking. At least a glimpse of a possible way forward is offered in them. In *El gesticulador* a revitalized César Rubio discovers that genuine political action springs from close contact with the populace. In *Un día de éstos . . .* the idealistic President Gómez Urbina takes a strong stand against foreign interference in the cause of national dignity. He also attempts to introduce the concept of government by consensus. This corresponds to Usigli's evident belief in the need for unity of purpose and effort among political leaders, which he again illustrated in the coalition government implied during the second act of *¡Buenos días, señor Presidente!* The later political plays therefore became less directly satirical and more overtly moralizing and didactic. Essentially, however, Usigli's pessimism did not abate, for the positive developments introduced in them are impeded and negative forces eventually prevail.

5
Social Drama: The Family at Home

For a dramatist who was to write a fair number of social plays, Usigli showed a surprising antipathy for pure realism early in his career. "El teatro realista no me interesa" ("the realist theatre does not interest me"), he wrote in 1937 in the prologue to *Medio tono* (Medium tone).[1] One of the creative problems he faced was the essentially nontheatrical nature of people when they are portrayed on stage without some kind of artistic enhancement. If he were to respond merely to his artistic instinct, he explained, he would make his characters exceptional rather than mediocre. But he recognized the needs for realism as a remedy for the poor health of the Mexican theatre. In his opinion, since the public had little opportunity to watch plays on national themes, realist drama offered the prospect of carrying "the majority" into the theatre—both on the stage and in the stalls. It is important to note that when he referred here to the majority, he actually meant the middle class, implicitly rejecting any idea of creating a drama for the proletariat. His project to attract the middle class involved giving them a representative theatre for the first time in his country. To write realist drama therefore meant to write middle-class drama, and it became a matter of public duty rather than natural inspiration.

Usigli's lack of emotional or instinctive involvement in the enterprise meant that he could apply a measured, analytical approach to his subject. Above all, he was determined to demonstrate that successful realist theatre did not mean the unselective reporting of events or the vulgarization of life but an attempt to capture the *spirit* of reality. He believed, moreover, that the dramatist's task was to study reality with a view to ennobling and improving it (TC 3 : 446). In *Medio tono* he fulfilled his pledge to represent the middle class in its essential mediocrity. But after that play his approach became more flexible. In 1942, writing his introduction to *La familia cena en casa* (The family dines at home), he insisted that invention and imagination were vital elements in the process whereby society was portrayed on the stage. The dramatist's art, he stressed, was "recordar con ayuda de la imaginación" ("to remember with the help of the imagination") (TC 3:608). He was not in favor of filling the theatre with what he called abnormal and unnatural subjects, such as "los seres que crecen, maduran y envejecen en seis años, los homosexuales, los enanos" ("beings that grow, mature and age in six years, homosexuals, dwarfs") (TC 3:608), since theatrical art was concerned not with the individual but with personal experience as a catalyzing element in collective emotion (TC 3:610). But he did believe it absolutely essential for the dramatist to avoid a literal representation of reality. His skill consisted in giving the audience the impression that it was watching reality itself, while in actual fact the events on stage were an amended version, raised above the level of banality. For the public, without realizing it, expected from the theatre both reality and miracle at the same time.

In this chapter I have chosen to examine two examples of his realist theatre, one boldly defying the dangers of banality and mediocrity, the other shamelessly mixing reality and miracle.

Medio tono

The Sierra family of *Medio tono* (Medium tone) enjoys a comfortable standard of living and a tolerable degree of harmony. In the course of the play, however, a series of crises subjects them to a testing experience. At the final curtain, the Sierras' material circumstances have deteriorated and many members of the family are going their separate ways, but the audience is left with the sense that most of the characters have emerged from their crisis with a positive outlook, and the family is more united than before.

The decor is carefully chosen to emphasize visually the social rank of these people, the significance of material possessions in their lives, and the hard times that they encounter. As the curtain lifts at the beginning of the play, the audience absorbs an impression of the moderate wealth of a middle-class household. Amid the ample furnishings, a baby grand piano and a Chippendale chair particulary draw the attention. A telephone and a refrigerator (off stage) are further indicators of class and living standards. At the beginning of act 3 a striking visual contrast with the previous acts immediately demonstrates the sudden change of circumstances. Gone are the grand piano, the radio, the suite, the Chippendale chair, the carpet, and other valuable items, and in their place we see old and poor-quality substitutes. It is not simply the image of an abstract or mental predicament, for the change of decor signifies, of course, the sale of furniture.

Business, employment, and money are subsidiary issues in the play that impinge on the action in a way that is emphasized by these visual effects. The head of the family, Sr. Sierra, is a civil servant who, after eighteen years working for a state politician, suddenly finds himself unemployed. The eldest daughter, Enriqueta, is married to a businessman who, almost simultaneously, goes bankrupt. A younger daughter, Gabriela, and her friend, Eduardo, lose their jobs after attending a political meeting. Money must be found not only to pay the rent but to finance the various needs of members of the family. David's ill health means that he requires a spell in a sanatorium. Sarah's pregnancy means that she must slip away to Oaxaca to avoid scandal. Julio requires the fare for his journey to Europe, and Víctor the expenses for an amorous adventure. In act 3 the actual sum of money appropriate to each item is discussed. In short, Usigli created a household that the audience could see to be dependent—to a considerable extent—on physical comfort and economic security, made the family aware of the precarious nature of those commodities, and examined their resilience when the fabric of their existence suddenly collapses.

The first act is built around preparations for a meal. As Sra. Sierra says, "El domingo es un día en que toda la familia cena en casa" ("Sunday is a day when the whole family dines at home") (TC 1:498)—words that were to form the basis of Usigli's 1942 play. An additional feature of this particular mealtime in *Medio tono* is the fact that a guest has been invited, so that the occasion becomes more of a display than is normally the case (with turkey as the main course). The meal, as an event which brings everyone together, becomes an institution that gives substance to the family's existence. Individual members acquire a collective identity, conform to a set of rules, confide in each other, and draw on each other for support. Differences among them are forced into the open and strains in the relationship produce moments of conflict. Sra. Sierra is the character who repeatedly affirms the family's importance: "¡Niños! Cada familia es un pequeño mundo" ("Children! Each family is a little world") (TC 1:504). This middle-class family becomes, in other words, a microcosm of middle-class society in Mexico.

Although the mood is on the whole cheerful and harmonious, we are permitted glimpses of the regular sources of tension: Sr. Sierra's philandering, Julio's affiliation to the Communist party, Gabriela's indecision over her romantic affairs, Victor's precociousness,

David's ill health, and Sarah's forbidden meetings with her boy-friend. Toward the end of the act a perceptible change in the atmosphere has been introduced, particularly as a result of Sierra's failure to return for the meal. Complaints against him are voiced by Gabriela ("Siempre hace lo mismo"—["He always does the same"] [TC 1:503]), Sra. Sierra ("Prometió venir, pero puede retrasarse." ["He promised to come, but he could be late"] [TC 1:512]), and Enriqueta ("Y . . . esto de papá" ["And . . . this thing about daddy."] [TC 1:513]), before various members of the family begin to quarrel and rebel. Gabriela casts the blame on her father for causing disunity by his bad example. Julio's reaction is more radical: they must split up; there must be no more disturbances in the name of family love (TC 1:514). However, the return of Sr. Sierra, even with news of their ruin, serves to contain the situation. The economic problem is set aside temporarily, the misconduct is forgiven, the meal unites them all.

> *Señora Sierra.* Anda, viejo verde, ven al comedor. Ya veremos mañana. El pavo se enfría.
> (*Se miran un momento. Se toman afectuosamente las manos*) (TC 1:518)

> (*Señora Sierra.* Come on, you dirty old man, come into the dining room. We'll see about it tomorrow. The turkey's going cold.
> [*They look at each other for a moment. They hold hands affectionately.*]

And the whole family enters the dining room.

The second act partly concerns the consequences of Gabriela's night in jail and Julio's continued detention. From the family's point of view, Julio's speech to a communist gathering and Gabriela's attendance at the meeting constitute a deviant or rebellious form of behavior. But this in itself is nothing compared with imprisonment. The social stigma is one cause of their disquiet, but what Usigli emphasizes is the individuals' separation and isolation from the home. It is recognized by both father and mother that every effort must be made to bring not only Gabriela but Julio back into the physical domain of the family. A second test for the very concept of a family comes with the news that the youngest unmarried daughter, Sarah, is pregnant. The immediate reaction is a mixture of anger and distress, but gradually feelings of understanding, compassion, and tolerance become dominant. Some credence is given to Sarah's explanation that the family are at fault for not permitting her to meet Alejandro openly at home. David acknowledges the existence of dual standards by which the men and the women are separately judged. And most importantly, Sierra himself recognizes his responsibility. It is he who finally puts an end to the discord by asserting his authority, rejecting hypocrisy, and ensuring Sarah's continued acceptance by the family. For the theatre audiences of 1937 in Mexico, there were one or two lessons in tolerance here. On the one hand, any innate upper- or middle-class prejudice against communist politics was implicitly questioned, while on the other hand any strict Catholic attitudes toward sexual behavior were countered by a strenuous liberalism.

The family's ability to survive is demonstrated in act 3 by a return to the setting of a mealtime. By contrast with his absence throughout most of act 1, Sierra is now on stage for almost the whole of the act. He deals with the problems of each member of the family in turn, showing a protective interest and a spirit of self-sacrifice. He places the family's needs above the demands of the rent collector. He makes a determined effort to understand Julio's beliefs and to accept his actions. At the end of the play the scene is set for the family's dispersal—a consequence of economic constraints and individual needs—but the crisis has served to strengthen the basis of their unity. In their final words the Sierras express their optimism.

> *Señora Sierra.* Estaremos separados de todos nuestros hijos casi, ellos estarán separados entre sí, y no sé por qué me parece que tú y yo y ellos estamos unidos por primera vez. No lo entiendo.
> *Sierra.* Yo tampoco. Probablemente porque no hemos matado los deseos de nuestros hijos. Creo que hemos hecho bien, pero no sé si habremos hecho bastante.

> (*Señora Sierra.* We'll be separated from all our children almost, they'll be separated from each other, and I don't know why I feel that you and I and they are united for the first time. I don't understand it.
> *Sierra.* Nor do I. Probably because we haven't killed off the wishes of our children. I think we've done the right thing, but I don't know whether we'll have done enough.)

In their different ways, both these characters are displaying a degree of self-assessment and self-awareness. Sra. Sierra juxtaposes her logical sense of things coming to an end, and entering a new era, with her intuitive feeling that the bond between them has been increased. Sierra recognizes that the fuller unity has probably been created by the parents' greater flexibility, tolerance, and understanding. His last clause sounds a note of caution, which has the felicitous effect of leaving the play on an acceptable level of realism, but the audience is given further cause to hope, as the couple look at each other and walk together into the dining room. Whatever their material circumstances, the Sierras have restored the harmony of their own relationship, and with this they are able to face the hardships of the future. In his prologue, Usigli admitted that the thesis implied in *Medio tono* was what he saw as a fundamental element in the Mexican family. It was, he explained, the clan instinct blended with the spirit of sacrifice and resignation that in the face of danger helps them to overcome personal differences (TC 3:445).

So far we have seen how the family faces these moments of danger and how most of the personal differences are overcome. But there is one kind of threat that we have not yet considered: the questioning of the theoretical concept of the family. This is a major reason for Usigli's decision to give the Sierras a communist son. Julio's first comment on the theme is stereotyped and fairly insignificant. "En el seno del partido no hay familia" ("In the bosom of the party there is no family") (TC 1:502). It occurs after a brief series of contentious and conspicuously anticapitalist statements, contrived to introduce him to the audience, and it is simply ignored by all his listeners on stage. Quickly, however, Usigli shows the family's meal interfering with Julio's plans to attend a communist meeting, and Julio interprets the meal as an attempt to buy him off. Still there is a lightness in the repartee, but a little later he adopts a more severe tone in his exasperation: "La familia, la familia, ¡la familia! No se oye más en esta casa, y estamos todo el día criticándonos unos a otros, molestándonos unos a otros . . . quizás odiándonos en potencia" ("The family, the family, the family! That's all you hear in this house, and all day we're criticizing each other, annoying each other . . . perhaps hating each other potentially") (TC 1:504). The most significant thing here is Julio's belief that the seeds of the family's destruction are already contained within it. The ensuing quarrel between Victor, Gabriela, and Julio himself, leading to Victor's haughty departure, provides him with the opportunity of expressing his most clearly doctrinaire statement: "Aquí puede usted ver un ejemplo de la disolución de la familia, esa institución burgués-canibalesca. No nos soportamos ya. Antes de mucho nos devoraremos" ("Here you can see an example of the dissolution of the family, that bourgeois-cannibalistic institution. We can't bear each other already. Before long we'll devour each other") (TC 1:505). It is important for us to notice that Usigli has introduced this communist forecast at a moment in the play when the discord is strident. In the following minutes the audience watches the effects as internal pressure increases and external factors intervene. Julio's words are therefore used by the dramatist as a challenge or test whose results are judged by the audience during the subsequent acts. The addition of a reference to cannibalism takes Julio's comment a step further than orthodox antibourgeois criticism. In a play where eating the Sunday dinner is presented as the symbol of family union, this gives the idea of self-destruction a useful irony.[2]

As we have seen, the family not only survives the stresses applied by internal strife and external misfortunes, it actually emerges strengthened by them. The meal sustains and supports each member. The validity of the family is proven. Julio himself reveals a deep-seated need for his father's affection, understanding, and approval. But a further criticism of a rather different kind is made by both Julio and David in the final act. From their different standpoints, both sons can see the mediocrity of their milieu. Julio is the first to make the point as a part of his explanation why he must fight with the Republicans in the Spanish Civil War. The key words are prompted by his father, confessing that he can not explain his thoughts clearly.

> *Sierra.* No sé por qué no puedo decirte lo que quería. Pensándolo bien, creo que eso es lo que me ha pasado siempre.
> *Julio.* Siempre, padre, y no solo a ti: a todos mis hermanos, a todas las gentes de nuestra clase. No hemos podido expresarnos, decir lo que queríamos. Todas las cosas nos quedan en no sé qué—en un medio tono que nos va bañando como metal, que nos va inmovilizando—y yo no quiero que me pase eso también a mí. No quiero *repetir,* ¿entiendes? lo que se ha repetido hasta ti, hasta tu generación. (TC 1:553)

> (*Sierra.* I don't know why I can't tell you what I wanted to tell you. On reflection, I think that's what has always happened to me.
> *Julio.* Always, father, and not only to you: to all my brothers and sisters, to all the people of our class. We haven't been able to express ourselves, to say what we wanted. Everything turns into, I don't know—into a medium tone that covers us like a metal, that gradually immobilizes us—and I don't want that to happen to me too. I don't want to *repeat,* do you understand? what has been repeated as far as you, down to your generation.)

Julio's decision therefore corresponds to his determination to express himself and thereby to live better. The father's generation participated in the Revolution in their youth (like Sierra himself), but they have lost the ability to act freely, to fulfill themselves, and to live according to their inclination. The new generation is following suit. It is, we notice, a problem attributed to their class. Usigli's use of the term *medio tono* intentionally alludes to common expressions such as *una familia de tono* (a good family) and *de buen tono* (elegant, genteel). In a literal sense the family is of medium social standing or of average refinement. But of course *medio* is also the identifying word to describe the class to which the family belongs; "middle class" and "medium tone" are thus made inseparable. If these criticisms were to be applied by Julio alone they would be perceived—like the attempt to undermine the family's validity—as a specifically communist point of view. The fact that David understands and supports him, however, converts this commentary on the middle class into a more neutral and therefore more influential criticism. David offers a perspective from which the various types of nonconformism by the younger generation in the Sierra family are seen as expressions of a need to avoid repetition of a pattern. It is an instinctive desire for change and a disillusionment with the world that their parents have handed down. David offers the audience a fuller understanding of the term *medio tono:* "Julio quiere salir del medio tono de la clase media de México—quiere ser cualquier cosa, menos mediocre y sofocado" ("Julio wants to get out of the medium quality of Mexico's middle class—he wants to be anything rather than mediocre and suffocated") (TC 1:554). Recognizing that this mediocrity means that the middle class's passions are stifled and that its capacity for action has been converted into dependency, Sr. Sierra recalls his own previous inability to handle the rent collector and his former employer with due severity. And to clinch the point, Usigli returns our attention to David, who actually broadens the scope of his criticism to embrace the whole of the environment in which they live: "la atmósfera de esta planicie de México, de la que debemos irnos todos. Es—medio tono" ("the atmosphere of this plain of Mexico, which we must all leave. It's—fair to middling") (TC 1:555). Only moments before, Víctor has expressed a similar feeling about the environment, complaining that Mexico's winter is imperceptible and wishing for a less benign climate for the sake of greater variety.

It is apparent from this analysis of *Medio tono* that Usigli was using middle-class characters to persuade a middle-class audience that they should examine the quality of their own lives. The play was in fact quite well received by the political left, who could sympathize with a number of its criticisms. For example, the play's journalist, Eduardo, acknowledges the tendency of Mexican newspapers to publish lies, reflecting the people's fear of truth and the nation's adhesion to the "Official Truth." The administrator collecting the rent is presented as unnecessarily harsh and ruthless, in a scene where Usigli exposes capitalism at its worst. Communism is treated on the whole with serious consideration. Usigli clearly disapproved of the idea of a communist meeting being deemed illegal. He was equally critical of the authorities who arrest those attending the meeting and the citizens who penalize them, in particular Gabriela's employer (who dismisses her) and her fiancé (who breaks off the engagement).

Our attention is briefly drawn to the northern origins of this family. Sra. Sierra jokes about the presence of Eduardo, a "civilized" guest surrounded by "savages" from the frontier. But there is some serious comment underlying the differences of character to which she and Eduardo refer: the tendency of people from the capital to smile rather than to laugh openly like the northerners. This smile becomes a disguise for their feelings. If there is some intention here to draw a link between this characteristic and the *medio tono* of the middle class, the question arises as to why Usigli chose to make the Sierras a northern family. The explanation gives us an important insight into his treatment of the middle class. In his prologue to the play, Usigli explained that the family was intended to appear frank, noisy, and likeable and that he chose characters from the north so that they would have a resistance and optimism not found among the native people of the high plateau in the center (TC 3 : 441–42).[3] This means that despite its negative characteristics (its *medio tono,* above all), Usigli's middle-class family possesses positive attributes and the potential to rise above its mediocrity. He uses northern characters to heighten the effects by adding their greater vigor to the typical Mexican middle-class family's capacity to make sacrifices and to face hardships with resignation. Far from condemning that social class, the play ultimately suggests that even within the mediocrity, sacrifice, and resignation there is something for us to admire.

Although the collective identity of the family, with Sr. and Sra. Sierra at its head, prevents us from isolating any character as the play's protagonist, there is an important subplot based in the relationship between Gabriela and Eduardo. Their romance not only helps to introduce us to the family as a whole but becomes the first major focus of interest. It is Eduardo's invitation to dinner that forms the core of act 1. (Only when the various crises are introduced at the end of the act does the emphasis change.) Gabriela encourages the attentions of Eduardo even though she is engaged to Carlos (who is never on stage). When Carlos breaks off the engagement, the way seems clear for the romance to blossom. But after a month Gabriela abruptly brings their relationship to an end. For a full understanding of the implications of this subplot, it is necessary for us to examine the nature of Gabriela's feelings toward Eduardo.

From the beginning, several members of the family allude to her duplicity. At this stage, she herself merely presents it as a precaution because Carlos seems capable of forgetting her. It is not long, however, before the audience is made aware of Gabriela's complex feelings. Now coquettish, now tender, now cool, she enjoys his kisses but dislikes the way he disturbs her: "Yo estoy disgustada conmigo, con mi debilidad" ("I'm displeased with myself, with my weakness") (TC 1:507). In act 3 she explains her reasons for breaking off their relationship. Her most forthright words concern the social and economic circumstances in which they both find themselves. He is out of work, whereas she now has a job. She cannot, she says, marry a man without money. Moreover, she points out the (slight) difference in their ages: she could not marry a man younger than herself. Besides, her family now depends on her work for their livelihood, and it is therefore a matter of survival. All of this constitutes a rational case, but, like Eduardo, we do not find it fully convincing. The missing truth eventually emerges in a more obliquely expressed fashion. After showing her desire for his embraces, she confesses: "No sabes cómo he pensado en ti todas las noches. No me dejas vivir ya. Tengo miedo de quererte demasiado. Miedo de mí. Yo no me casaría nunca contigo—después. Y no quiero eso" ("You don't know how I've thought of you every night. You don't let me live anymore. I'm afraid of loving you too much. Afraid of myself. I would never marry you—afterward. And I don't want that.) (TC 1:559). We have only to connect these words with her lack of interest in Eduardo as a partner in marriage to realize that her feelings are of sexual desire. Her passion, her temptations, and her fears belong to the sexual theme underlying various other facets of the play. Sarah's pregnancy and her father's womanizing are the notable cases.

In perspective, we are able to see Gabriela's dilemma as symptomatic of the drives and constraints shared by the family as a whole. It is Carlos, training to be an engineer, who attracts her to the idea of marriage, with prospects of security, comfort, and a good social status. Eduardo represents an alternative kind of attraction, away from the safe and moderate behavior encouraged by family life. Going to the communist meeting with Eduardo will, she says, be a pretext to escape from the family (TC 1:510). In the end, she comes to terms with her conflicting impulses. Having seen Carlos for the snob and hypocrite that he is, she is determined not to return to the hypocrisy of marrying him. On the other hand, she has also resolved not to compromise her moral status with Eduardo. Too weak to be confident of success, she refuses to give him her new address. Gabriela chooses self-control rather than passion, service to her parents rather than self-indulgence, and security, respectability, and morality instead of excitement. She opts, in other words, for the *medio tono* of her class. Since her decision becomes an aspect of the generally positive ending of the play, in which the family's *medio tono* enables it to overcome adversity, there seems little doubt that Usigli saw it as essentially correct.

The Church, however, denounced the play as immoral. At the time, a League of Decency made regular assessments of films and theatrical productions and distributed leaflets in churches to indicate its judgments. Usigli's play was classified as unsuitable for Catholics to watch. We might speculate on the reasons for such a censorship of *Medio tono*. In this play, the father figure has caused his wife and family great distress through his philandering. He and his wife seem to rediscover their love for each other. But his wife forgives and overlooks his past dismeanors while he himself fails to apologize or express any regret. Could it have been inferred that Usigli was, if not condoning his behavior, attributing little importance to it? The youngest daughter has committed the sin of intercourse outside marriage, simultaneously threatening the respectability of the family's name. After suffering a fairly brief period of hostility, she is treated gently by her parents and eventually restored to the family's embrace. Her conduct is partly excused in the light of her parents' admission of some responsibility, and her need for money receives the same generous response as those of other members of the family. In the eyes of the Church in 1937, this might have appeared too close to condoning her action. Of course, there are are other instances of sexual behavior with which the Church would not have wished the audience to sympathize: Gabriela's flirtatiousness; Víctor's readiness to follow his father's example. In fact, Sr. Sierra displays an understanding and generosity toward Víctor that exceeds expectation when he hands his son a large sum of money precisely to facilitate his success with a beautiful woman. And this, despite the fact that Víctor has refused to promise to reform. It is an attitude that the Church was bound to find too liberal.

Reviewing *Medio tono* in *El Universal Ilustrado,* the critic

"Marco Aurelio" faulted the play on numerous counts. He found it "una comedia de factura ligera y vulgar" ("an insubstantial and vulgar comedy") impaired by exaggeration in the portrayal of a northern family and by a lack of formal balance.[4] While admitting the lightness and the exaggeration, I would reject the idea that these features necessarily constitute a fault. They ensure that a potentially humdrum subject matter becomes entertaining on stage. As for the question of vulgarity, I would suggest that the complaint is symptomatic of the very prejudices (whether social, religious, or ethical) that the play was designed to examine. But in the last aspect of his criticism, Marco Aurelio has indeed made a telling point. *Medio tono* ambitiously attempts to depict a family of nine. Even the outsider, Eduardo, competes with the family for the audience's interest. Although Usigli did not attempt to give them all equal attention, he certainly failed to study some of them in the depth that they deserved (Gabriela and Julio, for example), while allocating more time than was necessary to others (David, Enriqueta, Víctor). The problem was created by the mistaken intention to introduce the greatest possible variety of psychological traits and emotional pred- icaments. As a consequence, the audience lacks a clear sense of focus. Another aspect of this deficiency is the slack correlation between the three acts. At first Gabriela's romance seems to be the play's main topic, but after the first act it yields to the theme of a family's reaction to a series of crises. We therefore miss the tautness that is a hallmark of Usigli's very best plays.

On the other hand, it can readily be understood why—according to the same critic quoted above—the opening night of *Medio tono* constituted an overall success for author and actors.[5] This, the first of Usigli's plays to be performed in Mexico City, already showed some of the talent that was to blossom later. The introductory scene is skillfully written to infuse a sense of expectancy and bustle. As Sra. Sierra and Gabriela prepare the table before the guest's arrival, they show their agitation and excitement by breaking a vase. This allows Usigli to use confused and interrupted dialogue, shouts from adjacent rooms, and constant movement as the two women repeat- edly hurry on and off stage—all of which serves to give the au- dience an impression of watching the routine activities of a household. Then the newcomer, Eduardo, fulfills a role on behalf of the audience by meeting and reacting to each member of the family in turn. Various types of humor serve to entertain us and to prevent the deepening crisis from creating an atmosphere of gloom. Humor based on character is typified by the behavior of Víctor when he first appears. He ignores the guest until prompted, shows him no courtesy, and jokes undiplomatically about the number of boy-friends that Gabriela brings home. Frequently it is the language that creates the humor. Julio, for example, playfully pretends to misunderstand his brother's abuse, thus scoring a political point.

> *Víctor.* Es una mujer de sociedad, idiota.
> *Julio.* De sociedad idiota. Es la primera cosa inteligente que te oigo decir en tu vida. (TC 1:513)

> *Víctor.* She's a woman of society, stupid.
> *Julio.* Society's stupid. That's the first intelligent thing I've heard you say in your life.)

Bathos sometimes introduces a mocking effect or relieves the tension of a situation, as in Sra. Sierra's response to Eduardo's passionate evocation of the effects of love on the young.

> *Eduardo.* Es amor nuestra mirada sana, son amor nuestros cabellos vivos y brillantes, nuestra piel sin arrugas, nuestros dientes sin caries, nuestras manos sin falta; nuestra risa más estúpida, nuestra palabra más vacía, es amor, fé en el amor, esperanza en el amor.
> *Senora Sierra.* Siento mucho que sea así, y que los cabellos de usted y sus dientes estén enamorados de Gabriela . . . (TC 1:530)

> (*Eduardo.* Our healthy gaze is love, our rich and shining hair, our skin without wrinkles, our teeth without decay, our hands without blemish are love; our most foolish laughter, our emptiest words, are love, faith in love, hope in love.
> *Sra. Sierra.* I'm very sorry that it should be so, and that your hair and your teeth are in love with Gabriela . . .)

Despite the general slackness of the play's structure, many individual moments can be enjoyed for their skillfully created dramatic tension. One of the most effective methods is for a character to hold his fellow characters and the audience in suspense. Sierra, for example, puzzles his wife with his moody reticence near the end of act 1. For a few minutes, the explanation is withheld and various theories are tested before he admits to being unemployed (TC 1:515–17). Clearly, the revelation is all the more forceful as a result of the delay. Another frequent and versatile use of dramatic tension occurs when the relationship between the characters on stage undergoes a sharp transition. Probably the best example is found in the third act, when the administrator's deceptively amicable disposition changes into ruthless arrogance, before Julio finally converts him into a terrified and humiliated spectacle (TC 1:549–52).

And a further indication of Usigli's finesse as a dramatist is the use of objects, situations, and behavior to encapsulate ideas. The quality of furniture strikingly represents the alteration of the family's fortune. Gabriela's framed photograph is used to heighten our awareness of Eduardo's shifting attitude to his love for her (at first he pockets it, and later he returns it with resignation to its place on the piano). But the most original of the devices is Martín's dog. The family's refusal to allow the dog in the house represents the rules and limitations binding Martín. At key moments in the play he attempts to bring in the dog, openly or stealthily. The two particularly effective instances occur at the end of acts 1 and 2. In the first case, the atmosphere is tense with news of Sierra's unemployment. Martín's arrival with his barking dog breaks the tension, causes a temporary sense of irritation, but finally helps to close the act with a spirit of family harmony. At the end of the next act the family has fallen silent over Sarah's pregnancy. Again the sudden appearance of Martín and his dog breaks the spell. But this time there is a continuation of the serious tone until the curtain. The young boy with his pet creates a sense of incongruity and bathos, his problem being reduced to genuinely insignificant proportions by the scale of Sarah's problem. His innocence contrasts vividly with the family's sense of scandal. Even the third act closes—or, rather, almost closes—with a recurrence of the same motif. Martín enters into the spirit of self-sacrifice by offering to sell his dog. But Sierra demonstrates that feelings are more important to him than money by refusing to accept the offer, and they all acclaim the dog's admission into the bosom of the family.

La familia cena en casa

Usigli's interest in the theme of the Mexican family continued with *La familia cena en casa* (The family dines at home) (1942). As in *Medio tono,* this comedy traces the course of a crisis in which the family comes under threat, saves itself, and, in doing so, learns something about itself. A mealtime is again taken as the focal point, the occasion that proves the family's reality and identity, and the forum for exchanges of opinion. But the comparison between the two plays goes little further. In *La familia cena en casa* the family is far from middle class, and the meals are large social gatherings attended by the nobility, the political élite, foreign businessmen, and celebrities from the world of entertainment. In the earlier play the main piece of misfortune (the fall from grace of Sierra's employer) has an external source and the virtual lack of plot is an important dramatic weakness. In *La familia cena en casa,* the misfortune derives directly from actions of members of the family, and a strong plot is created from their efforts to redeem the situation.

The setting for act 1 is a lavish social evening at the home of the Torres-Mendoza family. With her three daughters, Sra. Torres-Mendoza welcomes and entertains the high-society guests. When the party is in full swing, her son Carlos bursts onto the stage, half-drunk, and presents a tartily dressed cabaret dancer, Beatriz, as his new bride. The guests leave immediately, only one of them, Fernando, staying behind to toast the couple. But the scene has been a practical joke: Carlos has hired Beatriz to play the part of his bride in order to create a scandal. Sra. Torres-Mendoza then resolves to restore the family's tarnished prestige. Carlos and Beatriz will be married, and the cabaret dancer will be trained to become a lady. At a future social evening all those who have snubbed her will accept her gracefully and submissively. Act 2 occurs three months later, on the evening of this party. In the intervening period Beatriz has learned her new role to perfection and has been warmly accepted by the family (except Carlos). But Sra. Torres-Mendoza's son and daughters are preparing to boycott the occasion for a different reason. They believe that their dead father acquired the family fortune dishonorably. It was distress over this news that led Carlos to seek the family's humiliation. Promised a clarification later, all the family stay for the introduction of Beatriz to the social world and the consequent restoration of their good name. Act 3 presents the scene after the triumph of the evening and the departure of the guests. Sra. Torres-Mendoza produces evidence to satisfy her son and daughters that no dishonorable deed was committed by their father. For her part, Beatriz has been accepted by everyone, including Carlos, who now declares his love for her. She chooses, however, to leave the family, divorce Carlos, and make a new life with Fernando.

As this synopsis shows, although the heart of the play is the Torres-Mendoza family, a complementary theme is the progress of Beatriz. The two aspects combine on numerous levels. Firstly, the question of social class is treated in different ways by the Torres-Mendozas and Beatriz. Secondly, the response to men by the three daughters differs from that of Beatriz. Thirdly, the audience's curiosity is divided between the family's efforts to exact its revenge and Beatriz's transformation and emotional orientation. In the course of the action, both the family and Beatriz benefit from the exceptional circumstances that they have shared. Sra. Torres-Mendoza finally admits to Beatriz, "Tú pareces habernos enseñado muchas cosas, y en cambio nosotros no parecemos haberte enseñado nada" ("You seem to have taught us many things, and we on the other hand do not appear to have taught you anything") (TC 2:141). But as we shall see, Beatriz has been given new prospects and a chance to reassess her life by her association with the family. For the sake of convenience, I shall separate the two complementary aspects, beginning with an examination of the Torres-Mendoza family and their society.

The curtain rises to display an elegant set. In all three acts the action occurs in the main reception hall, whose marble fireplace, antique furniture, tapestry, and paintings contrive to persuade the audience that they are in an aristocratic household. Francisco, the butler, wearing a dinner jacket and white gloves, adds a good-natured gentility to the atmosphere. The opening of the play is dominated by the characters' excited and nervous anticipation before the arrival of the guests. With the exception of a short dialogue about Carlos, we notice that for several minutes the topic of conversation is thoroughly trivial: whether Sra. Torres-Mendoza ought to be wearing a dress that she has already worn in Paris and New York, how many pieces of jewelry are appropriate, which famous actor, bullfighter, or boxer they have invited, which guests have telephoned to give their apologies for not attending, and so forth. If Usigli delays the arrival of the first outsider, it is, of course, to give the audience an impression of the family itself: good-humored, preoccupied with their appearance and their status, wealthy, and banal.

In his letter to a fellow dramatist before the play's completion, Usigli foresaw technical difficulties: "Entre los muchos problemas que ofrece esta comedia figura la treintena de invitados del primer acto. Un absurdo cinematográfico, pero necesario a pesar de todo según creo. Sin esa treintena de invitados mixtos, todo está perdido, como puede usted ver. Pondré en resolverlo mi esfuerzo más auténtico" ("Among the many problems offered by this comedy are the thirty-odd guests in the first act. A cinematographic absurdity, but necessary in spite of everything I believe. Without those thirty-odd assorted guests, everything is lost, as you can see. To resolve the problem I shall apply the most genuine effort").[6] In the event, he overcame the problem in a masterful way. The guests arrive in groups, each of which is subjected to gentle satire. We observe the American relative who needs to have every joke translated, the Argentine diplomat who arrives in golfing clothes, the Countess who disguises her envy with slyly derogatory remarks, the French family with a pride in their name (la señora de Leclerc de Leclerc-Rocha and her daughter Graziella Leclerc-Rocha Leclerc), the boxer with a pride in his biceps, and so forth. Once they have been introduced, they move either to the back of the stage or offstage, forming larger groups, each of which holds its own conversation. If Usigli found this abundance of characters necessary, it was surely because he wished to overwhelm the audience, not only with the grand scale of the occasion but with the sheer vanity of social types welcomed by the Torres-Mendoza family. As we shall see later, the variegated nature of this social landscape is one object of his criticism. At first, however, the more obvious focus of the social comment is the ridiculous quality of the guests, reflected in the emptiness of their conversation and the affected nature of their behavior. Usigli's great dramatic talent is demonstrated here in a carefully orchestrated arrangement of conversations. Two groups in different corners of the stage speak simultaneously in loud voices; during a brief lull, words from the Torres-Mendozas' conversation intervene; two other groups then take over with their simultaneous dialogues; they are followed by the Torres-Mendozas, and then a further two groups, and so on. What emerges out of this patterned arrangement of noisy, confused, banal conversation is a vivid caricature. The audience is certainly left in no doubt about the pretentiousness, superficiality, and absurdity of the whole event. At this point Carlos drunkenly announces his marriage to a hostess from the Waikikí nightclub. A scandalized silence is a prelude to a few barbed comments from the countess and the hasty departure of the guests. With this display of snobbery, the visitors round off the unfavorable impression that they have been creating. It should be noted that Sra. Torres-Mendoza and her daughters behave differently from their guests. Their efforts to put Beatriz at her ease and make her welcome is not missed by the audience, who naturally mark this down as a point in the family's favor.

Having portrayed the broad characteristics of the Torres-Mendozas' society, and having established the audience's amused hostility toward that society, Usigli proceeds in the following acts to analyze it in greater detail through the dialogue between some of its members and two of its critics. One of the complaints that Beatriz makes after her successful debut—one of her reasons for being unable to feel at ease—concerns the hypocrisy of the guests, who disguise their base desires with a mask of respectability: "Mientras hablaba y bailaba esta noche con los invitados, me pareció que estaba yo de nuevo en el cabaret. Todos decían las mismas cosas y buscaban lo mismo, pero de un modo respetable y falso, que no me gusta" ("While I was talking and dancing this evening with the guests, I felt that I was back in the nightclub. They were all saying the same things and trying to get the same out of it, but in a respectable and false way, which I don't like") (TC 2:134). Sra. Mendoza gives this criticism her seal of approval. But Beatriz's discomfort goes deeper than this: "Pero, además, las bebidas eran auténticas, y, de pronto, me sentí insegura. Más que un cabaret, esto parecía otra cosa, y sentí miedo de ligarme a todas esas gentes . . . de estar condenada a ellas" ("But what's more, the drinks were real, and, suddenly, I felt unsure of myself. Rather than a nightclub, this seemed like something else, and I felt afraid of being associated with all those people . . . of being condemned to them") (TC 2:134-35). What preoccupies Beatriz is the sense that this high-society party has in some way been more squalid than a nightclub, its atmosphere perhaps more appropriate to a brothel. If a former hostess feels soiled by such company, the condemnation is powerful indeed. Moreover, Fernando adds the criticism that money has spoiled them (TC 2:137). This society recognizes that wealth is its pivot. The Torres-Mendoza family may have acquired its money only recently, but the nobility, the political hierarchy, the business community, and foreign VIPs readily admit them and even bow to their will. A good deal of attention is paid, moreover, to the source of these people's wealth. Usigli leaves us in no doubt that financial fraud has played its part. Faced with Carlos's anxiety over rumors that his father acquired the family fortune by theft, Sra. Torres-Mendoza comments revealingly, "En todo caso no seríamos los únicos ladrones que hay aquí. Fíjense en tantos de nuestros amigos" ("In any case, we would not be the only thieves here. Look at many of our friends") (TC 2:115).

It is interesting to consider how far Usigli exonerates or condemns the deceased Torres-Mendoza himself. Because of Carlos's shame and anguish, the audience becomes extremely curious to discover how the family came by its wealth. Although the issue is raised in the middle of act 2, it is not resolved until late in the final act—a suspension of information that increases the importance and the impact of the clarification when it eventually comes. Carlos has been told that his father stole from the Ramírez-Rosas family. His mother's first reactions are not to make an outright denial of the charge but to show her dismay that her children should lend credence to such a defamatory story. For the time being, she restricts herself to emphasizing the family's justifiable honor and affirming her pride in her husband. This hints at Torres-Mendoza's innocence, but I suggest that the effect of her making no clear statement at first is to leave a slight uncertainty with the audience, and that this uncertainty influences our ultimate judgment. In act 3 Sra. Torres-Mendoza reveals the full facts, substantiating her explanation with signed documents. Many years previously, the Torres-Mendozas were poor and the Ramírez-Rosas family rich. At the time of his death, however, Ramírez-Rosas had contracted so many debts that the family's fortune would be completely lost if they were repaid. To avoid repayment to his creditors, the dying Ramírez-Rosas came to an arrangement with Torres-Mendoza. The latter was to hold all the money until the debts were no longer legally redeemable and then return it to the Ramírez-Rosas family. This is precisely what Torres-Mendoza did. In addition, he skillfully invested his collaborator's money and made a fortune with it before returning the original sum. It is noticeable that in two ways Usigli shows the Torres-Mendozas' behavior to be generous. While the full amount was in Torres-Mendoza's hands, he regularly sent a proportion of the earnings to the Ramírez-Rosas family as living expenses. His widow has been continuing the practice. This information provides a more than satisfactory account as far as Carlos and his sisters are concerned, and young Enrique Ramírez-Rosas acknowledges his error and becomes humbly apologetic. The atmosphere of rejoicing (stipulated in the stage directions) leaves us in no doubt that the honor of the family is intact. There is more than a hint, however, that Usigli distances himself from this outright approval. In particular we notice the self-criticism of Sra. Torres-Mendoza, once she feels confident that the general effect of her explanation has been successful.

> *Carlos.* No sé cómo fui tan imbécil que pude creer. . . . ¡Perdóname, madre!
> *Sra. Torres-Mendoza.* ¿Por qué? La acción de tu padre al ayudar al padre de Enrique no fue muy limpia. Lo acusaron de ser demasiado ventajoso, demasiado . . . revolucionario en los negocios.
> *Carlos.* ¡Pero honrado! (TC 2: 132)

> *(Carlos.* I don't know how I could be so foolish as to believe. . . . Forgive me, Mother!
> *Sra. Torres-Mendoza.* Why? Your father's action on helping Enrique's father was not very honest. They accused him of being too eager to take advantage, too . . . revolutionary in business deals.
> *Carlos.* But honorable!)

There is, of course, a sharp contrast between Carlos's notion of honorable behavior and his mother's sense of integrity. According to Carlos, society can readily respect the family provided that the letter of the law is obeyed. Sra. Torres-Mendoza, on the other hand, acknowledges a criterion higher than the law. Let us make explicit what she presumably feels to be dishonest: her husband took part in a conspiracy to deprive creditors of money that was rightfully theirs. It is a criticism, therefore, of the double standards applied by that wealthy sector of Mexican society. Moreover, the use here of the term "revolucionario" should not be overlooked. Torres-Mendoza had been a revolutionary in his youth, we are informed in act 2. To their aristocratic colleagues, his being a revolutionary implied robbing and killing, but Sra. Torres-Mendoza feels the need to add that "También se puede ser revolucionario y gente decente" ("You can be a revolutionary and a decent person, too") (TC 2:114). To be revolutionary in business deals must mean—if we retain the aristocrats' use of the term—to be both unorthodox and fraudulent. But in Mexico, as we know from *El gesticulador* and other plays, "revolucionario" is also a euphemism that bestows respectability. The same process of distortion and hypocrisy that legitimizes the false use of that term validates fraudulent business affairs.

In describing the society that Usigli depicts in *La familia cena en casa,* it is difficult to use a more precise definition than "wealthy" or "upper class." The Torres-Mendozas are, strictly speaking, nouveaux riches, whereas their associates vary from the titled aristocracy to the political elite and national celebrities. This indistinctness of social class—this amorphous, tenuous, rootless quality—is one of the major objects of Usigli's criticism in the play. In Fernando's words, the Torres-Mendozas are like mercury, floating between all the social classes all the time (TC 2:123). When asked by Sra. Torres what he finds wrong with their social class, Fernando replies more explicitly: "Que no tiene clase, señora. Nunca saben ustedes de qué lado están, oscilando entre Porfirio Díaz y Plutarco Elías Calles, entre azul y buenas noches, entre el diablo y el mar azul" ("It's that you have no class, señora. You people never know which side you are on, wavering between Porfirio Díaz and Plutarco Elías Calles, between day and night, between the Devil and the deep blue sea") (TC 2:136). Mixing with both the surviving reactionary elements of pre-Revolutionary Mexico, and the brutal and authoritarian post-Revolutionary politicians, they have nothing but money to represent reality. As a middle-class family, they would be magnificent, continues Fernando, but instead they are lofty and ephemeral. In place of a thoroughly Mexican outlook, they have inclinations toward the United States and Europe. This indictment by Fernando is corroborated by the extraneous evidence in Usigli's prologue: "Es una familia venida a más, como las conozco, que . . . representa la falta de realidad y de raíces de las clases altas de México" ("It is a family that has struck it rich, like some that I know, which . . . represents the lack of reality and roots of Mexico's upper classes") (TC 3:610). In the final analysis, it would have to be admitted that Usigli's severe attitude to the family in this prologue—written at the planning stage—is considerably attenuated in the play itself. According to the prologue, the family attempts to put itself in order and discover its reality but finds itself humiliated and "condenada a substistir en el aire y a desaparecer con él" ("condemned to subsist in the air and to disappear with it") (TC 3:612). Such a conclusion would be fully consistent with the negative implications that I have discussed above. However, the final version of the play does not possess that degree of consistency. Beatriz's departure could be regarded as a humiliating development for the family, but Usigli makes no attempt to make it so. Instead he draws our attention to the family's various measures to reform and to come down to earth. Estela will open a children's hospital, Gilda will open an art gallery, Carlos will devote himself (perhaps) to his profession, and Sra. Torres-Mendoza will gradually bring her extravagant social life to an end. There is an emphasis on humility rather than humiliation, and a lesson appears to have been learned. This is consistent with the overall light in which the Torres-Mendozas are depicted. As we saw previously, it is the guests who receive the heavily satirical treatment, whereas the family emerges as a warm, generous, and lively set of people despite their faults. It may well be that the relatively benign approach grew out of the dramatist's own fondness for his creations. It is also possible that a harshly antagonistic attitude seemed counterproductive, given the presence of Torres-Mendoza types in the audience. For whatever reason, what the play gains in warmth, it inevitably loses in critical force.

Much of the explicit commentary on the family and its social background is voiced by Fernando Rojas. The Fernando who first appears on stage in act 1 is submissive and indecisive, an unenthusiastic suitor of Gilda—the eldest daughter—and a novelist who cannot bring pen to paper. With the bullfighter, the boxer, and the actor, he represents what Usigli called "la curiosidad y el esnobismo de las capas inferiores" ("the curiosity and the snobbery of the lower levels") (TC 3:610). It is only near the end of the act, when he demonstrates a fascination with Beatriz, that the audience begins to pay him any attention. His role in the play is to set an example by discovering his previous errors, to criticize high society from a new, detached position, and to complement Beatriz in the search for an alternative world. The agent of his reform and reassessment is Beatriz—or his love for her—and the first product is a completed novel. Both he and Beatriz, he argues, have remained servile in their respective environments; now self-expression, decisive action, and rebellion against formal constraints are his new ideals (which he attempts to communicate to Beatriz in act 2 and to Sra. Torres-Mendoza in act 3). The most satisfactory aspect of Fernando's role in the play is that he forms a contrast with the Torres-Mendozas and helps Beatriz to reject the family totally. The weakest feature is the vagueness of his alternative targets in life. At the end, he and Beatriz depart together to "inventar nuestra clase" ("invent our class") (TC 2:146). Theirs will be a "real" class of "real" people: "será viva . . . porque no partirá del dinero, y será fuerte porque cerrará las fronteras" ("it will be living . . . because it will not derive from money, and it will be strong because it will close all the frontiers") (TC 2:136–37). In other words, the "class" that he dreams of creating is the reverse of the Torres-Mendozas' society. It is not a social class in the sense of a layer or rank but a group of people with common values. In fact, we know from the prologue to this play that as a general principle Usigli lamented Mexico's lack of social classes. In his country, all that there had been were illusions of class and all that remained were "gentes dispersas sin un destino nacional, intenciones de clase, borradores de clase" ("people scattered with no national destiny, intentions of class, rough drafts of class") (TC 3:614–15). The Torres-Mendoza family therefore constitutes a specific instance of a more general national weakness. In his view, only through social classes can people unite in a common purpose for the national good. While it means that communism has lost all chance of success in Mexico, it also implies that politicians will continue their equivocal practices, favoring the poor at election time and the well-to-do afterwards (TC 3:615).

As I noted above, however, most of the play's emphasis is placed on the need to break with triviality in order to seek freedom of expression and self-fulfilment. A subsidiary aspect of this theme is love and desire, with their respective repercussions in male and female behavior and in social customs and values. The point of introducing a nightclub hostess into the family (rather than any other girl from the lower levels of society) is to draw out the sexual aspect of hypocrisy. Beatriz was thrown out of her middle-class family by parents scandalized by a single mistake committed with the young man whom she loved. Friends who had committed the same error took up prostitution in order to make a living, but she hunted for jobs. She lost one employment in a government office for rejecting the sexual harrassment of her boss, and everywhere else—she complains—she came up against the same kind of persecution (TC 2:108). At least in the nightclub she says that she has merely been acting a piece of fiction, whereas in the Torres-Mendozas' social gatherings the intentions—though respectably disguised—have an uncomfortable realism. One role of Beatriz in this play, therefore, is to expose the vulnerability of women to men's sexual advances.

It is female characters who dominate the stage during this play. Apart from Fernando Rojas, the men are noticed mainly in their relationship to women rather than in their own function as individuals. Some are thinking of marriage (Felipe, Fernando), while others are not (Carlos, the bullfighter, the boxer). The effect of this is to emphasize the various influences of men's attentions on different women. Sra. Torres-Mendoza's daughters offer three examples. In Usigli's careful stage directions, we notice the relative prominence given to degrees of sexual attractiveness. Gilda, "evidentemente fea, pero llena de simpatía" ("obviously ugly, but a thoroughly nice person"), is chosen as the one who will be neither desired nor married. Elena is described as "la beldad de la familia; alta, flexible, no podría decirse que es hemosa, pero tiene atracción y una sonrisa irresistible" ("the good-looker of the family; tall, supple, she could not be called beautiful, but she is attractive and has an irresistible smile"); she is the divorced daughter, unable to have children, and represents desirability rather than marriage. And the actress playing Julieta must have a plain face and a slim figure, her youth and overall charm being sufficient to suggest that Julieta is both desirable and marriageable.

Beatriz's experiences therefore highlight a feminine response to society. In addition, however, they reveal the differences that love makes to a relationship. Puzzled by Fernando's failure to show any desire for her, Beatriz believes his love for her to be incomplete (TC 2:138). But Fernando helps her to understand that desire does not need to be openly exhibited. Love and sexual attraction, he explains, are related in a special way. The desire that comes with love, as opposed to simple desire, has a certain intimacy and modesty. Besides, he continues, desire springs from love, but not the reverse: "El sexo no es una causa, es una consecuencia" ("Sex is not a cause, it is a consequence") (TC 2:138). But Fernando himself must learn a lesson: that he should show his desire for Beatriz more candidly. This romance is therefore linked to the central theme of the play in that it helps the couple to find their true selves and their true feelings at the same time as they recognize their relationship with others.

In his play *Pygmalion,* Bernard Shaw gave a modern social framework to the ancient myth in which the artist creates an image of his ideal and falls in love with his creation.[7] To this he added elements from the Cinderella fairy tale. A young girl, taken out of the poverty and ignorance in which her environment has confined her, is trained to speak and behave like a refined lady and accepted by the higher social class of her teacher. There is little doubt that Usigli—a profound admirer of Shaw's, as noted in chapter 1—had Eliza Doolittle's progress in mind when writing the part of Beatriz. Both girls become the object of an experiment whose success will be tested at a major social occasion (the Buckingham Palace garden and the Torres-Mendozas' evening meal). Both find themselves facing a small preliminary test before the big event (Mrs. Higgins's tea party and the countess's visit). Both reach a new point of self-assessment after their successful performance. Both come to terms with their feelings toward the creator of their new self (the counterparts of Henry Higgins being Carlos and Sra. Torres-Mendoza). *Pygmalion*'s ambiguous ending is resolved in Usigli's play by the girl's rejection of marriage to her "creator"—which is precisely the interpretation that Shaw himself recommended in his endnotes. (Even Shaw's Freddy has a counterpart in Fernando, the man preferred to this "creator.") According to critical opinion on *Pygmalion,* "The major didactic achievement of the play is its pointed objectification of the hollowness of social distinctions, and its assertion of the importance of the individual personality which such distinctions obscure."[8] Much the same might be said of *La familia cena en casa,* as the foregoing analysis has indicated. The two plays therefore share both didactic and structural features. In other respects, it must be said, they have quite different appearance and detail. Higgins as an individual is replaced by a whole family with social preoccupations; phonetics simply disappear; the varied ambience gives way to a single wealthy setting.

One feature that this brief excursion into Shavian studies has helped us to see is that Beatriz's transformation becomes the central action of *La familia cena en casa.* For much of the time, she is converted into an actress performing on behalf of the other people. In the nightclub she realized that she was helping to create fiction: "Una no es para ellos más que un manequí (*sic*). . . . Se hacen la ilusión de que están con una amiga. . . . Nosotras aceptamos al amigo y nos hacemos la ilusión de que tomamos una copa" ("For them one is no more than a dummy. . . . They imagine that they are with a girlfriend. . . . We accept the boyfriend and imagine that we are having a drink") (TC 2:109). As the play progresses, her role playing moves two stages further. Firstly, Carlos, who has pretended to love her, persuades her to act the part of his wife. The distortion of truth here operates on several layers simultaneously. Carlos does not love her yet, nor is his purpose merely to perform a practical joke, nor are his family and friends the only humiliated parties (for Beatriz's humiliation is intense). Secondly, Sra. Torres-Mendoza persuades her to take part in a huge charade in which the family and their guests become willing participants. It is important for us to notice how greatly reality is falsified in the course of this charade. Carlos and Beatriz actually attend a civil marriage ceremony, thus fostering the illusion that they love each other and wish to enjoy a life together. Sra. Torres-Mendoza and her daughters accept Beatriz as a member of the family, disguising as far as possible their prejudices against her (though the daughters' efforts are not entirely successful after the enthusiasm of the first night). The whole family creates the impression that the grand party is being held for the sake of its new member. But in reality, of course, it is an act of revenge against those who scorned the family, a measure to restore the Torres-Mendozas to their prime position, and an experiment to prove that any person from any background can eventually be absorbed by this Mexican high society. "Veremos cuál clase absorbe a cuál" ("We shall see which class absorbs which"), vows Sra. Torres-Mendoza (TC 2:100). And this leads us to the last participants in the charade. The guests are not a mere audience; without their willing involvement, the illusion would be incomplete and totally pointless. As Usigli triumphantly demonstrates, there is no problem because this society is perfectly accustomed to accepting superficial appearance as though it were reality. Beatriz looks and acts her part well, therefore, as far as they are concerned, she *is* what she purports to be. Although it is only three months since they abandoned the house to avoid association with a nightclub hostess, the guests succumb to the power exerted by the Torres-Mendozas' wealth and suppress their memory of the past in order to create a fiction from which they can all benefit.

The analysis of *El gesticulador* in chapter 3, showed how Usigli took advantage of metatheatre in order to suggest that Mexican political life involved a kind of theatrical performance. In *La familia cena en casa* Beatriz—like César Rubio—acts a role in a dramatic fiction within the play itself. The dramatic purpose is similar, except that in this case the comment is social rather than political. Let us imagine the Teatro Ideal in Mexico City during the performances of December 1942. That audience watched a theatrical work in which the Torres-Mendozas' grand hall became a stage and the family and guests—led by a fairly reluctant Beatriz—became actors. It was a clear indication for that audience that society tends to transform fiction into a substitute for reality, preferring to live a lie rather than to cope with the truth. The conclusion of *La familia cena en casa* offers some hope that the leading characters have become aware of their error. Beatriz attempts to explain her grasp of reality to Carlos in words that demonstrate the confused state of mind that she must shed: "Me parece ridículo que me ruegue usted, siendo quien es cuando yo soy lo que soy" ("It seems ridiculous to me that you should ask me, being who you are when I am what I am") (TC 2:141). And she tries to explain to him that he is still requiring her to give substance to his illusions, just as he did in the nightclub. Fernando reiterates his determination to free himself from the repetition of society's pattern (in other words, to avoid playing a part in society's script) and to find some basic truths (TC 2:137). Sra. Torres-Mendoza plans to bring her social life to an end, and each daughter chooses her own way to "llegar a alguna parte . . . como diría Beatriz" ("get somewhere, . . . as Beatriz would say") (TC 2:143). In other words, there is little doubt that the overall impact of the final scenes is to suggest the need to avoid merely acting the role that society has created for its members. However, Usigli still implies the need for *invention*. Each member of the family invents a course of action, while Fernando and Beatriz set off to invent their "class," taking with them the novel that one of them has written (that is, invented) about the other. Beatriz's words to Fernando emphasize the interrelation of the fictional and the real: "Llévese su novela . . . pero lléveme a mí con ella" ("Take away your novel . . . but take me away with it") (TC 2:146). She means that her true self will supplant the literary character. But she does not reject the novel; she recognizes it as a creation, a form of expression, and an achievement. We might therefore assume that she and Fernando are now about to create their own substitute for the fiction that society had previously forced on them. Whether it will be any more real is open to doubt.

The nature of this theme—the representation of social life as a form of acting—entails a different approach from the realism of *Medio tono*. In one respect, the play becomes less credible as a direct image of life itself. Can we believe, for example, that Carlos would contrive such a damaging scandal for the reasons given? Is it possible that Beatriz would so readily yield to Sra. Torres-Mendoza's persuasion and become the key figure in a new scheme to deceive others? But what *La familia cena en casa* lacks as a literal reflection of reality it gains in dramatic impact and entertainment. It proves to be a good vehicle for Usigli's doctrine that theatre should be "una forma reconcentrada, poética de la verdad" ("a concentrated, poetic form of truth") (TC 3:297).

Suspense is one of the play's greatest technical assets. Once the scheme to convert a nightclub hostess into a high-class lady is conceived, the audience is full of curiosity to discover whether it will succeed. Three moments are particularly worth attention: two arrivals by the ambassador and one by the countess. The ambassador's late entry in act 1 means that he has missed the scandal and knows nothing of Beatriz. Sra. Torres-Mendoza transforms the potential embarrassment into immediate verification of her claim that Beatriz will be accepted. She introduces her family to him, adds the plain truth that the girl is a hostess from the Waikikí night club, and sits down on the staircase. The ambassador, momentarily disconcerted, quickly accepts the situation and sits obediently beside her, as if to symbolize his willingness to descend to any level on which the family finds itself. With this, the meal is served and the curtain falls, leaving the audience intrigued by potential developments. At the end of act 2, with an artistic touch of symmetry, Usigli brings the ambassador back to the house—early to compensate for his previous error—face-to-face with the new Beatriz at the start of her great occasion. Again his role is to test the success of the ruse, and again he quickly overcomes his scruples and authenticates the scheme, bowing deeply, kissing her hand, and pronouncing the single all-important word, "Señora" (TC 2:126). The countess promises to be a harder case. As we remember, it is she who first rounds on Beatriz and draws attention to her alien qualities. If her prejudice and snobbery could be overcome, Sra. Torres-Mendoza would seem assured of success. Hence the importance of her unexpected appearance in act 2. Uninvited, but determined not to miss such a major social occasion, she seeks an invitation by ingratiating herself with the family. Her encounter with the transformed Beatriz is an entertaining scene, in which the following extract is the key moment:

> *Señora Torres-Mendoza.* Siéntate y respira, Carolina. *(Se acerca para saludarla.)* Conoces a Beatriz, ¿Verdad? Es la esposa de Carlos.
> *Condesa. (Viendo a Beatriz con incredulidad.)* ¡No! La . . . bueno, la chica que . . .
> *Beatriz. (Saludando.)* La cabaretera, señora Condesa.
> *Condesa.* ¡Ya lo creo! Lo que pasa es que no la reconocía. *(Le tiende las dos manos.)*
> *Beatriz.* ¿Cómo está usted, señora?
> *Condesa.* Yo estoy trastornadísima, pero tú estás preciosa, hija mía, ¡preciosa!
> *Beatriz.* Es usted muy amable.

Condesa. ¡Usted! ¡Usted! Tutéame, boba. Es lo que se hace en nuestra clase.
Beatriz. Entonces, lo mismo que la mía. (TC 2 : 118–19)

Señora Torres-Menoza. Sit down and catch your breath, Carolina. [*She goes over to greet her.*] You know Beatriz, don't you? She is Carlos's wife.
Condesa. [*Seeing Beatriz with incredulity.*] No! The . . . well, the girl who . . .
Beatriz. [*Greeting her.*] The nightclub hostess, Countess.
Condesa. Of course! The thing is, I didn't recognize you. [*She holds out both hands to her.*]
Beatriz. How are you?
Condesa. I am utterly dazed, but you look delightful, my dear, delightful.
Beatriz. That is very kind of you.
Condesa. You're so formal! Use the *tú* form with me, you silly thing. It's the done thing in our class.
Beatriz. So it's just the same as in mine.

Among the many gems worth picking out in this sparkling piece of irony are the stages in the Countess's change of attitude. Incredulity gives way to embarrassment and hesitation. Once the truth becomes comfortable, she commits herself to a wholehearted display of warmth and removes the social differences. But Beatriz's last comment is an amusing piece of veiled mockery, based on the irony that the Countess is being downgraded by the same process that promotes the nightclub hostess.

Our wish that Beatriz's test should not fail creates a tension that is intensified by a further device in act 2. As the act begins Usigli mystifies us with the signs that Carlos and his sisters are on the point of abandoning the project. For some moments the whole basis of the potentially entertaining scheme appears to be threatened. Later, several other kinds of tension are skillfully introduced into the play. Sometimes the source of the uncertainty lies in the character development and, in particular, in the question of whether Beatriz will choose Fernando or Carlos. A second type of uncertainty derives from misunderstandings, such as the disastrous error caused by Fernando's and Beatriz's misinterpretation of each other's feelings. Yet another technique used to great advantage is the suspension of information. It becomes a matter of great interest to the audience (as well as to Carlos and his sisters) to learn whether or not the family's wealth is based on theft. But instead of providing the answer in act 2, when the question is first raised, Usigli tantalizingly presents ambiguous leads (Sra. Torres-Mendoza's failure to make an outright denial, the proud and defiant placing of her husband's portrait on a prominent wall, and so forth) and withholds the full truth until the final act.

When the story of the family's wealth is eventually revealed, our curiosity is satisfied, even if we are left in doubts over the ethics involved. But the dramatist, as always, has something in reserve— an unexpected revelation that causes a further alteration of perspective. Surprise is used with its most sensational results in act 1, when Carlos scandalizes the guests at dinner. In a more subdued tone, surprise occurs with Beatriz's sudden revelation of her past, modifying the audience's attitude to her moral and social status (act 2, TC 2:107–9). And now, toward the end of the play, Usigli presents the audience (and all but one of the characters) with three consecutive revelations: that the deceased Torres-Mendoza treated the Ramírez-Rosas family with a proper adherence to the agreed conditions; that he was in fact unnecessarily generous with the other family; and that Sra. Torres-Mendoza herself has continued to fund that family through the years, maintaining secrecy to spare them humiliation. With this augmenting succession of disclosures, the dramatist releases powerful emotions. For the young Ramírez-Rosas, this is a moment of utter dejection; for the Torres-Mendozas, one of joy followed by compassion.

Visual effects serve Usigli, as usual, in a variety of ways. To the comments made above on the aristocratic appearance of the set it is worth adding the fact that careful attention is given in the stage directions to the characters' clothing. In general, the purpose is to ensure that the whole set exudes an air of elegance and formality. Against this background, a few individual cases become especially interesting. Harry, an American related to the family, comes to dinner dressed casually but carrying his dinner jacket in a parcel. When he sees what the other men are wearing, he changes into the dinner jacket. It is a sign used to illustrate the guests' desire to produce the correct visual image and the uncertainty caused by the mixture of social types. The Argentine diplomat's golfing clothes are a further amusing example. The matter of Beatriz's attire becomes highly significant. When Carlos carries her onto the stage and stands her on the table, what the audience must be made to see is a girl who "en toda evidencia, es una mujer de la calle" ("quite clearly, is a streetwalker") (TC 2:94). In order to convey this impression strikingly, Usigli requires that she should wear cheap and excessive make-up and a flimsy evening dress in gaudy red. The contrast with the black dresses and expensive jewelry of other women on stage could hardly be greater. Beatriz's appearance throughout the rest of the play reflects her change of status and attitude. For the grand party she wears a pink and black evening dress, which immediately conveys the idea that she has become a lady (though the colors contain a neat reminder of her past). At the end of the play the audience sees her once again in the red dress. Before any words are spoken, therefore, the visual image has made Usigli's point emphatically: Beatriz has rejected her noble identity and returned to her former status. As she explains to Fernando, this dress is her "uniform" (TC 2:146).

A few other visual effects are used to supplement the dialogue and, in some cases, to convey an idea that the spoken words alone could not communicate. There is the use of the staircase as a humble substitute for chairs at the end of act 1 and the use of Torres-Mendoza's portrait as an affirmation of family pride in act 2. But the most ingenious device is reserved for the end of the play. The party is over, the guests have departed, and the family has retired. Francisco, the butler, extinguishes all but one of the lights. But Beatriz encourages Fernando to join her in placing all the chairs on top of the round tables. "Así quedaba todo cuando salía yo del cabaret a estas horas" ("This is how everything was left when I used to leave the nightclub at this hour"), she comments (TC 2:146). The result is striking. Suddenly the aristocratic hall is converted into a nightclub while the audience watches. We vividly recognize the paramount social comment and fully understand Beatriz's rejection of the family. The butler extinguishes the remaining light, giving the audience a sense of witnessing the end of the performance. But then the curtain falls, to complete the idea of one show being contained within another.

While *La familia cena en casa* was still in the planning stage, Usigli considered the challenge posed by the highly serious theme that he had chosen. The social group that he was about to portray—unpopular with most people in Mexico—appeared to belong best in a sober, realist theatre. But with the mild cynicism of a dramatist who had seen the contradictions between ambition and public demand, he decided that one of the first priorities must be to make the public laugh. The play had to be a comedy (TC 3:613–14). I have argued that Usigli's technical expertise and sense of humor served him well in writing a play that is both amusing and thought provoking. Its main inconsistency lies in the treatment of the central family. At times, the evidence suggests that Usigli would have liked to criticize them more severely and satirize them more ruthlessly; in the end, however, he seems to hold a grudging affection for them. It was the inevitable consequence of his choice of comedy, for, as he admitted almost twenty years later, once the process of composition was underway, the characters escaped from his hands and began to live independently (TC 3:618).

6

Psychological Drama: Two Faces of Usigli's Success

In the three-and-a-half years between July 1950 and January 1954, Usigli saw the first performances of no fewer than seven of his plays in Mexico City. Two of them broke records for national theatre. *El niño y la niebla* (The boy and the fog) lasted eight months in the small Teatro del Caracol in 1951, enjoying 450 performances and earning its author twelve thousand pesos (TC 3:720, 722). The following year, *Jano es una muchacha* (Janus is a girl) brought similar receipts with its first hundred performances alone at the Teatro Colón. Usigli's career had undoubtedly reached its apogee. Even then, however, that success was not free from controversy, for although *El niño* was favorably received, *Jano* caused a public scandal and gave rise to accusations that the dramatist was tastelessly seeking a box-office triumph. Historically, therefore, the two plays represent two faces of Usigli's achievement.

But there are anomalies. Although their appearance was separated by only a few months, their composition belonged to different epochs (*El niño* was written as early as 1936). And although the critics regarded one as serious drama and the other as a potboiler, they have certain important features in common. For all its gravity, *El niño* deals with an extraordinary case of pathological madness; and for all its sensational appeal, *Jano* makes a frank and highly serious examination of sexual behavior. Both plays, moreover, take a family as the framework for their action. And finally, both counterbalance a social theme with individual psychological analysis.

With only half of his plays written, Usigli thought that he could see a pattern forming in his dramatic production, a single line with three branches: politics, the Mexican family, and psychopathological cases (TC 3:610). This eventually proved to be an inadequate classification of his work, but it is certainly a useful indicator of his earlier trends.[1] At this point in his career, three of the eighteen plays could possibly be classified as psychopathological: *El niño y la niebla* (1936), *Mientras amemos* (For as long as we

131

Love) (1937–48), and *Otra primavera (Another Springtime)* (1937–
38). A little later, his interest in abnormal psychology was to combine with a historical theme in *Corona de sombra (Crown of Shadows)* (1943). It was also a dominant feature of his entertaining novel
Ensayo de un crimen (Rehearsal for a crime) (1944), where the
psychological causes of the protagonist's determination to commit
the perfect gratuitous murder are unclear until the final pages.[2]
After this, madness itself was not to figure prominently in his
theatre, though the exploration of psychological complexes continued in several plays: old age and solitude in *La función de
despedida* (The farewell performance) (1949); the process of aging
in *Los viejos* (Old people) (1971); the anxieties of motherhood in
Las madres (Mothers) (1949–60); and sexual drives and inhibitions
in *Jano es una muchacha.*[3]

In perspective, it can be seen that rather than constituting a
category in their own right, the plays dealing with mental illness
belong to the important branch of Usigli's dramatic production that
might be termed—more broadly—psychological. The two works
chosen for detailed examination in this chapter are representative
of this aspect of his theatre.

El niño y la niebla

During his period of study in the United States, in 1934 Usigli
heard of an unusual murder case. A woman contrived the death of
her husband by taking advantage of her son's somnambulism to
arrange for him to kill his father while sleepwalking (TC 3:435–36).
The story attracted Usigli for its potential as dramatic material.
Although he made a fundamental alteration to the anecdote, he
developed it into the core of a play about passion and madness. But
he was not intent on converting the sensational features of the real
court case into a light melodrama. The actual event inspired a
meticulous character study, in which a thoroughly humdrum situation develops toward a somber outcome. It is not so much what
happens as why it happens that interests us. In the course of intense
domestic strife, Usigli's characters gradually reveal their psychological problems. Not until the final act do we realize to what extent
pathological mental conditions have determined events.

As the curtain lifts for act 1 we immediately notice a careful
attempt to convey a particular social ambience by means of the set.
The stage is the living room of a wealthy provincial family (in the
script, Durango is named as the location), with nineteenth-century

architecure, violet curtains, and Chippendale-style furniture. However, a certain shabbiness pervades the room, suggesting possible
financial constraints and a definite lack of family pride. Dim lighting
caused by a power cut enhances our sense of disorder (besides
giving us an early visual representation of the fog of the title).
Within a few minutes we know from the conversation that the
action is taking place on the night of 21 May 1920, twenty-four
hours after the assassination of President Venustiano Carranza.
What we are watching on stage therefore acquires an air of authenticity as the image of life in a Mexican family during the post-
Revolutionary period. Eventually we are able to recognize other
reasons besides the search for social realism for this historical
precision. A change of government means new opportunities for
Guillermo Estrada to advance his stultified career. The violent and
disruptive political event in the background serves as a calatytic
agent, hastening an alteration in the family's relationships. The
world outside the domestic scene becomes gradually more remote,
however, until we realize its ultimate irrelevance to private lives and
the individual psyche.

There is a distinctly humdrum air about the situation that develops before our eyes. A husband and wife, married for almost
sixteen years, quarrel bitterly. The immediate causes of their argument—how much freedom to give their teenage son and whether to
move to the capital—prove to be symptomatic of a deeply rooted
resentment. The boy is caught between his father and his mother.
He receives contradictory instructions and a mixture of affection
and indifference. At times he is used as a weapon by one parent to
spite the other. A love triangle completes the ordinariness of this
situation. The wife and her husband's friend secretly desire an
opportunity to start a new life together, but they are unwilling to
seek recourse in a professionally damaging divorce. Into this thoroughly conventional plot, Usigli introduced a unique variation suggested to him by the court case in the United States. The teenager,
who has already shown a tendency to walk in his sleep, approaches
his father in a somnambulent condition and directs a pistol at the
man's head. An involuntary movement from the unsuspecting father causes the boy to stop, turn, and leave the room. A shot off
stage marks the boy's suicide. The mother confesses to her would-
be lover that she attempted to use her son to kill her husband. She
informs him, moreover, that her son had been fully conscious when
he shot himself and that she had done nothing to prevent the
suicide. While the boy's father vainly seeks an explanation, offers
his wife her freedom, and diminishes his career prospects by re-

maining in the provincial town, the mother relinquishes all aspirations for a new relationship and willingly resigns herself to a resumption of married life.

Clearly, the routine nature of the plot is destroyed by the boy's somnambulance and suicide and the woman's attempted murder. Yet the action that we witness on stage rarely looks irrational. Only at the very end of act 1 do we see the first indication of any abnormal behavior, when the boy sleepwalks in the presence of his mother and her friend. Throughout act 2 the action reverts to normality until the last minute, during which the critical murder/suicide episode occurs. And act 3, though amply provided with surprises, contains nothing but arguably rational behavior from beginning to end. On the other hand, the two extraordinary episodes emphatically draw our attention to the problem of understanding these characters. We are already extremely curious to know more about the boy's psychological condition throughout act 2. In the final act Usigli intensifies the investigative atmosphere by endowing the father with that same curiosity. Eventually the focus switches from the boy to the mother, whose own mental state dominates our attention for the last minutes before the curtain falls. In perspective, therefore, we can see that the play's principal source of interest is psychological and that Usigli's dramatic success lies in the convincing revelation of motives.

Guillermo Estrada is presented as a man dominated by a sense of frustrated ambition and failure. In his own eyes, instead of realizing his potential as an architect, he has been limited to menial building work in a provincial town. To the audience this might well seem scant explanation for the depth of his feeling, but more to the point, in his wife's eyes he is a failure (TC 1:467). Marta herself admits that his career has made no progress because he has always yielded to her will to live in isolation. For this submission of his will to hers she calls him cowardly (TC 1:467). Guillermo's invitation from the new president to work at his side in Mexico City is therefore both an immense career success and a symbolic triumph over Marta. His impatience to share the news with their son, Daniel, demonstrates his need not only to be admired by his son but also to be adjudged the victor. Failure in almost sixteen years of marriage has created a sadness and bitterness in him. Void of love, lovemaking, further children, affection, and even mutual interest, the marriage is worth preserving only because of the basis that it offers for Daniel's upbringing. (There is perhaps a hint, too, of the damage that a divorce would cause to Guillermo's career.) Guillermo's relationship with Daniel offers another explanation for his sense of personal failure while illustrating his need to compensate vicariously. Anxious about his son's poor health and physique, he has become overprotective, inhibiting Daniel's freedom of movement and reducing his pleasures. He seems to be striving for an unusual degree of control over Daniel's behavior, as though he were attempting to use his son's life as a substitute for his own diminished prospects.

In his relationship with both Marta and Daniel, Guillermo reveals a conspicuous lack of understanding. How is it, we wonder, that he has never investigated the cause of her anxieties about her family? Is it possible for him not to suspect amorous feelings between his wife and his good friend when they have been meeting for two years in his house? Such ignorance about Marta can be ascribed only to a form of self-centeredness. We know that he once loved her and suffered because of her rejections, and yet Marta is quite convinced about his essential inability to take her feelings into account: "Allí habla tu egoísmo, como siempre" ("That's your selfishness talking, as always") (TC 1:469). In his treatment of Daniel, this egoism becomes all too evident. Insensitive to the boy's self-esteem, he speaks in public of his thin physique and lack of strength (TC 1:454). Insisting on the importance of academic achievement (at the expense of such pleasures as horse riding), Guillermo appears determined to impose his own values on his son and to seek his own fulfillment through him.

This is the psychological position of Guillermo during the first two acts. Daniel's suicide, however, leads to one or two fundamental changes. In act 3 the most conspicuous difference in Guillermo—apart from his grief—lies in a tormented desire to understand the reasons for his son's death. There are still vestiges of egoism in this: an unclear sense of guilt, a suspicion that he drove his son to suicide, and above all, the absurd thought, "¿O se mató por vergüenza del fracaso de su padre?" ("Or did he kill himself out of shame for his father's failure?") (TC 1:490). But on the whole, this tragic event has caused him to think deeply about another person's problems—perhaps for the first time in his life. His investigation into Daniel's behavior, interests, and acquaintances reveals the full extent of his ignorance and simultaneously produces a kind of self-assessment. It is noticeable that he treats young Felipe with understanding and sympathy, and if he still shows Marta no warmth, he also spares her any vindictiveness. Finally, his opportunity of beginning a new and highly promising career loses its priority. His plans, his dreams, his building (to borrow Marta's words) are all replaced by the need to stay close to Daniel's grave. In this we recognize yet another sign of the inability to overcome obstacles; but at the same time we acknowledge the sheer size of those barriers. To relinquish everything in order to stay "with Daniel" is to reduce his life to an experience of perennial anguish and uncertainty, as the stage directions testify: "Está pensando, interrogando; se siente que pasará así el resto de su vida" ("He is thinking, questioning; he feels that he will spend the rest of his life like that") (TC 1:491).

However difficult it may be for us to understand Guillermo's state of mind during the final act, Daniel presents us with a far more complex problem. This is partly due to his dual function. On the one hand, he has a dramatic role at the center of a conflict, serving as an instrument to bring about a crisis and a subsequent change in the disposition of his parents. On the other hand, he is a strikingly unusual character, interesting and important in his own right. The title of the play itself contains a duality: *el niño–la niebla*. As the action unfolds we see Daniel at first as an apparently normal— though weak—adolescent who is suffering disturbing influences at home, and only later do we realize that he has a hereditary mental illness. In assessing this character, therefore, we must decide both what his instrumental role is and whether the pathological madness is convincingly presented.

Daniel's function as an instrument or agent consists of three aspects. Firstly, each parent works through him against the other. Guillermo cultivates a special rapport with his son that excludes Marta, while the latter contradicts her husband's orders and turns Daniel against his father. The murder plan is the culmination of this process. Secondly, in the context of social drama, Daniel represents the most vulnerable element in a situation of constant domestic strife: the child who suffers untold psychological harm. Audience sympathy is inevitably aroused by his need for affection, his confusion over loyalties, and his partial awareness that Mauricio is a rival to his father. Ostensibly, his suicide has its direct cause in this confusion. Daniel's third function is to embody Marta's fears. She has treated him as an alien phenomenon in her life, but when he dies, he takes with him her obsession with insanity. Through his suicide Daniel brings his mother and father together. Irrespective of his intrinsic interest, therefore, Daniel proves to be an indispensable agent of the basic dramatic forces.

As a character in his own right, Daniel interests us both for his normal behavior and for his pathological abnormality. At the age of fifteen (his birthday is the day after the action of act 1), he is undergoing some of the recognizable problems of adolescence. His voice is breaking, he insists on being treated as an adult, and he strains for greater freedom from his parents' control. In certain respects he could be considered an unusual rather than an abnormal boy: highly intelligent, extremely sensitive, petulant, moody, with a frail and unhealthy physique. His great need of maternal affection combined with his gradually increasing antipathy for his father (which almost culminates in his father's death) temporarily suggest to us that he may be suffering from an Oedipus complex. However, this proves to be a false lead, presumably introduced by the dramatist to contrast with the greater abnormalities revealed at a later stage. Daniel's somnambulism is the first clear indication of a psychological disturbance. Only during act 3 do we learn from Daniel's schoolteacher, schoolfriend, and mother the serious extent of his pathological condition. Assembling the various pieces of information, we are able to form a picture of abnormality. He undergoes capricious changes of disposition, from a habitual silence to occasional spells of garrulity, and from moments of intense interest to periods of thorough indifference. He has experiences of dislocation that make it difficult for him to grasp the real connection between things. For example, if flowers can change their appearance, he does not see why words should not vary their spelling (TC 1:478). Altered behavior is another symptom of his illness: the spirit of friendship toward his father becomes gradually transformed into antipathy; he develops false convictions about the way Guillermo treats him; and he begins to talk obsessively about killing. (Of course, we discover that Marta has inculcated these ideas.) Dreams provide an insight into his state of mind. In one in particular, he sees his mother crying without tears, indicating a subconscious awareness of her duplicity. From a kind of sleepwalking that is harmless to others there is a sharp transition to the hypnotic state in which he is on the point of shooting his father. And his suicide is an ultimate abnormality—the mad act that destroys insanity itself. Marta's confession to Mauricio, almost at the end of the play, completes the picture of a child manifesting symptoms of a hereditary madness.

These psychological traits are authentic enough to persuade a theatre audience that the strange events on stage are plausible. Daniel's sleepwalking is consistent with medical accounts of the phenomenon as "an imperfect form of sleep, in which the muscular apparatus, and the portion of brain controlling it, remain awake though the intellectual faculties are buried in slumber . . . those who suffer in the most aggravated form, rising from bed and going through complicated movements. . . . In many cases, some of the organs are also awake, and the somnambulist may see and avoid objects in his path, or may hear and answer questions, though seldom with coherence. These active dreams are, as a rule, totally forgotten on awakening."[4] At the end of act 1 Daniel visibly falls asleep, rises from his chair, automatically picks up his school cap and books, hears Marta's questions, responds to them in a rambling fashion, and obeys her commands. It is therefore possible for us to believe that Marta subsequently takes advantage of his semi-consciousness to condition some of his attitudes and to suggest certain actions. We can accept the plausibility of Daniel's sub-conscious indoctrination and virtual hypnosis as readily as we recognize the verisimilitude of his somnambulism. The fragility of the sleepwalker's state and the theoretical danger of awakening a person in that state (mentioned by Mauricio in act 1, TC 1:459) explain Daniel's behavior when Guillermo's slight movement of the hand suddenly brings him to consciousness and abruptly makes him aware that he has been on the verge of shooting his father.

If Daniel's patricidal behavior is explained by these details, his suicide deserves further consideration. In his fully conscious state he frequently witnesses the quarreling between his parents. His mother's unwillingness to touch him or even to be close to him presumably helps to create the impression that she does not love him. When he is in his somnambulent state, Marta talks to him about the need to kill Guillermo, and this explains his obsession with death and with killing, which could feasibly be converted into a death wish during a psychological crisis. But toward the end of the play Usigli strongly hints that Daniel may have subconsciously absorbed some of the conversation between Marta and Mauricio while apparently asleep (at the end of act 1). Guillermo suspects it; Mauricio and Marta are almost certain of it (TC 1:483–84). Let us imagine that Daniel is not fully asleep during the critical conversation and that a part of his mind is able to assimilate the information that is inadvertently transmitted. He would "hear" his mother speak some extremely painful words:

> "Oh, todo sería tan fácil—y tan justo—si Guillermo pudiera morirse." ("Oh, everything would be so easy—and so fair—if Guillermo could only die.") (TC 1:457)

> "Me gustaría vivir aquí contigo, Mauricio. . . . Te he elegido a ti." ("I should like to live here with you, Mauricio. . . . I have chosen *you*.") (458)

> "No quiero a mi hijo . . . siento como si no fuera más que una duplicación de su padre." ("I don't love my son . . . I feel as though he were just a duplication of his father.") (458)

"Mauricio . . . Te juro que tú eres todo para mí . . . que no tengo marido ni hijo." ("Mauricio . . . I swear that you are everything to me . . . that I have neither a husband nor a son.") (459)

"Seremos libres, seré tuya, Mauricio." ("We'll be free, I'll be yours, Mauricio.") (459)

To discover that his mother wished his father dead, loved another man, planned to free herself to live with that man, rejected him, Daniel, and above all did not love him—all this would destroy the basis of his life. Moreover, noticing the way in which he is identified with his father, Daniel would associate his father's death with his own. In short, there is ample evidence here to explain the suicide of a tormented, hypersensitive, insecure, and mentally sick adolescent.

Whichever explanation we accept, responsibility for Daniel's death must be attributed especially to his mother. Marta, the main character of the play and the most difficult to fathom, undergoes a distinct change once her fear of madness is removed. In order to understand her fully, we need to consider three phases in her development. The first of these might be called the status quo. In her midthirties (presumably, though no age is actually stated), Marta has a manifestly negative outlook. She already feels old (TC 1:455), and she faces domestic life with a mixture of indifference, tedium, and frustration. Her husband fills her with a deep resentment, both because of his egoistic career interest and because of his dominance over their son. Moreover, she is contemptuous of his limited achievements, and she spitefully humiliates him in front of Daniel. It is eventually revealed that she has been selfishly controlling events in their lives to avoid the threat of madness. There is more than a hint that she has used their sex life as a bargaining point and that now she despises Guillermo for what appears to be his impotence. For her part, she declares, "Soy incapaz de esa pasión en que estás pensando, pero no de otras más—naturales" ("I am incapable of that passion that you are thinking of, but not of others that are more—natural") (TC 1:446), implying that her inability to love him does not mean sexual incapacity. Her relationship with Mauricio is not permitted to vindicate this claim. Although she loves him, recognizes him as her one hope (TC 1:455), and is ostensibly prepared to murder for him, she conspicuously fails to display any passion for him, she lies to him, and she eventually acknowledges that if Guillermo were killed, she would have to remain with Daniel rather than marry Mauricio (TC 1:490). And her lack of motherly feelings toward her son—whom she is loath to touch—is a further indication of an unusual coldness. Much of this is explained, of course, by her obsession with hereditary madness, which has dominated her life. She reacts with excessive sensitivity to Mauricio's casual exclamation, "¡Marta! Estás loca" ("Marta! You're mad") (TC I:457). In her constant fear of becoming a victim of her family's insanity she has actually developed a pathological state of mind, as she eventually confesses: "Era una persecución implacable, otra locura" ("It was a relentless persecution, another madness") (TC 1:488).

The second phase of Marta's development begins when this status quo is subjected to new pressures. With the increasing strain of having to keep her romance a secret, with Mauricio impatient to take her away, and with Guillermo announcing plans to move with the family to Mexico City, a solution becomes imperative. In the course of this phase, the changing psychological situation gathers an irresistible momentum. The idea of killing Guillermo is conceived little by little during the conversation at the end of act 1. Mauricio speaks (metaphorically?) of wishing that he could settle things by means of a duel. Marta rejects the proposal, but after some hard thinking she expresses the wish that Guillermo could die. Then, without formulating a plan, she becomes determined: "Te juro que será pronto, pronto. Encontraré un medio y será bueno, eficaz" ("I swear it will be soon, soon. I'll find a means that will be good, effective") (TC 1:459). At this juncture, Daniel walks in his sleep. Noticing that he obeys her commands as though he were hypnotized, Marta sees her opportunity and becomes afraid of her thoughts (TC 1:460). At the beginning of act 2, with the murder plan now secretly in operation, Marta tests her son for signs of any change in his disposition toward Guillermo. Throughout this act we notice a crescendo of pressures: Mauricio insists that she should leave with him; she has an exceptionally acrimonious quarrel with Guillermo; Guillermo refuses to grant her a divorce; Guillermo denies loving her (which means that she has lost her control over him); the telegram from the new president represents a triumph for Guillermo and makes the family's departure imminent; Mauricio desperately declares, "Me siento capaz de todo—de matar a tu marido, Marta" ("I feel capable of doing anything—of killing your husband, Marta") (TC 1:472); and finally, Guillermo loses his self-control and hurts her arm. The criminal intent, therefore, is convincingly explained by a combination of her profound psychological disturbance and the mounting pressure from external circumstances.

In her last phase (act 3) Marta is justified in claiming to be a different woman (TC 1:485). As the audience soon notices, there is a visible difference in the way in which she behaves. The stage directions describe this new Marta as "serena, fría, fuerte" ("serene, cold, strong") (TC 1:484); "lenta, firme, lejana" ("slow, firm, distant") (TC 1:490); and "erguida" ("erect") (491), reflecting her self-confidence, her sense of freedom, and her strength of will. For the first time, she is able to face her previous fears and speak honestly about them. Her disposition toward Mauricio has undergone an important change: she has developed the altruistic awareness that she could never risk having children with him and that he would do better to find another woman. Even more significant is her change of disposition toward Guillermo. Although she does not love him, she feels that the barrier between them—her fear—has been removed. She has a sense of debt toward him, a desire to help him to achieve something constructive in compensation for having deprived him of his son. This is such a powerful resolve that it endures even a last-minute opportunity for her to change her mind. If she wishes to compensate, it means that she has acquired a new sense of justice and morality. To some extent there seems to be an inclination to sacrifice herself for him and to inflict a form of punishment on herself. This becomes particularly apparent when, realizing that she will not be given an opportunity to help Guillermo to build, she accepts the less attractive option of helping him to endure. In a supportive role she can achieve something positive with her life, though it will be a form of imprisonment for her to live in Daniel's shadow, with madness always threatening (TC 1:491, 489).

There are some grounds for arguing that the portrayal of Marta is flawed, from the psychological point of view, by the strength of character displayed in the final minutes of the performance. Just as the earlier negative behavior—including her plan to murder her husband—is convincingly explained by her pathological fear, so, too, the new serenity and clarity of vision spring logically from the removal of that fear. We can readily accept, moreover, that she must suffer immense guilt and that, consequently, she feels constrained to undergo some form of recompense or retribution. Usigli's solution—imprisonment in a loveless marriage—has abundant moral and artistic consistency. But he chose to bring about this solution through a totally new and extraordinarily powerful sense of justice and altruism within his protagonist rather than through the more credible means of irresistible circumstances. It is probably more in line with his ambition to use the theatre constructively than with the expression of a psychological truth.

In the performances of *El niño y la niebla* at the Teatro del Caracol in 1951 a slight modification was made to the ending. Usigli's original version, in which a group of women arrive to mourn Daniel in the traditional way, excludes Marta from the stage (once she has decided to stay with her husband) and focuses on Guillermo, who is resigned to living with his burden. It also introduces a vaguely religious atmosphere—the kind that Usigli believed conducive to fruitful audience participation similar to the experience of catharsis in classical tragedies.[5] The director, José de J. Aceves, avoided the use of such extraneous material and achieved a greater internal logic. In his amended version, Marta remains on stage, sitting down with her sewing. Instead of bringing mourners onto the scene, the director simply focused on the new and perhaps mutually helpful relationship between Marta and Guillermo. At the same time, he created a pleasing balance with the opening of the play, where Marta sets aside her sewing and then, with the entry of Guillermo, picks it up again. Her future is symbolized—in this new ending—by the resumption of a dull routine, while Guillermo's future is represented by thoughts of Daniel shrouded in a haze of cigarette smoke.

I have not included Mauricio in this analysis because Usigli left him as little more than the stereotype of a married woman's lover. In *El niño y la niebla* he resisted the temptation to explain *every* character's motives in depth, avoiding the dramatic problems that he was to create for himself in *Jano es una muchacha*. On the whole, *El niño,* though an early work, shows considerable technical accomplishment.

Let us consider, for example, the simple matter of stage lighting. In order to establish a somber atmosphere at the beginning of the play, Usigli prescribes a single oil lamp. An electricity failure becomes the external representation of an inner malfunctioning, whose result is the psychological fog experienced by Daniel and Marta. But a subtler idea is associated with this. As Marta's maid Jacinta reveals, both the power cut and the death of President Carranza bring to mind the violent events of the past: "Parece que ni pasa el tiempo: estamos como en los días de la revolución, niña" ("It's as though time didn't pass at all: we're as in the days of the Revolution, miss") (TC 1 : 443). In the course of the play, both Marta and Guillermo will think back to the early period of their marriage and will take part in a violent and radical revolution in their domestic affairs.[6]

The structure also deserves comment. According to Usigli's prologue, the third act was written before the first and second (16, 26, and 29 February 1936) and slightly amended in 1949 (TC 3:434). It is not his normal method, and he does not recommend it, but in this instance at least it has produced an exceptionally compact arrangement of material. The key to an understanding of the action—the information about inherited madness—is provided exclusively in the final act. By writing this first, Usigli ensured that it would form the very basis of each scene in the previous acts. In fact, the play's success is derived from the skillful interrelation of a gradual unveiling, the withholding of information, the creation of mystery, the introduction of surprise, final revelation of the answers, and a constant uncertainty in the denouement. In act 1 the status quo is unveiled through a series of scenes calculated to maintain interest: the discord between husband and wife, their respective relationships with their son, the wife's secret love. Into this steadily developing situation Usigli introduced a sudden heightening of the tension with the threat that Marta and Mauricio might be overheard. The final scene of the act is a masterful climax to that threat, enabling the audience to be aware of a danger unnoticed by the characters and leaving unresolved the question of whether Daniel has heard anything. The sleepwalking incident—the act's great surprise—formulates an effective enigma at precisely the best moment to ensure that the audience will not leave the theatre. In act 2 the principal sources of interest are the rapidly escalating crisis and the significant change in relationships. Here we notice how Usigli introduced signs of Daniel's new attitude to his father—an important preparation of the audience for the later revelation that Marta has been misleading him. The sleepwalking at the end of the act forms a neat parallel with the end of act 1, not only satisfying our aesthetic sense but also reinforcing the causal link between the two episodes. Of course, the main effect is achieved by a pistol shot off stage, raising a number of urgent questions for the play to answer in the final act. Even in act 3 there is ample variety in the manner in which the solutions are provided. The explanation for Daniel's behavior is settled by means of his teacher's professional judgment, then by his schoolfriend's intimate confession, and finally by his mother's revelation of the murder plot. Attention turns next to Marta herself. True to form, Usigli reserved until late the information that is most important to us (her fear of the family's history of madness). And he devised a means of sustaining the tension until the very end by introducing Guillermo's abrupt change of mind and by giving Marta, too, an opportunity to reverse her decision.

Unusually for an Usiglian play, *El niño y la niebla* does not contain a single comic line. But the naturalness of the unremittingly serious dialogue is one of its most successful features. Without any personal experience of married life by that time, Usigli managed to capture the painful reality of domestic quarrels, proving his undisputed skill in transferring the commonplace to the stage. He acknowledged a combination of factors in explaining the play's success—the public's preference for a theatre of characters and the author's notoriety being the chief among them (TC 3:436). But the important factor, surely, was that the play is finely balanced between the portrayal of everyday life and the investigation of psychological abnormality. Its realistic and serious theme contains the exceptional ingredients that Usigli always believed to be desirable in the theatre.

Hereditary madness forms the basis for a less striking treatment in *Otra primavera*. The illness that threatens a family could be interpreted at first as a metaphor for the economic changes being forced on them by land redistribution. But the socioeconomic dimension gives way to the psychological. The young generation learn that they must leave the house and find their independent way in life. The older couple, only one of whom suffers from the mental disease, resolve to face the future with mutual help and with optimism. In the end, insanity becomes a less important theme than old age and the shadow of death. By contrast with this play, *Mientras amemos* is lightweight. In it, Usigli took advantage of an abnormal mental condition to create a highly melodramatic plot. This leaves *Corona de sombra* as the only rival to *El niño y la niebla* in the dramatic portrayal of insanity. As will be seen in chapter 7, Usigli proved a master in taking historical veracity and psychological verisimilitude as his basis, and in developing parallel themes of national sovereignty on the one hand and individual ambition, insanity, and poetic justice on the other. Meanwhile, it is important to note that although he showed a diminishing interest in the use of pathological cases for dramatic material, he continued to find inspiration in the study of subconscious influences on people's behavior.

Jano es una muchacha

The audience remains puzzled by the title of this play until the second act, when the middle-aged professional writer, Felipe Regla, explains why the Latin god Janus ought logically to be a female divinity. Displaying a helpfully encyclopedic knowledge of Roman mythology, Felipe enables the audience to perceive various levels of meaning in the statement "Jano es una muchacha" ("Janus is a girl"). According to some authorities, Janus was the god of all beginnings. Others believe him to be empowered to see—simultaneously—the past and the future, life and death, what has been forgotten and what has never happened. He is the god of entrances. He is always between the world that one leaves and the world that one enters. And that is why the Romans depicted him with two faces. At this point in Felipe's reasoning, part of the sense is already clear: the seventeen-year-old Marina, who is now sitting demurely in her aunt's living room, has shown her other face to Felipe in a brothel, where she called herself Mariana. The mythological intention is, however, a good deal more profound than this: "Marina . . . parece llevar en sus diez y siete años toda la sabiduría del mundo cuando calla, toda su puerilidad cuando habla, es decir: el pasado y el porvenir, pero sin un presente definido, sin una realización en el presente" ("Marina . . . seems to bear in her seventeen years all the wisdom of the world when she is silent, all its childishness when she speaks, that is to say: the past and the future, but without a definite present, without any fulfillment in the present") (TC 2:415). In other words, Felipe's thoughts about Janus and the girl are inherently connected with a longing for universal knowledge, a nostalgia for childlike innocence, an awareness of transitory experience, and a preoccupation with the process of aging.

But there is a further stage in his reasoning. A girl of that age, he explains, with Marina's depth, mystery, uncertainty, and formlessness, is capable of turning the head of any experienced man. The girl's aunt contradicts him.

> *Eulalia.* Una niña no es más que el vacío. Una puerta que se abre sobre el vacío.
> *Felipe.* ¿Conoce usted un vértigo mayor?
> *Eulalia. (Suavemente.)* Cállese pecador. En fin, usted lo ha dicho: una niña así es Jano. (TC 2:415–16)

> (*Eulalia.* A girl is no more than emptiness. A door opening onto emptiness.
> *Felipe.* Do you know of any greater vertigo?
> *Eulalia. [Gently.]* Quiet you wicked man. All right, it's as you say: a girl like that is Janus.)

The audience realizes, as Eulalia does, that Felipe has converted her innocent remark into a sexual innuendo, based partly on the idea of Janus as the god of entrances.[7] This central discussion touches therefore on the essential nature of *Jano es una muchacha.* It is a play about duplicity and about aging, but it is especially a study of the sexual drive, which Usigli called "el problema más viejo del mundo" ("the oldest problem in the world") (TC 3:696).[8]

Condemned by the League of Decency, advertised as unsuitable for children and young ladies, parodied in other theatres (*Jano es un muchacho* [Janus is a boy]; *Jano es una borracha* [Janus is a drunken girl]), the play earned plenty of money but little approval by theatre critics looking for a work of art.[9] Usigli was not particularly resentful that it should be regarded as a mere potboiler. He cited Bernard Shaw's use of the term (for *Pygmalion* and other plays) as evidence that dramatists of the highest repute legitimately wrote some works principally to earn a living. In the analysis below, I shall be mentioning a number of features of *Jano es una muchacha* that unmistakably demonstrate his conscious resort to salacious material (both verbal and visual). Two points deserve to be made immediately, however. Whatever its aesthetic faults, the play is on the whole excellent theatre. And however scandalous the subject matter, however melodramatic the plot, Usigli's intention was to approach a taboo subject with a serious and candid frame of mind.

In plays that I have examined elsewhere, signs of Usigli's recurrent interest in sexual problems have been evident: Julia's preoccupation with her physical appearance in *El gesticulador;* Gabriela's fear of yielding to desire to *Medio tono;* Sarah's pregnancy in the same play; Beatriz's insistence that desire be a part of love in *La familia cena en casa.* Other instances through the whole range of Usigli's work reinforce the argument that this was a topic not frivolously or artfully chosen but deeply important to him. In fact, the idea of *Jano* had been at the back of his mind for ten years (TC 3:696). It was, he claimed, an especially difficult play for him to write, but one that he felt compelled to tackle: "Casi podría decir que me fue dictada por fuerzas que las conveniencias sociales envuelven en bellas palabras y expresan, a veces, en feísimos actos" ("I could almost say that it was dictated to me by forces that social proprieties wrap in beautiful words and express, at times, in the ugliest of acts" (TC 3:711).

Usigli was intent on ensuring that *Jano* was seen in the context of world theatre. In his prologue he declared that sex had been inseparable from drama but rarely treated candidly. The range of disguises extended from amorous sentiment to religious vocation and psychopathological heredity. At the end of the nineteenth century he found exceptions in Becque's *La Parisienne* and Shaw's *The Philanderer* and *Mrs Warren's Profession* (though even Shaw, he added, converted sex into an *idea*). Expressionism produced Ernst Toller's *Hinkelman*—a frank treatment of a sexual issue but a bad play. During the 1920s the influence of Freud led to a universal acceptance of sexual themes on stage provided they were (or seemed to be) the subject of scientific analysis or research. A few more recent dramatists had drawn closer to his criterion (O'Neill in particular), but on the whole sex in the theatre had been "disfrazado de amor, envuelto más tarde en celofán psicoanalítico y atado con hilos de sueños" ("disguised as love, later wrapped in psychoanalyatical cellophane and tied up with threads of dreams") (TC 3:700). As for Mexico, Usigli singled out Gamboa's *Teresa o la carne* from the end of the last century and two more recent plays, *El pobre Barba Azul* and *El caso de don Juan Manuel,* though he found them rather imprecise (TC 3:700). His own play would attempt to deal with sex without the customary disguises.

What he set out to write was a concrete rather than an abstract treatment of the theme, with a specifically Mexican context. He believed that in his own country sex tended to be confused with prostitution. Compared with men of other countries, Mexicans were unusually boastful about their visits to brothels (and incidentally, Usigli readily admitted firsthand experience in a place similar to that in his play when he was still a bachelor [TC 3:715]. To a large extent, the boastfulness was, he thought, a form of hypocrisy, a display of machismo that exceeded the essential reality of the experience, though these men would nevertheless neglect their business, their political affairs, and their friendships in favor of a woman who fulfilled this need—"una mujer que reconcentre por un minuto en su sexo el amor propio de toda una larga y mexicana vida" ("a woman who might concentrate for one minute in her sexual organ the self-esteem of a whole, long Mexican life") (TC 3:704). For Mexican women, on the other hand, sexual matters were private and intimate. With the exception of a few cases of prostitution, nymphomania, and infidelity—no more, he believed, than in other countries—they set their minds on marriage and became the slaves of their husbands. This willing submission was their way of owning a man.

Usigli also explained his views on the fundamental truths of sexual experience, in which he found an abundance of contradictions. The seductive appeal and the brevity of the sexual act contrasted, he argued, with its enormous importance in creating, reproducing, and improving people (TC 3:709). Awareness of the full significance of sex—by which he meant its capacity to produce children and thus contribute to the world's vital movement—arrived only when people's faculties were ebbing and the living force was being replaced by a merely conceptual power. As we shall see in *Jo   es una muchacha,* Felipe Regla's attempt to detain the process of aging seems to be symptomatic of this awareness. One further contradiction impressed Usigli: sex implied many positive values, yet it had a negative side represented by sterility, torture, and destruction. The ambivalence of Marina/Mariana, which is the reason for Felipe's resort to the image of Janus, therefore becomes an expression of the more general ambivalence of sex itself. For sex—as Usigli wrote in his prologue—"tiene, como Jano, también dos caras" ("also has, like Janus, two faces") (TC 3:709).

To reject the disguises used by other dramatists inevitably entailed contravening the standards of decorum that usually applied in the early 1950s—a time when the strict rules of Hollywood in the cinema were transferred to most types of public performance. What the audience heard and saw during a performance of *Jano es una muchacha* was calculated to produce an experience of shock, which could be instrumental in compelling people to face the truth. This play therefore has an audacity that is immediately visible in the setting and the characters and soon perceptible in the conversation. It opens in a brothel. The slightly seedy decor is matched by the fading beauty of the woman who welcomes a prosperous client. Three prostitutes are introduced to the visitor in turn, each displaying a different character and—thinly covered—a different figure. It is worth remarking that these features of the first scene are of interest both to the innocently curious and to the voyeur. But there is no attempt to arouse any erotic instinct in the audience or to glamorize the occasion. On the contrary, there is every effort to suggest an atmosphere of disillusionment and vulgarity. The strikingly ungraceful speech of Obsidiana, the more than ample proportions of Alejandra, and the loquacious hypocrisy of "La casta Susana" ("chaste Susana") are all calculated to help the audience to appreciate the client's dissatisfaction. Usigli vigorously reminds us of the commercial basis of the establishment. Each prostitute discusses the price of her services, which is always more than previously announced (but never, incidentally, more than the cost of a bottle of whisky). Since the actual sums are stated (two hundred pesos for the whisky, for example), Usigli was clearly intent on encouraging the audience to sense the realism of events and simultaneously recognize the presentation of sex as business.

The realism of language was another of his concerns. Although his plays normally avoid the use of words that are, as he put it, "funcionales, pero sin curso *social*" ("functional, but not in *social* currency") (TC 3:711), *Jano es una muchacha* was by necessity a special case. The vulgarity of the prostitutes needed to be expressed by word of mouth as well as by action and demeanor. Usigli set to work with gusto in the short speeches of Obsidiana, transforming the provincial expressions, the uneducated accent, and the crude words into something amusing rather than scandalous.

> *La Mujer.* El señor es muy fino, Obsidiana. No vayas a hacer de las tuyas. *(Sale por la izquierda.)*
> *El Hombre. (Sirviendo un whisky.)* ¿Por qué esa recomendación?
> *Obsidiana. (Con fuerte acento pueblerino.)* ¿Eh?
> *El Hombre.* ¿Por qué la señora . . . te hizo esa recomendación?
> *Obsidiana.* Vieja jija. Siempre está fregando con eso de que yo soy muy mal hablada.
> *El Hombre.* ¿Y no?
> *Obsidiana.* Pos yo soy de pueblo, soy de los Altos, y cuando no me gusta algo, pos lo digo clarito pa que no se equivoquen, 've? (TC 2:395)

> (*The Woman.* The gentleman is very fine, Obsidian. Don't get up to your tricks. [*Exit left.*]
> *The Man.* [*Pouring a whisky.*] Why that recommendation?
> *Obsidian.* [*With a strong rustic accent.*] Eh?
> *The Man.* Why did Mrs. . . . the lady make that recommendation?
> *Obsidian.* The ol' bag. She's always bleedin' on abaht me speakin' bad.
> *The Man.* And you don't?
> *Obsidian.* Well, Oi'm from a village, from up in Los Altos, an' when Oi don't loik summat, well Oi say so lahd an' clear so there's no mistake, see?)

In a play contrived to break through social hypocrisy, Usigli needed to call things by their name. He introduced the words *putitas* (little whores), *prostíbulo* (brothel), and *burdel* (bordello) at the appropriate moments (though we also find the usual euphemisms *profesoras* [teachers] *pupilas* [pupils] and *casa* [house]). To encourage the audience to share his candid approach from an early point in the play, he allows a short digression in which the client explains the etymology of the word *burdel* to the woman who runs one (TC 2:394). And lastly, the play abounds in sexual innuendos of the kind frequently encountered in conversation, particularly conversations on sexual topics: "Ya todo se hace a máquina" ("Now everything is done by machine") (TC 2:393); "En este cementerio enterré un poco de mi juventud" ("In this cemetery I buried a bit of my youth") (TC 2:394); "¿Eres cazador? Qué usas, escopeta?" ("Are you a hunter? What do you use, a shotgun?") (TC 2:432); "Me salí de mi casa con un muchacho que iba a hacer una película . . ."—Te puso en cinta, ¿no?" ("I left home with a boy who was going to make a film . . ." "And he got you in a home movie, eh?") (TC

2:433); "Ya estoy hasta aquí de esta vida de puro manoseo."—
Digamos: una vida a tientas, ¿no?" ("I've had it up to here with this
life of nothing but groping." "So you've been sort of feeling your
way along, eh?") (TC 2:434). This list of examples is long enough to
show that the expressions range from simple puns to unmistakably
erotic allusions capable of offending chaste ears. Some of the outrage produced by the play as a whole was caused specifically by the
inclusion of such linguistic material. But Usigli mounted a strong
defense: there was no such thing as bad language if it was in
common use; Bernard Shaw had put swear words in the mouth of
his professor of phonetics in *Pygmalion*; a dramatist ought always
to call a spade a spade; and in short, "no es la palabra, sino aquello
que la palabra describe, define y *clasifica,* lo que importa" ("it is
not the word, but what the word describes, defines and *classifies*
that matters") (TC 3:712).

Usigli called *Jano es una muchacha a pieza* (dramatic piece)—
the word also used for *El niño y la niebla, El gesticulador, Corona
de sombra,* and a few other dramatic works of an essentially serious
nature. He might almost—and I emphasize the word *almost*—have
called this play a *melodrama.* A man enters a brothel to find a girl to
remind him of his past. One young girl measures up to his hopes but
slips away after no more than a tantalizing conversation with him.
The following day, in the house of friends whom he has not seen for
twenty years, he meets the same girl. She is the daughter of his old
friend. That night they meet again in the brothel, where the girl
proves to be a new arrival. The brothel owner, who has heard about
the novice, calls to claim his right to initiate her in the profession. It
is her father. The girl threatens to kill herself unless her father
leaves and asks the man to take her away. At this point in the
development of the plot—the end of the second act—the scandalous events and the strong emotions have introduced a melodramatic dimension. But it is worth pausing to consider the technical
qualities of the play so far.

Acts 1 and 2 constitute an almost autonomous structure within
the play, with a symmetrical arrangement and an action that is
complete in itself. This action moves between two settings in a
sequence of reversed pairs.

Act 1	Act 2
Scene 1—The Brothel	Scene 1—The House
Scene 2—The House	Scene 2—The Brothel

The main enigmas posed in the first scene are resolved in the last.
Meanwhile, Usigli created powerful dramatic tension counter-

balanced by periods of slow release and moments of explosive impact. A sequence of questions and answers could be used to demonstrate his carefully wrought framework:

1. Will Felipe's quest be fruitful? No sooner does Mariana seem to provide the answer than she disappears (act 1, scene 1).
2. What are the reasons for Felipe's quest? Conversations with Eulalia and Víctor gradually fill in the details from his past (1.2, and 2.1).
3. Is Marina the same person as Mariana? Her dress and the setting are strikingly different; she treats Felipe as a stranger; but the name is similar, and Felipe seems confident that she is the same girl (1.2).
4. Will their secret be exposed? Felipe discreetly supports her pretense in public but directs his intimate thoughts at her while seeming to address her Aunt Eulalia (1.2, and 2.1).
5. Will Marina admit her secret identity once they are alone? She remains totally indifferent at first (1.2) but gradually betrays hidden feelings (the choice of piano music, the brief kiss) before renewing the enigma (2.1).
6. Will Felipe rediscover Mariana in the brothel? People there deny all knowledge of her, but at the last moment she makes her entry (2.2).
7. Will Marina (Mariana) be subjected to the brothel owner's will? In his fury at the way she has tormented him, Felipe seems ready to step aside. Only the fact that it is Víctor prevents the potential disaster (2.2).
8. How will Víctor react when he discovers his daughter in his brothel? The effect of his astonishment and rage is offset by his daughter's own extreme reactions (2.2).

Some of the moments of surprise and revelation are calculated to cause as much impact on the audience as on the characters. Marina's arrival home (1.2) produces a situation that the audience can share with Felipe at the expense of the girl's family; Víctor's arrival at the brothel (2.2) provokes such a degree of shock that the audience feels an empathy with the characters in the emotional outburst that ensues. Equally skillful is the creation of the greatest enigmas (or suspense) at the end of the first three scenes: Mariana's disappearance (1.1); Felipe's whispered exhortation "Esta noche, Marina, ¡esta noche!" ("Tonight, Marina, tonight!") (1.2); and Marina's kiss and display of innocence (2.1). In contrast, the scene that brings act 2 to a close rises to its climax during the last few minutes, but as the curtain falls, Felipe's coldly spoken words "Será mejor que todos tomemos una copa. Salud" ("It will be best if we all have a drink. Cheers") (TC 2:441) release a little of the tension and prepare the way for a solution.

It should be added that the two acts have been admirably strengthened by the striking contrasts in scenery and atmosphere, the amusing presentation of the prostitutes, and several pieces of humorous dialogue. Moreover, some piano music in the second act is used to extremely good effect. At the simplest level it provides aesthetic pleasure. But it also provides psychological insight and theme enhancement. Marina begins by playing light music reflecting her youth and femininity (for example, Dubussy's *La Fille aux cheveux de lin*). When the conversation between Felipe and Eulalia broaches the question of marriage, Marina abruptly changes to Beethoven, introducing a more serious tone. Eulalia's departure from the room marks an important transition in the scene, which Marina punctuates by switching to Bach, whose air of propriety and formality helps her to create a protective screen around herself. Finally, thinking that she is alone, she plays a waltz entitled *Memory*, which then serves as a stimulus for a dialogue about the past. To sum up, then, the play thus far functions smoothly and powerfully, and the action and emotion are harmoniously blended with the ideas expressed in the dialogue (of which I shall have more to say later).

Commenting on the structure of Shaw's play on prostitution, Arthur Ganz echoes other critics with the view that *Mrs. Warren's Profession* "seems to be, from one point of view at least, finished by the end of Act II."[10] The same might be said of *Jano es una muchacha*. Certainly there are several unresolved issues, but not even with an assiduous determination to defend Usigli's third act—which, he confessed, was unanimously condemned (TC 3:735)—could we accept his need to resolve them all, or argue that he did so artistically.

The main problem with act 3 is that, though set entirely in the Iglesias family's house, it has two separate focal points. The matter deserving some kind of resolution is the one that has concerned us during the first two acts: Felipe's relationship with Marina. Before attending to this, however, Usigli leads us into an exploration of Víctor's life. For one-third of act 3 we are required to develop an interest in a dialogue between Víctor Iglesias and his sister-in-law Eulalia. We must learn how he loved Eulalia but married her sister, Arcelia; how Eulalia disguised her love for him to avoid a conflict with her sister; and why after twenty years of a platonic relationship he now asks Eulalia to marry him. The arrival of Felipe and Marina then introduces some welcome tension. Their version of events at the brothel is at first denied by Víctor, but Dora and Camila—both from the brothel—substantiate it, leaving Víctor to offer some further clarification. More of his past comes to light: his neglect of his wife, Arcelia, his nightly visits to the brothel, Arcelia's search for him there, her employment there, Víctor's visits to her in the brothel, the birth of Marina, Arcelia's illness and death, and Víctor's purchase of the brothel. As will be seen, information about the different responses to sexual matters by the various characters does enhance the main theme. But it is presented in a way that digresses from the plot, weakening the play's dynamic composition.

A secondary problem is the improbable and sometimes melodramatic nature of the action. Felipe and Marina call at Víctor's house merely to collect Felipe's luggage and a photograph of Arcelia. This is transparently a pretext to bring them face-to-face with Víctor again, and the clumsiness of the arrangement is evident in the fact that Felipe's suitcases have only just been transferred to the house from the hotel where he has been staying. But Usigli requires yet more suspension of disbelief on the part of the audience. One moment Eulalia listens placidly to Víctor's reminiscences, and the next moment she invites him to take his own life. His refusal and his brutal kiss leave her apparently unmoved, but within seconds (off stage) she shoots him. Finally, the whole business is too quickly and dubiously settled. Felipe arranges for the shooting to look like suicide, and he and Marina agree to marry in due course. A more logical solution might have been for Felipe and Marina to elope while Eulalia punished Víctor by scorn instead of death. But in perspective, we can readily understand why Usigli shunned it: he was looking for something closely resembling a newspaper scandal.

In response to the harsh criticism that this act received, Usigli offered two explanations. One was that Víctor gained an autonomous identity while the play was being written, controlling events more than the dramatist intended. At times this kind of admission is impressive; on this occasion, however, it must be concluded that an unwavering authorial tyranny was required. His other point was that he was searching for psychological verisimilitude. This alone, of course, cannot compensate for an inept dramatic technique; in act 3 too many facts are simply narrated by the characters. It does help us to appreciate, however, that Usigli was not merely interested in providing an entertaining evening at the theatre but also in exploring the effects of the sexual drive from a variety of viewpoints and in some detail. The weakness of this final act detracts from his success but does not destroy it.

The two male characters are in several respects contrasting and complementary types. Felipe Regla is the artist, the wanderer, the man with a reputation for wild behavior, the Don Juan who openly discusses sexual matters and unashamedly visits brothels. His surname, with its suggestion of moderation, orderliness, and normality, stands in ironical antithesis to these salient characteristics (although the other meaning of *regla*, "ruler" or "measure," contains the appropriate phallic symbolism). Víctor Iglesias is the notary, the leading citizen, the respectable man (with a surname that enhances his saintly air), the man whose appearance of respectability, convention, and abstemiousness in sexual matters belies his indulgent private life. The two men have many contrasting attitudes, therefore, but they have an important feature in common: they both express their powerful sexual drive in a brothel rather than within the context of marriage.

It is above all through Felipe Regla that Usigli conveyed his candid ideas about the function of brothels in the lives of Mexican men. As a youngster, Felipe and his friends used to visit Encarna's place, "pensando que buscábamos una mujer para hacer la vida, cuando en realidad nos buscábamos a nosotros mismos, el secreto de nuestra fuerza" ("thinking that we were looking for a woman so as to make something of life, when in reality we were looking for ourselves, for the secret of our strength") (TC 2:409). With hindsight, Felipe can recognize that the romantic motive was confused with the basic machismo that dominated them. Now, after his experiences throughout the world, he can explain the advantage that brothels have over those love affairs in which sexual fulfillment, and not love, is the objective: "No hay que jurar, ni que mentir, amor; no hay que hacer promesas ni hay que incubar engaños. Todo es limpio y claro, sin complicaciones, sin humillación, sin fraude" ("You don't have to swear to love, or to lie about it; you don't have to make promises or hatch deceits. Everything is clean and clear, without complications, or humiliation, or fraud") (TC 2:394).

Usigli chose to create a character who is at a critical moment in life. In several respects the forty-three-year-old Felipe is emblematic of the male menopause. From the opening dialogue with Dora he reveals a preoccupation with the time that has passed, an inclination to reminisce nostalgically, and a wish to recapture his youth (TC 2:394). In his subsequent conversation with Eulalia he immediately displays a self-consciousness about the signs of aging (his loss of hair, his wrinkles) (TC 2:404). Disillusionment with his career augments the problem. Although he has become a highly successful writer, he has decided that literature never prevented a war, saved lives, or improved human nature, and so he has stopped

work. In an important speech describing his sense of tedium, satia-
tion, and lingering hope, he reduces all his experiences to sexual
relationships: "Ciudades y ciudades y ciudades . . . Y todo igual
siempre: todas las mujeres iguales, todas las noches semejantes
. . . La mujer elegida está en uno, como una ilusión primero; luego,
como un deseo, y luego sólo como una nostalgia" ("Cities and
cities and cities . . . And everything always the same: the women
all the same, the nights all alike . . . The chosen woman is within
us, like an illusion at first; then like a desire, and then only like
nostalgia") (TC 2:430–31). The aspiration for fulfillment, the dream
of reaching a destination and discovering an ideal are converted
into a quest for the right woman. But time has persuaded him that
the target will always remain elusive, for it is essentially no more
than the embodiment of his psychological needs. In the torment of
his bitterness and self-denigration, Felipe refers to his grotesque
resistance to inevitable physical decay, encapsulating his thoughts
in imagery that evokes his diminishing sexual powers: "Y no se
decide uno a envejecer, a abatir la cresta de gallo como una bandera
a media asta por la muerte del gobierno" ("And we don't make up
our minds to grow old, to lower the cockscomb like a flag at half-
mast for the death of governing powers") (TC 2:431). And his
stream of self-criticism eventually leads to a new and negative
attitude to brothels as "falsos lechos en infiernos de cinco minutos"
("false beds in five-minute hells"), where emotion is petrified and
the visitor ends up no different from the woman: "el hombre se
emputece" ("the man becomes a whore") (TC 2:431).

Although Felipe has preoccupations typical of men of his age, his
ability to express them is exceptional rather than typical. Moreover,
he is not an average customer at Encarna's brothel (as Dora herself
remarks [TC 2:392], and his visit after twenty years of traveling
around the world is not treated as a typical case. He rejects the
opportunities to satisfy mere sexual appetite because he is looking
for a memory and an illusion, "el regreso al amor y a la limpieza"
("the return to love and cleanliness") (TC 2:730). Marina combines
both features. She has an extreme youthfulness, displayed in her
appearance and occasional childlike behavior, but an unfathomable
depth, suggested by her capricious actions and her secret thoughts.
In her role as Mariana she entices Felipe coquettishly, speaking the
words of eternal womanhood while acting the part of a small girl. In
her father's house she intrigues him with her innocent and guarded
responses but, above all, with the intense silence that seems to form
a veil of mystery (see TC 2:414). As youth, she represents his past,
and as the unknown, she is his future (facing both directions simul-

taneously, like Janus). Marina arouses in Felipe an intense sexual desire as well as unexpected thoughts of marriage. She restores his motivation and creativity, not only by enabling him to rediscover the will to write but by offering him her fertility. At the final curtain Felipe accepts the risk implied by her ambivalence. His sexual passion has now been supplanted by long-term considerations, with the result that he can resist her appeal for an immediate elopement and await the day when her wedding arrangements are complete. An alternative future is offered to him, of course, by an older woman, who represents a safer and more predictable life-style. But Felipe rejects this possibility in favor of youth, arguing that only the blending of maturity with youth can produce "un hijo nuevo que contenga la madurez y la inocencia del mundo" ("a new child containing the world's maturity and innocence") (TC 2:454).

Unlike Felipe, Víctor is not at first involved in any midlife reassessment. More significantly, unlike the male without sexual inhibitions, Víctor represents men whose sexual lives are dominated by unhealthy complexes. In order to explain his psychological formation, Usigli presents the audience with an extensive record of his past. As a young man Víctor—studious, athletic, solemn, and ironical—gave his friends an impression of saintliness. Never joining them in their nights at the brothel, he seemed to have a marvelous girlfriend and a uniquely pure and harmonious sexlife (TC 2:408–9). The truth was a picture of frustrated romantic aspirations and a damaging confusion of love and sexual impulse. Víctor loved a girl (Eulalia) whose responses were cool. He married the girl's sister (Arcelia) as a substitute (TC 2:444). This may be intended as support for Felipe's defence of brothels, suggesting that Víctor's failure to satisfy his early sexual needs in Encarna's place led directly to a disastrous marriage. Whether or not this is the case, Usigli certainly emphasized Víctor's increasingly dominant need for sexual experience that his wife was incapable of providing at home, "protegida por estas paredes tan limpias" ("protected by such clean walls") (TC 2:457). The word *limpias* that Víctor uses here reveals as much about him as his description of Arcelia as *mármol* (marble) (TC 2:456). Having failed to achieve a harmonious erotic relationship based on the union of love and desire (with Eulalia), he sought sexual gratification devoid of all romantic associations, impersonal at first and then tinged with brutality and bestiality. All this may be inferred from his own account of his neglect of Arcelia and nightly visits to the brothel, and his renewed desire for her after she had been raped (TC 2:456). Subsequently, the will to *possess* led him to purchase the brothel. Víctor is a character who represents the violent transition from restraint and frustration in youth to harmful complexes and sordid excesses.

In another aspect the mature Víctor epitomizes the hypocrisy of middle-class men. Outwardly he has become a pillar of society: the most respected solicitor in the city, hardworking, helping to promote culture, on good terms with the governor and other political figures, devoted to his daughter—in Eulalia's words, "ha llevado una vida ejemplar" ("he has led an exemplary life") (TC 2:404). Even Felipe thinks that he can perceive a saintly halo (TC 2:409). But Víctor's private life threatens to subvert all this. He claims to be no different from Felipe or any other men in his sexual behavior (TC 2:440), but there is a hint of overcompensation for a sense of inferiority in his insistence on exercising his droit du seigneur with the new girl. And what is perhaps most difficult for him to cope with is the sense that the brothel (and all that it represents) is ultimately shameful. Confronted with the sight of his daughter in Encarna's house, he reacts not only with amazement and anger but with a sense of being contaminated. He rejects Marina as though he were the innocent party: "¿Mi hija una mujer de éstas? ¡Qué inmundicia! ¡Qué vergüenza! . . . basura. No te reconozco" ("My daughter, a woman of this type? It's filthy! It's shameful . . . trash. I don't recognize you") (TC 2:440). Usigli leaves us with a clear impression of distaste for the double standards implied here.

Despite their contrasts, Felipe and Víctor essentially complement each other in the dramatic presentation of male sexual behavior. They offer different examples of the *expression* of libido (Víctor's youth excepted) rather than the more complete contrast between—say—a profligate and an ascetic. Marina and Eulalia, however, are far closer to representing female opposites.

In terms of dramatic structure, the role of Eulalia is to serve as a foil to Marina (and in a different respect, to Felipe and Víctor, too). But Usigli has developed her into a character of some depth in her own right. Reminiscences permit us to form an impression of Eulalia during her youth. She emerges as a beautiful woman who in some way discouraged the men who desired her. She claims to have felt the same urges as any other person, and to have held them in check by sheer strength of will. But we notice something revealing in her question to Víctor: "¿Qué sabes tú lo que es el freno del deseo, la pausa, el silencio, la abstención del agua inmóvil frente al agua que corre? Te creía sediento de Arcelia, y mi sed se aplacó a la fuerza" ("What do *you* know about restraint of desire, respite, silence, the abstention of still water in front of running water? I believed you to be thirsting for Arcelia, and my thirst was soothed out of necessity") (TC 2:455). It is clear here that she recognizes a difference between her own nature ("agua inmóvil") and her sister's ("agua que corre"). In these words, as in other parts of the dialogue, there is a hint of a coolness that might be taken for frigidity. If she can describe her sister as cheerful and full of the joy of living (TC 2:404), Eulalia seems to create a more somber and restrained image of herself. For Víctor the problem is summed up by her resolute sangfroid, the temperament that permitted her to kill her favorite horse and threaten to kill herself rather than yield to an exigent foreman: "Eso fue lo que no me dejó acercarme a ti entonces" ("That's what stopped me from getting close to you then") (TC 2:457).

Eulalia's exceptional restraint and self-control have led her to suppress her love for Víctor in memory of Arcelia and to accept a patient, supportive, platonic role in his house. Without actually marrying him, she has in fact achieved what she regards as the main benefits in marriage: "La mujer es siempre más vieja que el hombre, y cuando se casa quiere sentir fortaleza, seguridad, apoyo" ("The woman is always older than the man, and when she marries she wants to feel strength, security, support") (TC 2:417). Her religious faith adds to her strength and capacity for abstinence, while a shield of jocularity holds potentially harmful topics of conversation at a distance. In act 3 we have ample opportunity to watch her head overcome her heart. When Víctor, after twenty years of disguising his love for her, declares his feelings, asks her to marry him, and embraces her, she begins to yield ("¡Víctor, al fin!") but suddenly resists ("No. Espera") because a sense of logic sounds a warning in her head ("Tenemos que pensarlo los dos un poco más" [We must both think about it a little longer"] (TC 2:444–45). At the age of forty, Eulalia, though still beautiful, no longer seems to believe in her capacity to respond to sexual desire, warning Víctor to think hard about the fact that she is an old maid. She has already responded to Felipe's lighthearted idea that he might propose to her as "como la declaración a la muerte" ("like proposing to death") (TC 2:416). In a sense, this half-joking remark captures the essence of Eulalia's role in the play as the sterile and fatal aspect of sexual attraction. Her self-denial and her rejection of men's approaches lead not only toward her own sterility but to a fruitlessness in the lives of the men drawn by her beauty. (Víctor is the main case, but Felipe is another with his prolonged bachelorhood.) Having already been an indirect cause of her sister's anguish and heart failure, she now becomes the direct agent of Víctor's death. Usigli arranges the shooting in such a way that the symbolic aspect becomes absolutely clear. It is not simply a matter of justice or revenge, for Eulalia twice informs us that she has killed Víctor while in the act of kissing him. It is a question of making death the substitute for love's fruitfulness.

Most of Eulalia's characteristics may be readily seen in direct contrast with those of Marina, whose dramatic function is—ultimately—to illustrate feminine sexuality. As opposed to the middle-aged spinster, Marina represents adolescence emerging into maturity. In order to understand her, we need to take into account the peculiarities of her background. She has been brought up under the benign but strict regime of her aunt, ignorant of the circumstances of her mother's life and death, and almost estranged from her father by his permanent mask of irony and humor. More recently she has been living in a convent school. It is therefore a basically secure background, in which we notice more than a hint of moral discipline and sexual repression. However, Marina has already begun to break free from the restraints and to discover the power of her instincts. During a brief holiday from the convent, she has been recruited to attract men into the brothel in her hometown. Outwardly the conflicting psychological forces are represented to the audience by a dual personality, beginning with her alias:

Marina	Mariana
convent/home	brothel
child	woman
navy dress and ankle socks	low-cut dress and high-heeled shoes
solemn	vivacious
innocent	worldly-wise
attracted by marriage	promiscuous

It is a highly effective dramatic technique to diagnose a young woman's complex behavior. But ultimately what interests Usigli is not so much the superficial manifestations as the composite personality. Marina confesses that she has enjoyed acting as a procuress: "Era igual que un juego. Y me dieron trajes y joyas y plumas" ("It was like a game. And they gave me dresses and jewels and feathers") (TC 2:454). In the brothel we see the evidence for this view of sexual foreplay as little more than a game. She creates a false image of herself (as a prince's consort, a femme fatale) based on romantic dreams, adopts a posture of elegance and culture (with schoolgirl French), transforms her juvenile innocence into worldly wisdom, and claims a perfect sense of ease in the brothel. After tantalizing Felipe with her coquetry, she intensifies his sexual desire by promising her body (TC 2:402) and by inviting him to join her in a game that he might hope to win (TC 2:437). Some of these provocative skills reappear in the Marina seen at home. Instead of plainly discouraging Felipe's attentions, she carefully offers isolated hints of enticement (particularly the pretext that she contrives in order to kiss him [TC 2:425]). Throughout the scenes in her home she maintains an enigmatic quality calculated to stir his interest in her.

Yet Marina is in total control neither of the situation nor of herself. The true dangers of her game are exposed when the brothel owner asserts his rights. Felipe's charms, moreover, create a form of compulsion within her: "Quise irme, tía; pero no pude. . . . Creía que tenía una cita implacable con Felipe" ("I wanted to leave, auntie; but I couldn't. . . . I thought I had an unavoidable date with Felipe") (TC 2:448). She is capricious both in the brothel and at home, as though subject to unpredictable impulses. Most importantly, she admits to being drawn remorselessly toward the brothel: "Y yo volví a sentir la atracción de aquella casa, sin entender por qué; el vértigo, la cosa que me había hecho daño desde chica—un arrebato" ("And I felt the attraction of that house again, without understanding why; the sense of vertigo, the thing that had harmed me since I was a child—a sudden impulse") (TC 2:454). In this effort to explain the compelling force Usigli first suggests a hereditary characteristic, expressed in psychological rather than physiological terms. It is clear, however, that he believes the explanation to be an irresistible sexual drive, to which Marina alludes in words that are as delicate as possible: "No sé todavía si lo que me atrae es la casa mala. Si casada con un hombre no me iré a buscar a otra casa así" ("I still don't know whether what attracts me is the whorehouse. Whether as a married woman I shan't go off looking for a another place like it") (TC 2:454). This is also suggested by her sense that virginity is a regrettable condition (TC 2:459). On the other hand, she is aware of having other needs. In her fear of being alone she asks for Felipe's company. She is swayed by Felipe's talk of marriage, and her final words to him convey the possibility that the instincts to have a family, help others, build for the future, and give herself to one man may become dominant: "Mi sangre tiene manos para ti, Felipe. Tendremos un hijo, por mi tía. Haremos un mundo nuevo, ¿verdad?" ("My blood has hands for you, Felipe. We'll have a child, for my aunt. We'll make a new world, won't we?") (TC 2:459). The dichotomy is not fully resolved because to fulfill the dramatist's purpose, Marina must continue to suggest the essential ambivalence of the feminine personality. In this play the general emphasis is placed on feminine enjoyment of sexuality and the strength of sexual drives (in Marina's case, possibly a propensity to nymphomania). But to make the picture more complete, Usigli used the third act to introduce (briefly but strongly) the idea of marriage and family life as an alternative to profligacy and prostitution.

When the final curtain falls on *Jano es una muchacha,* we are left with an uncomfortable sense that Usigli has tried to tie up the loose ends too neatly. Marina will fulfill Felipe's need for rejuvenation; he will give her sexual experience, protection, and security (always bearing in mind the danger of her becoming promiscuous). Víctor has received the ultimate punishment for ruining people's lives. And Eulalia, pardoned for killing him, will continue (temporarily) in her quasi-maternal role. We are surely unconvinced that Marina could show so little emotional and psychological response to her traumatic experiences during the past twenty-four hours (culminating in the violent death of her father). Most of act 3, moreover, suffers from the effort to explain the present by reference to the past, causing a digression from the tense situation skillfully and entertainingly built up during the first two acts.

On reflection, however, we are able to recognize the depth and scope of Usigli's analysis. With Felipe and Marina he portrays the uninhibited expression of sexual drives, male and female, in middle age and adolescence. With Víctor and Eulalia he explores the complexes arising from sexual inhibitions. Manifestly, the picture is incomplete and selective, and perhaps it is not surprising that some of the play's critics protested that the types chosen for illustration were not average cases in the Mexican population. But Usigli found a persuasive response: "Estoy . . . lejos de imaginar que mi pieza represente la realidad sexual del cincuenta por ciento de los matrimonios mexicanos. . . . Pero . . . en el teatro es necesario amplificar el ejemplo que se presenta. Por excepcional que parezca lo que sucede en *Jano,* ha ocurrido y puede repetirse: es *probable,* y esto basta para admitirlo dentro del teatro" ("I am . . . far from imagining that my play represents the sexual reality of fifty percent of Mexican married couples. . . . But . . . in the theatre it is necessary to amplify the example that is being presented. However exceptional the events in *Jano* may appear, they have happened and they can happen again: they are *probable,* and this is sufficient to admit them within the theatre") (TC 2:713–14). Although he denied attempting to promote any particular moral thesis with the play, his general attitude can easily be discerned. Felipe advocates freedom of expression as a means of avoiding ruined lives: "Construyamos sobre la verdad. La prostitución debe exhibirse, no esconderse"

("Let's build on the basis of truth. Prostitution must show itself, not hide away") (TC 2:455). If the play's action tends to support this idea, the fact of *Jano*'s performances in the Teatro Colón put theory into practice. Usigli was convinced that his play portrayed more than ninety percent of Mexican males and that it uncovered their "hipócrita doble vida sexual" ("hypocritical sexual double life") (TC 2:714). While deploring the press reaction to the public performances and propaganda claiming that the play exploited scandal and lowered theatrical standards, he was more than satisfied with the general response from the theatregoing public. And he acknowledged the correct attitude of the Mexican authorities, who refrained from imposing an official censorship.

In this section I have attempted to give *Jano es una muchacha* the serious treatment that it deserves. I do not deny that Usigli foresaw the box-office potential of a play on sexual behavior or that he intentionally introduced salacious material, and it is not difficult to understand why some of his contemporary dramatists suspected the corruption of his integrity. But with the perspective of several decades, a reassessment is deserved. I would argue that the play makes an important contribution to Usigli's survey of Mexican social and psychological reality. It is a thoroughly sincere examination of a sensitive subject, fully consistent with the dramatist's project to create a middle-class realist theatre. Within this overall context, *Jano* belongs to the category of psychological drama. Unlike *El niño y la niebla,* it does not deal with pathological cases, but it does conform to the principle that for the purpose of transferring reality to the stage it is necessary to enhance the material and heighten the effects. As a work of art, it is marred by the clumsy effort to increase verisimilitude and develop psychological analysis in act 3. But both the aesthetic and entertainment qualities of the first two acts are extremely high. In view of its overall theatrical merits, both as a spectacle and as a form of communication with the people, the play deserves—even today—to be performed more often and studied more widely.

7

History and Sovereignty

When Usigli wrote *Corona de sombra (Crown of Shadows)* in 1943 he was responding to an old personal fascination with the figures of Maximilian and Carlota.[1] In previous years what had appealed to him as potential dramatic material was the death of Carlota after sixty years of insanity (TC 3:620). By the time he had written the play, however, he had introduced a completely new dimension into the theme. An individual's suffering was integrated with a nation's struggle for independence, the empress's madness was interconnected with the emperor's execution, and the present time was illuminated by a reassessment of the past. Eventually he saw this play as a contribution to his *Gran teatro del Nuevo Mundo,* one of a series of three dramatizations of key episodes, "tres coronas que me parecen fundamentales para el destino, ya no de México, sino del Continente" ("three crowns which I believe to be fundamental for the destiny, not merely of Mexico, but the Continent") (TC 3:673). As I have remarked in previous chapters, he was to relax this emphasis on a Continental scope for his drama, but he never lost his belief in the national symbolism of the three incidents. They were, he insisted, "los tres elementos básicos de nuestra soberanía" ("the three basic elements of our sovereignty").[2] In 1960 he completed *Corona de fuego* (Crown of fire), on the execution of Cuauhtémoc by Cortés, and in 1963 the last of the trilogy, *Corona de luz* (Crown of light), on the subject of the Virgin of Guadalupe. This group of plays reveals Usigli at his most intensely serious in the use of theatre to explore and influence the Mexican psyche. In his own words, "Cuauhtémoc representa el factor culminante, el mito . . . de la soberanía material; la Virgen de Guadalupe . . . , el mito . . . de la soberanía espiritual; y Maximiliano . . . y Carlota . . . los elementos determinantes de la soberanía política de México" ("Cuauhtémoc represents the culminating factor, the myth . . . of national sovereignty; the Virgin of Guadalupe . . . , the myth . . . of spiritual sovereignty; and Maximilian . . . and Carlota . . . the determining elements of Mexico's political sovereignty").[3]

Usigli's view of these dispersed events as in some way interrelated by a deep and hidden substructure corresponds to what some historians would call an "organicist" approach.[4]

We may refer loosely to these as Usigli's three historical plays (excluding from the category *Los fugitivos* [The fugitives], set in 1908; *Las madres* [The mothers], set in 1915–17; and *El niño y la niebal* [The boy and the fog], set in 1920—all of which are plays dealing with the recent past and quite different in their intention). In his studies of the threatre Usigli made it clear that he was fully aware of the tradition of historical drama, particularly in its connection with Greek, Roman, Shakespearian, and modern tragedy. Yet he chose to apply the label *"antihistórica"* to each of the three *Coronas*. It is a term that appears to indicate negation while simultaneously and paradoxically insinuating that each play does indeed have a historical ingredient. Conveniently preempting any complaint about the inaccurate representation of actual events, he threw the emphasis on his deliberate inclusion of nonhistorical elements. Since he was not interested in writing either dramatized versions of historical record or drama documentary whose primary function might be to illustrate and inform, literal exactitude became irrelevant. He admitted of *Corona de sombra,* "he cometido diversas arbitrariedades e incurrido en anacronismos deliberados" ("I have acted in an arbitrary manner on several occasions and created deliberate anachronisms") (TC 3:625), and the same admission would be valid for the other plays in the trilogy. On the respective importance of historical fact and artistic imagination he insisted, "El poeta no es el esclavo sino el intérprete del acontecimiento histórico" ("The poet is not the slave but the interpreter of the historical event").[5] In this attitude he was, of course, following both Aristotelian and Spanish Golden Age tradition. As A. A. Parker wrote, "the principal condition that the seventeenth century, following Aristotle, demanded of historical drama was that its theme would, where necessary, be 'emended' in order to satisfy the requirements of poetry."[6] For Usigli, therefore, it became a matter of using the dramatist's technique and the artist's imagination to adjust literal facts in order that a play should capture the essence of a situation. Moreover, one of the fundamental points to remember when considering Usigli's historical drama is that he was always interested primarily in the present and the future. If he dealt with the past, it was only to show it in perspective and to demonstrate its continuing influence.

Two things in particular are of concern here. One is the nature of the theatre produced from this historical material, the other the ideas that Usigli was attempting to communicate. I propose to undertake an analytical correlation of historical records and dramatic representation, and then to determine the new perspective that he was attempting to give to key moments in Mexico's past in order for his twentieth-century audience to have a better understanding of their country's identity. When these two features have been taken into account, I can more fruitfully assess the quality of the works as dramatic pieces. The chronological order dictated by the historical events themselves is: 1525, the execution of the last Aztec ruler, Cuauhtémoc, by Hernán Cortés during the expedition to Honduras *(Corona de fuego);* 1531 or 1555, the beginning of the pious tradition of miraculous appearances of the Virgin Mary of Guadalupe to the Indian Juan Diego on the hill of Tepeyac *(Corona de luz);* 1864–67, Maximilian's occupation of the Mexican throne and his execution by Juárez *(Corona de sombra).* But a better order to follow is that of the appearance of each play, for this will help to show how Usigli's purpose gradually crystallized and how his methods of adapting history to the theatre evolved.

Corona de sombra

The dramatic basis of *Corona de sombra* is a (fictitious) Mexican historian's visit in 1927 to the Château de Bouchout (Belgium), where the former empress of Mexico has been living since the onset of insanity some sixty years before. This encounter prompts Carlota to remember scenes from the time when she and her husband, Maximiliano, became rulers of Mexico, and these selected episodes from the past are re-created on stage to form the bulk of the play's action. A final return to the twentieth century allows Usigli to give the events a new interpretation before drawing the final curtain with Carlota's death.

During the first half of the nineteenth century Mexico lost roughly half of its territory to the United States. The deepening crisis in political and social affairs during the middle of the century was punctuated by the beginning of the Reform movement in 1855, under the leadership of Benito Juárez; the framing of a new constitution in 1857, under the auspices of his Liberal party; and the War of the Reform in 1858, a civil war between the Liberals (reformists who had set up their government in Vera Cruz) and the Conservatives (supported by the Church, landowners, and traditionalists, with a government established in Mexico City). After three years Juárez and the Liberals emerged victors. Short of financial resources, Juárez declared a moratorium on foreign debt repayments in 1861, provoking hostility from France, Great Britain, and Spain. In 1862 French troops sent by Napoleon III invaded the country, and by June 1863 the French army occupied Mexico City. With the cooperation of Conservative elements among the Mexican population, Napoleon set up a monarchy dependent on the French Empire. He invited the Archduke Maximilian of Austria—who was married to the Belgian princess Charlotte—to take the throne as emperor of Mexico. It is the subsequent events that Usigli traced in *Corona de sombra,* reflecting the general development of the situation as historians record it and highlighting specific episodes for which there is ample evidence. The broad correlation between historical reality and the dramatic work is as follows:

Historical Record	*Corona de sombra*
1864 (10 April) In Miramar Maximilian officially accepts the invitation and is proclaimed emperor of Mexico.	act 1, scene 2 (9 April: the decision).
(12 June) Maximilian and Carlota enter Mexico City.	act 1, scene 3
1865 (2 October) While Juárez continues to wage guerrilla war, Maximilian offers the choice of an amnesty or the death penalty to those possessing arms.	act 2, scene 1
1866 (13 July) With the rising costs, Napoleon III is proposing to remove French troops from Mexico, Carlota embarks for France to seek his continued support.	act 2, scene 2 (7 July: the decision).
(August) Carlota obtains three interviews with Napoleon but fails to achieve her purpose.	act 2, scene 3
(27, 29, 30 September) Carlota has three audiences with the pope but fails to win the Church's backing.	act 2, scene 4

(October)
Carlota is examined by the alienist and nerve   act 3, scene 1
specialist, Dr. Riedel of Vienna.

Carlota is taken to the Château de Bouchout,
Belgium. French troops under General Bazaine
withdraw from Mexico.

1867 (14 May)
Maximilian captured by Juárez while defending
Querétaro.

(19 June)
Maximilian is executed.   act 3, scene 3

1927 (19 January)
Carlota dies in the Château de Bouchout, during   act 1, scene 1;
the presidency in Mexico of Plutarco Elías   act 3, scene 2;
Calles.   act 3, scene 4

1943
Manuel Avila Camacho is president of Mexico.   Usigli writes
                                                   the play.

1947 (11 April)
Miguel Alemán is president of Mexico.   First night of
                                                   *Corona de
                                                   sombra* at the
                                                   Teatro Arbeu.

A closer comparison shows that not only the play's events but the characters, too, have a basis in history, as do their foibles and preoccupations, and the matters that they discuss. (All, that is, with the exception of Erasmo and his visit to Carlota. As we shall see, it is this exception that provides the key to the play, opening up Usigli's dramatic purpose for us.) Historians agree that in 1864 Carlota was bored and discontented in her luxurious residence at Miramar (on the Italian Adriatic coast), dreamed of greater things, was driven by restless ambition, and played an important part in persuading Maximilian to accept the Mexican throne. (The account by Richard O'Connor entitled *The Cactus Throne: The Tragedy of Maximilian and Carlota* is particularly illuminating. His version of events on pages 74, 87, and 91 compares with *Corona de sombra*, act 1, scene 2.)[7] There is agreement, too, that when Napoleon was arranging for the withdrawal of French troops from Mexican soil in 1866, Carlota urged her husband not to relinquish the struggle and made the decision to go on a personal mission to win support for their cause in Europe (1.2). Her interview with Napoelon III at Saint Cloud in August 1866 (2.3), his refusal to support the Mexican intervention any longer, her wildly agitated behavior, and even the glass of orange juice that she rejected in the belief that it was poisoned—all these details have been reported by eyewitnesses.[8] Usigli may well have read the memoirs of Maximilian's private secretary, José Luis Blasio, who was sent to Europe to assist Carlota and report back to the emperor.[9] Blasio's account confirms the essence of the interview with Pope Pius IX in the Vatican in 1866. It is worth adding that even the scene where Usigli's Carlota is examined by an alienist (3.1) is based on fact. In October of 1866 the celebrated alienist and nerve specialist Dr. Riedel of Vienna examined the empress and was compelled to admit that he saw no hope of curing her mental disorder.[10] She was transferred to the Château de Bouchout, north of Brussels, where she remained until her death in 1927.

Although Maximilian's role in *Corona de sombra* is less important—in purely dramatic terms—than that of Carlota, his function in the ideas conveyed is equally significant. It is worth pointing out, therefore, that his stage personality, too, has some of the best-known traits of the historical figure. There is ample evidence that Maximilian demanded proof of the Mexican people's wish for him to be their emperor and that he vacillated greatly before accepting the throne, having received warnings from a variety of notable sources (1.2). Historians acknowledge the reputation that he had already formed in Europe for his progressive ideas, and his efforts—once in Mexico—to seek an end to hatred between the political parties, to obtain their collaboration, and to introduce liberal measures, such as an amnesty for political offenders, the removal of press censorship, and freedom of worship, which made it difficult for him to sign the decree that those who failed to hand in their weapons would be executed if captured (2.1).[11] Several aspects of the execution scene (3.3) bear comparison with historical record: Maximilian, having resolved to lead his troops in the campaign against Juárez's republican forces, faced the death sentence with dignity and a heroic sense of self-sacrifice. He asked (in vain) for Generals Miramón and Mejía to be reprieved and yielded the central position before the firing squad to Miramón. According to one version, he declared: "Voy a morir por una causa justa, la de la independencia y libertad de México. ¡Que mi sangre selle las desgracias de mi nueva patria! ¡Viva México!" ("I am going to die for a just cause, that of the independence and freedom of Mexico. May my blood put a seal on the misfortunes of my new country! Long live Mexico!")[12] Some of his words are echoed by Usigli's character (TC 2:216, 220).

This does not exhaust the points of comparison between the play and historical records, but rather than make a systematic listing of the details, I prefer to undertake a more revealing operation: to note the deliberate divergences. There are essentially two types of divergence—or, to use A.A. Parker's term, emendment—introduced by Usigli. One is a process of simplification, the other a more fundamental modification corresponding to the author's personal interpretation.

Let us consider briefly two examples of the first of these types. In the scene at Miramar in 1864 (1.2), Usigli gives no sign that Carlota had second thoughts about the Mexican venture; in reality, however, she had her doubts but subsequently overcame them. This is a case where the dramatist has concentrated on the character's dominating force—her ambition—in order to capture the essence of the situation. Despite the risk of doing his character an injustice, he was guided by his instinct to avoid excessive subtleties and to drive home salient points. A different kind of change is made with the interview at Saint Cloud (2.3). Historically, Carlota had three interviews with Louis Napoleon in August 1866. In the first of them she managed to control herself; when a second meeting was refused, she gate-crashed and behaved in a wild and melodramatic manner, finally rejecting a glass of orange juice and fleeing from the palace; the third meeting (at the Grand Hotel) ended with Napoleon admitting that France was withdrawing its support and with Carlota exploding in a vitriolic verbal attack against him. Ever the skilled craftsman, Usigli captured the gist of the three interviews, with their tenor and development, in one single, taut encounter. (Similarly, the scene with the pope is also a compressed version of three separate audiences.) Clearly, what these examples involve is a matter of dramatic technique rather than interpretation.

Emendments of the second type, however, actually entail a modification of the essential truth. For example, Usigli tends to gloss over the fact that there was something wrong with the marriage between Maximilian and Carlota: the word had passed around that they were sleeping separately, and "childlessness after seven years of marriage had become a very sensitive subject at Chapultepec."[13] The historian tends to reject the romantic picture of Maximilian and Carlota: "It was a love story with human flaws, that of a prince to whom casual infidelity was a princely privilege and a princess whose intense pride would not allow her to grant it."[14] The dramatist, on the other hand, though hinting lightly at this, prefers the romantic picture. It is in keeping with his general intention to gain sympathy for the couple; it makes their separation all the harder and more worthy of the audience's pity.

Usigli's treatment of the decisions concerning Carlota's mission to Europe and Maximilian's continued occupation of the throne in Mexico is highly significant. In 1866, with the prospect of the French troops' departure, Maximilian had—according to some versions—decided to abdicate. Carlota dissuaded him.[15] Moreover, she wrote a memorandum for Maximilian in which she voiced her opinion that abdication amounted to failure, cowardice, or error: "I say that emperors do not give themselves up. So long as there is an emperor here, there will be an empire, even if no more than six feet of earth belong to him."[16] Usigli, on the contrary, made his Maximilian say, "Estoy clavado en esta tierra. . . . Mejor morir en México que vivir en Europa como un archiduque de Strauss. Pero tú tienes que salvarte" ("I am firmly rooted to this earth. . . . Better to die in Mexico than to live in Europe like one of Strauss's archdukes. But *you* must save youself") (TC 2:186), transferring to him a spirit of resignation and sacrifice. There seem to be two important inferences to be made here. Usigli was surely trying to make of Maximilian a figure more heroic, more sympathetic to the Mexican people. At the same time, he was deliberately reducing—though without removing—Carlota's culpability concerning her husband's execution. He seems intent on generalizing her guilt so that it concerns not merely her role in bringing Maximilian to his death but her part in a black episode in the nation's history.

Equally significant are the changes that Usigli introduced to portray Carlota's insanity. According to Maximilian's private secretary, the first signs of madness appeared on the journey from Mexico to Vera Cruz, where she was to embark for Europe. There were rumors indeed (for which Blasio finds no foundation) that at Puebla and Cuernavaca "she had been poisoned by being given . . . doses of toloache," an Indian herb said to be capable of producing insanity.[17] As opposed to this evidence, another source, the historian Arnold Blumberg, considers that "it was on the journey to Rome that the first serious evidence of psychosis began to manifest themselves," and not until the first audience with the pope did "the full force of her paranoid convictions became apparent."[18] In Usigli's play, the theme of madness is obliquely foreshadowed in the dialogue with Max at Chapultepec, when Carlota suddenly opts to seek aid in Europe. She says at one point, "Ya sé que parece una locura . . . " ("I know that it looks mad . . ."), and furiously begins to imagine wild plans against France until Max intervenes with the words "No digas locuras, amor mío" ("Don't be mad, my love") (TC 2:187, 188). However, the audience first notices symptoms of genuine insanity in Carlota's interview with Napoleon. Failing to achieve any positive response to her demands that France should treat the Mexican emperor and empress justly in fulfillment of promises made to them, she becomes nervous and fatigued, she finds her head spinning, she lets loose a storm of abuse, she claims to have been poisoned by the drink of orange juice offered to her, and she leaves the stage with a display of highly agitated behavior. The great importance of this consists in the fact that Usigli was intent on linking the onset of her madness firmly and distinctly with her frustration in the attempt to gain cooperation from Napoleon. Her insanity is therefore made to derive not only from the confrontation of her personal ambitions and desires with an inflexible opposition but from the treachery of France, the evil of Napoleon, and the sense that Mexico was betrayed.

Some historical reports suggest that when Carlota reached Rome, she had lost sight of her principal objective. In her first audience with the pope, for example, she is thought to have forgotten "that she had come to plead a truce between church and state," and "she had cried out that agents of Napoleon and Eugénie were trying to poison her."[19] The pope called at her hotel two days later and found her calm, but the following day she demanded admittance to the Vatican and papal protection, creating a scene until the pope allowed her to spend the night there. Although we may presume that she did mention her mission at some point, it looks as though her principal concern was for her own safety. Yet Usigli makes the issue of the concordat prominent in the opening of his Vatican scene (2.4). Again, therefore, we realize that the dramatist was determined to diminish the purely personal aspect of Carlota's situation in order to emphasize her role as a national emissary.

What followed was more melodramatic in reality than anything that Usigli included in his play. Back at her hotel, Carlota accused the lady of her bedchamber—whom she had known for many years—of selling herself to Napoleon's agents. She dismissed her and told her to flee or else she would be arrested. She then filled a jug with water at a public fountain, bought a stove and some cooking equipment, two live chickens, and a basket of eggs, took them to her room, and ordered her maid to kill the chickens and dress and cook them immediately. From that day, she reportedly ate only things cooked in her presence. When Blasio went to take dictation from her a few days afterward, an extraordinary sight met his eyes: "There was . . . a table, on which was the charcoal stove used by Mathilde in cooking the Empress's meals. Some hens were tied to the legs of the table, and on it were eggs and the pitcher of water which Carlota procured for herself."[20] Such material would have been appropriate for a drama showing the disintegration of a personality, but it did not form part of Usigli's plan for a drama with a national focus. Nor did it suit the elegant, dignified portrayal of insanity that he wished to give of Carlota.

In his handling of this insanity, Usigli maintained an essential verisimilitude. His Carlota appears to suffer from a functional psychosis, which is manifested in symptoms that correspond with those that psychologists would expect to find in a genuine case. Schizophrenia in general is described in the following terms: "Usually young people are affected, once ill they show an inclination to withdraw and as the illness progresses the personality, though not the intellect, shows signs of dilapidation. The schizophrenic's inner life becomes of more concern to him than objective reality, against which he does not check his ideas."[21] The subgroup of schizophrenics to which Carlota would seem to belong, the paranoid schizophrenics, "are notably hallucinated (perceiving—usually hearing—things when there is nothing there) and deluded (possessed of false beliefs of a fixed and pathological type."[22] The evidence shows that the real Carlota had "periods of withdrawal from reality."[23] When the Empress Elizabeth of Austria visited her at Bouchout in 1875, she found "a gloomy salon with draped windows, which had been converted into Carlota's throne room. . . . Carlota sat on her mock throne, wearing a tinsel crown, toying with a bowl filled with fake jewels."[24] She was known to write letters in which she called Maximilian "Lord of the Earth" and "Sovereign of the Universe."[25] The Carlota who we see in the opening scene of *Corona de sombra* is similarly hallucinated. She expects to be treated like a monarch (her servants address her as "Majestad") and she believes—after seeing Erasmo's book—that Maximilian is alive and that she has returned to him in Mexico. Her demand for more light, when the sun is pouring in through the windows, manifests a lack of awareness of objective reality. Her sudden change of mood as she contemplates the Mexican history book is symptomatic of an unstable mental condition. In one or two details the connection between the dramatic character and the real Carlota is remarkably close. The scene confronting the audience when the Dama de Compañía has drawn the curtains and lit the

candles bears a striking resemblance to the sight witnessed by t
Empress Elizabeth. Carlota expresses an anguished preoccupation
with time: "¿Y qué es el tiempo? ¿Dónde está el tiempo? ¿Dónde
lo guardan? . . . Max, Max, Max. El tiempo está en el mar, natural-
mente" ("And what is time? Where is time? Where is it kept? . . .
Max, Max, Max. Time is in the sea, naturally") (TC 2:158–59),
calling to mind words that the real person is reputed to have spoken
to Elizabeth: "Love makes time pass. . . . Time makes love
pass."[26]

The treatment of Carlota's insanity therefore both imitates reality
and creates a convincing dramatic character. But Usigli introduced
a major innovation: he finally gave his protagonist full lucidity. The
consequences of this emendment of reality are far-reaching. His
Carlota achieves a new insight into her past, and by this means she
is released from the enduring torment of her life. The extent of this
departure from historical fact could be justified both on the grounds
that it contains more than a grain of underlying truth and because it
is vital for the dramatist's moral purpose. We know that from 1866
to 1927 the real Carlota "endured alternating periods of sanity and
insanity."[27] A few weeks after Maximilian's funeral she sent a
photograph of him to Blasio inscribed, "To Don José Luis Blasio
. . . Pray for the repose of the soul of His Majesty, Ferdinand
Maximilian Joseph, Emperor of Mexico,"[28] proving that she knew
of his death even though at other times she seemed to think him
ruler of the Earth. Usigli transferred this pattern of alternating light
and darkness into one single change from darkness to light. There is
no evidence of such an illumination for the real Carlota at the time
of her death. In January 1927 she caught influenza and, after willful
resistance, finally died of the ensuing pneumonia. The play's version treats her death as the direct outcome of the traumatic experience of reliving painful scenes from her past and of her new insight
into the meaning of Maximilian's execution.

This innovation by Usigli acquires its full dramatic effect through
a second invention: the Mexican historian, Erasmo. In *Corona de
sombra* this fictitious character—playing the dramatist's role within
the play—is intrigued by the idea that the inability of Carlota to
meet a definitive death for so many years implies some supreme
design or justice in control of events: "Yo no creo como todos en mi
país, que Carlota haya muerto porque está loca. Creo que ha vivido
hasta ahora para algo, que hay un objeto en el hecho de que haya
sobrevivido sesenta años a su marido, y quiero saber cuál es ese
objeto" ("I do not believe like everyone in my country that Carlota
has died because she is mad. I believe that she has lived until now

for something, that there is an object in the fact that she should have survived her husband by sixty years, and I want to know what that object is") (TC 2:158). When he eventually discovers the missing explanation, he is able to speak on behalf of the dramatist, revealing Usigli's message to the audience. In act 1 Erasmo categorically summarizes the typical Mexican perception of Carlota's wrongs: "Esta mujer era una ambiciosa, causó la muerte de su esposo y acarreó muchas enormes desgracias. Era orgullosa y mala" ("This woman was full of ambition, caused her husband's death and brought about many great misfortunes. She was haughty and bad") (TC 2:151). By the time the action returns to 1927, three scenes from the end of the play, we are able to see—with Erasmo—that her main errors have each brought an appropriate punishment. For her excessive ambition, which led her to interfere with the affairs of Mexico, she has been punished with personal frustration and sixty years of insanity. For driving Maximilian to his death (though we remember that Usigli carefully does not emphasize this point), she is punished with sixty years of remorse. The moment of enlightenment, when she realizes the full extent of her wrongs and simultaneously becomes aware of the magnitude of her suffering, is itself a final punishment. Indeed, it is possible to make the case that she has been subconsciously avoiding this moment since 1867, and to see her insanity as a form of flight from the reality that causes her pain. Alternatively, the madness could be considered as a form of self-inflicted punishment, as Usigli himself suggested in his prologue: "Edipo se arranca los ojos y . . . Carlota se arranca la razón" ("Oedipus tears out his eyes and . . . Carlota tears out her reason") (TC 3.:629).

In this scene, however, Erasmo is still not quite satisfied with the extent of the revelations. Intuitively we might already sense some extenuating circumstances that he has overlooked. When the pope says of Carlota, "su corona es de espinas y de sombra" ("her crown is of thorns and of darkness") (TC 2:202), he calls to mind an extra dimension in the symbolism of the crown. It is not difficult to see that the crown symbolizes the darkness of insanity, distress, and torment while also serving as an ironical reminder of her frustrated dreams of empire. Carlota herself calls it her "corona de sombra" (TC 2:214, 221) and her "corona de pesadilla" ("nightmare crown") (TC 2:215). But the pope's use of the image "espinas," with its obvious allusion to Christ's crown of thorns, suggests not only mockery and suffering but also the notion of sacrifice. It is possible, therefore, to see Carlota as a sacrificial victim who wears her crown on behalf of Mexico, as Christ wore his on behalf of mankind. In act

3, scene 2 Usigli allows her to argue that there has been a divine purpose and justice in everybody's fate except her own. She hints at the disproportion between her punishment and the crime: "¿Cometí un crimen tan grande para merecer esta separación?" ("Did I commit such a great crime as to deserve this separation?") (TC 2:213), she asks Erasmo; "¿Y no bastan acaso sesenta años de vivir en la noche, en la muerte, con esta corona de pesadilla en la frente, para merecer el perdón?" ("And are sixty years of living in the night, in death, with this nightmare crown on my brow, not enough perhaps to merit pardon?") (TC 2:214–15). At this moment the figure on stage becomes pitiable, and the audience surely feels some compassion. But before we are fully ready to grant our own pardon, we await the reaction of Erasmo, whom Carlota herself has called "la mirada de México" ("the eyes of Mexico") (TC 2:215).

Erasmo remains uncertain until one further scene is re-created. Only the execution of Maximilian is capable of giving the events their full symbolic meaning. After learning how her husband faced the firing squad and what he said about his execution, she lucidly recognizes that his death had an essential integrity. To this peace of mind is added the spiritual comfort derived from her hope of being reunited with Max in death. Her own death then ensues, releasing her simultaneously from the crown of darkness, the agony of separation, and the sense of guilt. If this dramatic transformation in Carlota and this romantic idea of reunion go dangerously near to the melodramatic and the sentimental, it is because Usigli wished to drive home the point that the real Carlota underwent a greater punishment than was fitting in the light of his own understanding of her role in Mexican history.

This intepretation is enhanced by the way in which Maximilian is treated in the play. Although he has some of the weaknesses that history imputes to him, our reaction to him is complicated by Usigli's emphasis on certain ennobling traits. He is seen to be devoted to his wife, yet he will not place state affairs in jeopardy for the sake of his love for her (he postpones their meeting in the wood [2.2]. He is an anguished thinker who seeks a meaning for his life, a man of courage and dignity even in the face of death. And most important of all, he develops a sense of dedication to Mexico's interests. In the context of my earlier reasoning, if Carlota is punished by being *denied* for sixty years a death that is a solace, Maximilian is permitted that early death because his crime was less serious. Although his execution punishes his interference in Mexican affairs, the absence of suffering corresponds to the absence of any blameworthy motivation. Not only Carlota but he, too, emerges from the play in a more favorable light than that in which Mexican history tends to represent him.

On the whole, historians regard the Second Empire as an interlude in the period dominated by Juárez and the Reform. As an indication of the relative unimportance attached to the roles of Maximilian and Carlota, El Colegio de México's *Historia general de México* devotes a mere twenty-four of its fifteen hundred pages to the entire topic of the Second Empire.[29] Elsewhere, in a colorful sentence, L. B. Simpson declares that he prefers to leave the pageantry, romance, and tragedy to others and to "name the affair for what it was: a desperate gamble on the part of the dying colonial elements of Mexico to regain their lost advantage by means of a puppet prince whom they hoped to dominate; a cynical grab of territory by Napoleon the Little; a novelesque adventure by a foolish young man and his power-mad wife, who saw themselves as exponents of Divine Right in the Western Hemisphere."[30] This is a fairly typical attitude. In more neutral language the usual assessment of the period may be summarized in three items: *(a)* Mexico's own Conservatives saw Maximilian as their opportunity to win back lost power; *(b)* Napoleon III, ambitious to extend his French empire, used the nonrepayment of debts as a pretext for invasion; *(c)* Maximilian—with no hope of acquiring a throne in Europe—pursued his ambition to act as a progressive, idealistic, liberal ruler, while Carlota sought the power and glory of being an empress. There is nothing here to suggest that Usigli could have been looking beyond the "pageantry, romance, and tragedy" when he chose to write a play on this theme. It certainly does not explain why he should regard this as one of the keys to Mexico's sovereignty. However, some historians acknowledge actual advantages for the country in the episode. These may be summarized in another three items: *(a)* it unified the country against foreign interference (in 1861 Juárez's problems looked insurmountable, with anarchy threatening; in 1867 he was the leader of a far more united people, great though his problems remained); *(b)* it finally brought Mexico its full independence (since independence from Spain in 1821, Mexico's sovereignty had continued to be threatened by colonial powers including France, Spain, and the United States); *(c)* it taught the world at large that bad debts cannot be collected by the costly and unjust use of force. Alluding only vaguely to the last of these, Usigli resolved his play with a focus on the first two items. It is these explanations that satisfy Erasmo at last that he has discovered the elusive meaning: "Decid a Maximiliano de Habsburgo"—he says to the dying Carlota—"que México consumó su independencia en

1867 gracias a él. Que gracias a él, el mundo aprendió una gran lección en México. . . . La revolución acabará un día, cuando los mexicanos comprendan lo que significa la muerte de Maximiliano. . . . Si el Emperador no se hubiera interpuesto, Juárez habría muerto antes de tiempo a manos de otro mexicano" ("Tell Maximilian of Hapsburg that Mexico consummated its independence in 1867 thanks to him. That thanks to him the world learned a great lesson in Mexico. . . . The revolution will end one day, when Mexicans understand what the death of Maximilian signifies. . . . If the emperor had not intervened, Juárez would have died before his time at the hands of another Mexican") (TC 2:220).

In his prologue to *Corona de sombra*, Usigli adopted an even wider perspective. He explained the historical events of the period concerned as a contrast between the forces of good and evil, or, as he put it in more vivid terms, between "el acto del diablo y el acto de Dios" ("the act of the Devil and the act of God") (TC 3:636). When his Carlota speaks to the pope, therefore, she is not merely using figurative language, nor is she simply demonstrating her insanity, when she claims, "Yo sé que fue el diablo el que nos llevó a México, Santidad, lo sé ahora—y el diablo es Napoleón" ("I know that it was the Devil who brought us to Mexico, Holiness, I know that now—and the Devil is Napoleon) (TC 2:201). There is indeed a basis for this use of terms in a letter written by the real Carlota to Maximilian after her failure to gain reassurances from Napoleon. She wrote of the latter: "He has Hell on his side. . . . He is the reincarnation of villainy on earth and means to destroy what is good. . . . For me, he is the Devil in person."[31] Instead of treating these as the words of a woman gradually losing her reason, Usigli took them as essentially reasonable. They became a kind of insight into an underlying reality. In his prologue, therefore, he argued that the Devil had been triumphant in taking over Europe. In Mexico, however, God had intervened. The choice of Maximilian, the pope's rejection of the concordat, the execution of Maximilian, and the insanity of Carlota—all could be explained as divine intervention to save Mexico: "La muerte de Maximiliano, que es uno de los medios divinos, parece un castigo; pero es, en realidad, la única forma en que Dios puede salvarlo" ("Maximiliano's death, which is one of the divine measures, seems to be a punishment; but it is really the only way in which God can save him") (TC 3:637). According to the same criteria, Usigli saw Carlota's madness as the means by which God prevented her from continuing with the struggle and from possibly taking the Devil to Mexico.

Since this interpretation of history visualizes Maximilian and

Carlota as mere pawns in a contest between the powers of good and evil, it correspondingly reduces the personal responsibility of the two human beings involved. As Usigli explained in the prologue, "Carlota es castigada por lo único irredimible: por el tiempo. Pero el tiempo, que es su castigo, se convierte al final en su perdón—prueba de perfección cíclica—puesto que antes de morir ella pudo saber, aunque sólo fuera en el último fondo de su subconsciencia, que el tiempo había segado a todos los héroes y a todos los villanos de la tragedia, y que el acto de Dios había borrado totalmente el acto del diablo" ("Carlota is punished by the only irredeemable thing: by time. But time, which is her punishment, is converted at the end into her pardon—proof of cyclical perfection—since before dying she was able to discover, even if it were only in the very depths of her subconscious, that time had cut down all the heroes and all the villains of the tragedy, and that the act of God had totally wiped out the act of the Devil") (TC 3:637). In other words, the dramatized version of these events shows the sixty years of madness as a kind of poetic justice in history.[32] Erasmo—who represents the rewriting of Mexican history—completes the enactment of this poetic justice by helping Carlota to return to sanity, easing her conscience, and releasing her from the punishment of survival. As though he recognizes that Carlota had suffered more than is fitting, Erasmo finally corrects the balance.

✱   Besides being the key that opens up the play's historical meaning, Erasmo is the key to its success as theatre. In literal terms, *Corona de sombra* could be considered as the dramatization of his visit to Bouchout and conversation with Carlota. The duration of the play is that of their dialogue. The scene is that of Carlota's final hours. All the rest is flashback, like an insight into Erasmo's imagination as he listens to Carlota's memories. The device is, of course, carefully introduced by her words "Aquella noche" at the end of 1.1, and continued by her voice off stage at the beginning of 1.3, 2.2, and 2.3. And there are neat links between the two time planes, such as the repetition of the words "Se me ha olvidado" ("I have forgotten") at the end of 3.1 and the beginning of 3.2. One scene is actually the reenactment of an episode "narrated" by Erasmo to Carlota—the execution of Maximilian (3.3). Erasmo's importance in relation to the theme is that he resembles Juárez, looks at Carlota with the eyes of Mexico, and revises the history books. But he also performs the vital dramatic roles of provoking and precipitating the action, and of guiding the audience's responses into the right channels. Finally, he determines the play's structure.

The bulk of *Corona de sombra* consists of lively scenes from

Carlota's distant past, always sharpened by interacting personalities and conflicting interests. The history is never dull. For example, the process whereby the young couple came to a decision over the invitation to rule in Mexico is compressed into a single discussion between them, in which Carlota's heady eagerness confronts and gradually overcomes Max's hesitant circumspection (1.2). The vast political, religious, and cultural difficulties in Mexico, focused on the antagonism between its Indian heritage and European colonialism, are presented by means of General Miramóm's dream (1.3). A whole range of complex issues relating to the French presence in Mexico are encapsulated in the personality of Major-General Bazaine, for whom the empress entertains a virulent disdain (2.1, 2). This exemplifies Usigli's dramatic technique. Rather than expecting the audience to respond to ideology, he fascinates us with the clash between Bazaine and Carlota as individuals. In fact, in some of these scenes the private domain assumes a greater impact than the public. The Second Empire is represented almost entirely through the relationship between the married couple. All the Mexican scenes end with a focus on their love, particularly to show how state affairs intervene between them, and the idea of resuming their intimate walks in the wood of Chapultepec becomes an important motif, finally suggesting the solace of death (TC 2:181, 189, 221).

But these scenes from the past are never quite autonomous. Encompassed by a "present time," they are subservient to those set in 1927. Visually, the impact of the structural features is enhanced for the audience by the way in which the set is constructed. Usigli stipulated that the stage should represent a double room, divided by a glass screen. In the first and last scenes of the play the whole double room is used; in all the others only the right or the left section is used. The first advantage of this arrangement is that it helps to overcome the problem of unusually frequent and large-scale changes of location and time, since no two consecutive scenes are set in both the same place *and* the same year. It is worth noting that Usigli resisted the obvious possibility of identifying one side of the stage with Europe and the other with Mexico. Instead he chose to locate scenes alternately right and then left (irrespective of their geographial setting) in order to create what Dennis Perri aptly calls a feeling of "movement through time and space."[33] In addition, we have the sense that only the full stage offers a full reality, while the half-stage reduces the action to the half-reality of memory or imagination. Only the first and last scenes possess this whole dimension. The incompleteness of the action is at once apparent when we return to 1927 temporarily in 3.3 because although we know that we are back in the castle in Belgium, we are expecting a double room occupying both sides of the stage.[34]

The great success of Usigli in planning *Corona de sombra*'s structure was to contrive a constant source of tension. From the beginning of act 1 the audience, immediately drawn into the same spirit of inquiry that has brought Erasmo to Bouchout, is eager for numerous explanations, and the flashbacks satisfy this need. Above all, the opening scene of the play establishes our interest in Carlota. It creates an image of her and provokes a response toward her before events from the past modify our impression. The porter's veneration for Carlota is the first influence upon us, the concern for her health expressed by the lady-in-waiting and the doctor is the second. Carlota's psychology intrigues us. Far from appearing simply a mad old woman, she strikes us as a figure at once strange and dignified, senile and vital, tentative and imperious. Her anguish over the passing of time elevates her suffering and enhances our tendency to feel pity for her. Because of this preparation of the audience, Carlota's youthful personality in the first scene from the past—at Miramar—creates a sharp contrast. Quickly, some of Erasmo's preconceptions are confirmed: she is ambitious, vain, impatient, proud, and, by twentieth-century standards, racist and politically unscrupulous. Like Erasmo, however, what we are most curious to know is how her madness interrelates with the rest of her life. And this is the aspect of the theme that Usigli reserves until the second half of the play. Her return to Europe forms a pivot in the middle of the central act, after which he gives us scenes that show insanity beginning to take hold of her (2.3, 4). Act 3 opens with an alienist confirming her pathological condition. When Bernard Shaw read *Corona de sombra,* his one mild reservation concerned the possible superfluousness of this scene.[35] But he perhaps overlooked the importance of focusing the audience's attention on the issue that was to remain crucial until the final curtain. Usigli takes us from insanity in 1866 to lucidity on 19 January 1927 by interlocking the four alternating scenes from "past" and "present" in act 3. The first return to Bouchout is a skillfully arranged false lead, temporarily creating the sense that questions have been answered. Up to a point, they have. We now understand some of the origins of Carlota's madness and sense some of the poetic justice in her long period of suffering. But the matter of paramount importance to Erasmo—and ultimately to the audience, too—remains unsolved: is there not a disproportion between the extent of her torment and the scale of her culpability? and does this not suggest that her survival until the postrevolutionary period must have an underlying explanation? The fact that only a final flashback to the execution of Maximilian can provide this explanation is what definitively fuses the historical and psychological themes of the play. Moreover, having allowed Erasmo to convey the political message, Usigli removes him from the stage and closes with the focus on Carlota's individual plight. Her new understanding and spirit of self-sacrifice have created a positive attitude toward her. The stage lighting—so effectively used in act 1 to communicate her madness—is dimmed to coincide with her death and then abruptly turned up to bathe her figure in brilliance. The audience therefore experiences a certain pity and sadness but is compelled at the end to react positively, feeling Carlota's death as a benefit and sharing some of the quasi-religious sentiment introduced by the sight of the king of Beligum, the lady-in-waiting, and the porter kneeling beside her.

Corona de sombra is justly ranked as one of Usigli's best plays. Some critics have found its scope excessively ambitious. I would argue that the only serious reason for its failure to gain an even greater international prestige is the esoteric nature of the historical basis for non-Mexican audiences. Apart from this, it is surely first-rate theatre, with a multiplicity of levels ranging from the universal to the national and from the political to the private. There is tension in every dialogue, and the suspense is sustained from the moment when Erasmo fires our curiosity to the last minute of Carlota's life. Moreover, the play is a striking spectacle, with period costumes, frequent scene changes, a split stage, and unusual lighting effects. The theme is both entertaining and thought provoking. At a simple level we have an unusual love story, and at a deep level a reinterpretation of history. Affairs of state are skillfully blended with intimate lives. Above all, however, *Corona de sombra* impresses us for the powerful study of insanity in its central figure. It is she who dominates the play, unifies the diverse elements, and endows it with the particular quality that for Usigli was the difference between humdrum reality and good theatre. She deserves to be regarded as the outstanding dramatic character of all his plays.

Corona de fuego

In chapter 1 it was noted that Usigli harbored a long-standing ambition to write a tragedy. He liked to think of *El gesticulador,* of course, as a tentative first effort, but in chapter 3 I argued that the term "tragedy" could be applied only very loosely to that play.

Corona de sombra also contains tragic ingredients, particularly in the scenes set in the castle of Bouchout in 1927, with their focus on a Carlota who has fallen from great heights as a result of a flaw in her character and who appears to be suffering a severe punishment. Moreover, the emotional effect of Carlota's death as the curtain falls bears some resemblance to tragic catharsis. But she has insufficient greatness and the wrong kind of reputation to be a tragic heroine in the classical tradition, and in any case, before she dies she has been released from her affliction and has already ceased to be tragic in the sense of suffering more than she deserves. In 1962, with *Corona de fuego* (Crown of Fire) (his only serious play in verse)[36] Usigli finally met the necessary criteria. It proved to be one of the most ambitious of all his ventures, for it represented an attempt to combine his search for tragedy with his mission to explain the essence of national sovereignty. In the following pages, I hope to show how these aspirations led him to deviate from the theatrical norms that he had always advocated.

The execution of the last Aztec ruler in 1525 was seen by Usigli as the earliest key to Mexico's sovereignty. After the deaths of Moctezuma and his successor, Cuitlahuac, leadership fell to the next in line, Cuauhtémoc. By all historical accounts, Cuauhtémoc led a heroic resistance against the Spanish invaders until the eventual fall of Tenochtitlán in 1521, when he was taken prisoner. He is revered for further heroism, moreover, in his refusal to divulge information about lost treasures. It is his torture by fire that provides Usigli with the title *Corona de fuego*. The play's action, however, is a reenactment of the events culminating on 27 and 28 February four years later, during Hernán Cortés's expedition south towards Honduras—a journey on which the royal prisoner was taken for security reasons—and the geographical setting is the territory then occupied by the Chontales and the Moctunes. The plot may be summarized as follows: Cortés and his Spanish troops, after a long, hard march, are given an ambiguous reception by the Chontales and the Moctunes. Informers tell Cortés of a threatened uprising by the Indian peoples under the leadership of Cuauhtémoc. Despite the lack of clarity about Cuauhtémoc's complicity, Cortés decides on a show of strength and executes the Indian monarch with two other Aztec nobles.

The first point to make about his play's action is that once again Usigli followed recorded events with remarkable care and insight. His version is, to a considerable extent, an imaginative synthesis of the various accounts of Cuauhtémoc's execution.[37] Even some of the smaller details of the play are based on those accounts. As far as the plot is concerned, for example, Usigli took advantage of the deceptiveness or devious behavior on the part of the Indian cacique Pax Bolón Acha. According to some records, the chief's son, Paxua, was sent to greet Cortés and to impart the false information that Pax Bolón himself had just died. In the first act of *Corona de fuego,* the reproduction of that scene is clearly designed to introduce as early as possible the sense that conspiracies might be in the air. This subterfuge over a small thing (Pax Bolón was actually concerned only to keep Cortés away from his rich lands) paves the way for Cortés's later readiness to believe in subterfuge on a major scale. To take an example of a different kind, we notice how one or two of the play's most important speeches are quite closely based on the words attributed to the actual historical figures. Some of Cuauhtémoc's bitter remarks to Cortés after he has been sentenced to death are remarkably similar in the play and the eyewitness account in Bernal Díaz's *Historia verdadera de la conquista de la Nueva España:*

Usigli	Bernal Díaz
Cuauhtémoc. Hace ya muchos días, oh Malinche, vine a entender que me darías muerte, la muerte que me das en esta ceiba. Muchos días que sé que tus palabras son falsas . . . . Muchos días supe que tú habrías de matar sin justicia al jefe de los hombres de la tierra de Aztlán. Que, tuyo o mío, Dios te demande esta muerte injusta que yo me debí dar en la batalla cuando venció tu fuerza venenosa. (TC 2:836)	Y cuando le ahorcaban, dijo Guatemuz: "¡Oh, Malinche!: días había que yo tenía entendido que esta muerte me habías de dar y había conocido tus falsas palabras, porque me matas sin justicia! "Dios te la demande, pues yo no me la di cuando te me entregaba en mi ciudad de México."[38]
(Cuauhtémoc. Many days ago, oh Malinche, I came to understand that you would put me to death, the death that you give me on this ceiba tree. For many days I have known that your words are false. . . . Many days ago I knew that you would kill without justice the leader of the people of Aztlán. May God require this unjust death from you, since I should have put myself to death	(And while they were hanging him, Guatemuz said: "Oh, Malinche: For days I have understood that you were going to give me this death and known your false words, for you kill me without justice. May God require this death of you, since I did not put myself to death when I surrendered to

in the battle when your venomous   you in my city of Mexico.")
strength prevailed.)

The main purpose of paying such careful respect to historical record is, of course, to endow the whole play with the authenticity that is essential for communicating a national message to the audience. But naturally this play, like *Corona de sombra,* becomes in certain respects *"antihistórica"* when the artistic imagination sets to work on the material. Dramatic structure determined one kind of deviation from literal reality. In sharp contrast with the previous *Corona, Corona de fuego* takes place in less than twenty-four hours. Moreover, whereas the former is located in various European settings as well as in Mexico, the latter is restricted to a single neighborhood (two separate places in act 1, two adjacent sites in act 2, and a single location in act 3). According to Cortés's fifth letter, at least five days were involved and at least five leagues separated the sites.[39] The changes are immaterial, however, in terms of overall veracity. What Usigli gained in dramatic effect was a heightened tension and a concentrated intellectual focus on the major issues.

As in the case of *Corona de sombra,* the more interesting alterations are those that involved the manipulation of material in order to transform it into the dramatist's chosen shape. In part it was a question of taking full advantage of ambiguities and discrepancies in the various known versions. In the accounts by Cortés, Gómara, and Ixtlilxóchitl, the informer is named as Mexicaltzinco; the version by Bernal Díaz names Tapia and Juan Velázquez; and a *Relación de servicios* of 1605 claims that doña Marina uncovered the plot.[40] Usigli put all these figures together in the play: the conspiracy is "uncovered" by Mexicaltzinco, with the help of additional reports by Tapia and Juan Velázquez, and in the presence of doña Marina. The consequence is a clear focus on the idea that a conspiracy certainly did exist. One of the most important discrepancies among the different sources is over the extent of Cuauhtémoc's own involvement in the conspiracy. In Cortés's letter to Charles V and Gómara's account, he is actually presented as the leader of the plot (not surprisingly, since both had an interest in justifying his execution). Bernal Díaz, however, quotes Cuauhtémoc's denial that the plan was his and that he had any intention of putting it into operation. Fray Juan de Torquemada reports no plot but merely complaints that were maliciously repeated to Cortes.[41] In order words, Usigli showed a bias here against the prejudiced accounts by Cortés and Gómara, for in his play the idea of a rebellion comes not from Cuauhtémoc but from Pax Bolón. Cuauhtémoc himself seems reluctant to take part, defers a decision, and merely plays a game in which he and his companions imagine the division of land among themselves. Usigli's purpose may be interpreted as that of underlining the harshness of the Spanish case against the Aztec leader, and of hinting at its possible unjustness.

Act 3 derives symbolic effect and emotional impact from a spectacular set, in which the key images are the silhouette of a huge cross counterbalanced by a great ceiba tree (representing the indigenous element). This appears to be a careful readjustment of the information conveyed in Bernal Díaz's account: "Y Cortés les mandó hacer una cruz en un árbol muy grande que se dice ceiba, que estaba junto a las casas adonde tenían los ídolos" ("And Cortés ordered them to make a cross in a very large tree that is called a ceiba, which was next to the houses where they had the idols").[42] The details of the execution itself, however, are even more revealing, for it is clear that Usigli chose the most barbaric and emotive of the versions. Cortés, Gómara, Díaz, and Ixtlilxóchitl all agree that Cuauhtémoc and other Indian leaders were merely hung. But a Mexican manuscript—the Mapa de Tepechpan—shows Cuauhtémoc's decapitated body hanging by its feet; and a Chontal text refers to his head being cut off and spiked on a ceiba tree.[43] It is the minority version that Usigli favored. His Cortés sentences the convicted prisoners as follows: "Sus cuerpos serán de estas ceibas colgados / por los pies después de ser decapitados" ("Your bodies shall be hung from these ceiba trees / by the feet after you are beheaded") (TC 2:834). The play therefore engages the audience's hostility toward the Spanish conquistador and sympathy for the dignified and unjustly treated Aztec leader. In perspective, we can see how Usigli set out to foster the notion that Cuauhtémoc was not so much punished as eliminated (and sacrificed).

Before the final curtain, *Corona de fuego* emphatically transcends the domain of history. With the light casting the cross's shadow on the ceiba tree, Usigli's character Bernal Díaz warns Cortés: "No mires atrás: / esa ceiba ha tomado la forma de una Cruz" ("Do not look back: that ceiba tree has taken on the form of a cross") (TC 2:839). Coming from Díaz, they are words evoking a sense of historical perspective that the characters themselves cannot share with the audience. But they also serve to guide our perception of the union between Christian and Indian deaths: the parallel between Christ's crucifixion and Cuauhtémoc's execution, and Christ's sacrifice for all mankind and Cuauhtémoc's sacrifice for his people. Above all, the associated concepts of resurrection and immanence are transferred by Usigli from Christianity to his

Mexican victim. The voice of the dead Cuauhtémoc counteracts the voice of Cortés; and then the chorus of Mexicans drowns the chorus of Spaniards with a final assertion that Cuauhtémoc lives on. Their words contain the essence of Usigli's message.

> Esos pies que quemaste caminan todavía,
> las manos que cortaste construyen todavía.
> Caminará Cuauhtémoc por esta que soñaba
> compacta, unida, y única y una,
> su nación mexicana. . . .
> Revivirán los ídolos como parte de Dios
> porque no ha muerto nuestro mundo de Anáhuac;
> porque, al morir, Cuauhtémoc le da vida y sentido.
>
> (TC 2 : 840)

(Those feet that you burned walk on, those hands that you cut off still build. Cuauhtémoc will walk on through this his country, the Mexican nation that he dreamed of, compact, united, unique and one. . . . The idols will live again as though a part of God because our world of Anáhuac has not died; because, on dying, Cuauhtémoc gives it life and meaning.)

It is a return to Usigli's favorite ideal of a united Mexico, this time with a specific emphasis on the persistence—we might almost say the supremacy—of indigenous culture.

Before making a full assessment of the idea of sovereignty and the success of the play, we need to take into account the chosen dramatic form: a tragedy in verse. Usigli's decision to write what he called (with misleading false modesty) a "Primer esquema para una tragedia antihistórica americana" ("first sketch for an antihistorical American tragedy") reflects an interest in dignifying the status of the indigenous culture. As we know from his "Primer ensayo hacia una tragedia mexicana" (First essay toward a Mexican tragedy),[44] he believed that tragedy as a fundamental artistic mode became extinct after the time of the ancient Greeks. It had flourished only while it was a living part of national religious expression, showing the struggle between man and the gods and the destruction of the former by the latter. There were no Roman tragedies (even by Seneca) because the mythology was borrowed from another culture (the Greek). No tragedy could ever arise under the auspices of the Christian religion because the principles of an immortal soul and the redemption of mankind ran counter to the fundamental tragic notion of the destruction of mankind by the gods. Racine's and Corneille's attempts to write tragedies were nullified by the fact that they merely transferred ancient tragic figures to their own era; twentieth-century efforts by Giraudoux, Cocteau, Anouilh, and O'Neill (among others) have failed for similar reasons. Usigli conceded that Shakespeare's *Hamlet, Lear,* and *Macbeth* were the best efforts to resurrect the genre, but even they contained elements extraneous to tragedy. Ibsen, too, came close to meeting the requirements, but he converted the struggle of man with the gods into the struggle of man with nature and the environment. With this line of reasoning, Usigli rejected all claims to tragedy in the last twenty-four hundred years. Although these are highly contentious views, many of them have been expressed in more cautious form by other writers. George Steiner, for example, in *The Death of Tragedy* finds no tragic drama since the seventeenth century, and among the points that he discusses is the lack of any modern equivalent to the essentially tragic mythology that was accepted by the ancient Greek audiences as a common sense of values. In the modern era dramatists are in a dilemma because the classic mythology "leads to a dead past," whereas "the metaphysics of Christianity and Marxism are anti-tragic."[45] For Usigli, too, this is one of the fundamental issues. The tragic author should deal with his own national themes, and the historical events should be incorporated into the *sangre nacional.* His belief that tragedy could be resurrected in Mexico stemmed from this condition. Mexico offered what the rest of the world lacked: mythical and historical material comparable to that of the ancient Greeks. The national heritage had Quetzalcóatl, Tollan, the fall of Tenochtitlán, and Cuauhtémoc. In Mexico, moreover, another essential condition persisted. All the old Indian myths were a living part of contemporary Mexican people, and the religious sentiment persisted. He promised to use these ideal tragic themes one day if he felt capable of facing the challenge, and within a decade he had fulfilled his plan. *Corona de fuego* must be regarded, then, as both the realization of a long-standing personal ambition and a nationalist enterprise.

It is not difficult to see that in *Corona de fuego* Usigli made strenuous efforts to construct a tragedy reminiscent of Aeschylus, Sophocles, and Euripides. In the first place, his play is—to borrow words from Aristotle's *Poetics*—"the imitation of an action that is serious and also, having magnitude, complete in itself."[46] As already noted, the action "imitated" is a highly important episode in national history, and the characters have a suitably elevated stature. Aristotle's principles of ethos and *dianoia* are also fulfilled, for the characters have great decisions to make (ought Cuauhtémoc to seek rebellion or accept his inevitable death? ought Cortés to act with severity or with justice and compassion?) and the capacity to express the thoughts that are fitting to be said in the situation. In his notes to *Corona de fuego,* Usigli stipulated that for tragedy to exist in full it must represent the destruction of mankind in the eternal struggle with the gods (TC 3:793). One of the priests brings this mythic dimension into the play in the first act: "Esta no es una guerra entre los hombres / sino mortal batalla entre los dioses" ("This is not a war between men / but mortal combat between the gods") (TC 2:97). The battle is between the Indian gods and the Christian God, with men as pawns in their game, and Cuauhtémoc laments that his gods have caused or permitted his own destruction and the slavery of his people (TC 2:106–7).

Cuauhtémoc is a hero on whom the destiny of a race depends. He has fallen from the condition of sovereign and military leader, been denied a quick, early death in battle, been tortured and held prisoner for four years, and is now unjustly judged and executed. Moreover, he has the kind of human weakness that Aristotle considered vital to tragedies: his hamartia is indecisiveness. Despite Usigli's qualms on the matter (TC 3:805), he has the essential attributes of the classical tragic hero. There are good grounds, too, for arguing that the play produces a cathartic effect. Tragic catharsis arises from the audience's involvement in the action to the extent that the suffering and downfall arouse emotions of pity and fear while effecting a purging and a relief. Usigli's audience is dismayed at the miscarriage of justice, impressed by Cuauhtémoc's dignity, and saddened by his plight. The severity of Cortés's judgment inspired fear. But what clinches the effect is the relief implied by the transcendence of Cuauhtémoc's sacrifice, enhanced by the sight of the cross and the mystical effect of his voice ringing out beyond death.

One means by which Aristotle thought a tragedy attained magnitude or elevation was through language with a rhythmic, harmonious, musical quality. Usigli sought to fulfill this qualification by writing his play in verse. The Spaniards speak in rhymed lines of twelve syllables, the Indians in blank verse. Equally bold was his use of a chorus. In the *Oresteia* trilogy, Aeschylus used a chorus of Argive Elders (in *Agamemnon*), a chorus of captive women (in *Choephoroe*), and a chorus of Furies (in *Eumenides*), choosing in each case a group that would represent a standpoint from which the action might be judged (and in the third case, a group that could also become the agents of judgment). In *Corona de fuego,* Usigli used a chorus of Spaniards and another of Mexicans, each to represent a point of view. The tension between the two factions, the relative ideologies, the assessment of Cuauhtémoc's execution—all are expressed by the two choruses. Further choruslike effect is achieved through the use of a Coreuta Moctún and a Coreuta Chontal, each of whom gives voice to the feelings of individual Indian peoples as opposed to Indian Mexico as a whole.

There is ample justification, therefore, for conceding that the play represents a successful attempt to write a tragedy. Far more of a problem is presented when we consider whether, as a tragedy, the play works well. Two great faults arise directly from the search for tragic qualities, and Usigli showed in his notes that he was aware of both. He confessed to suspecting that "lo que puede encontrarse a faltar en mi esquema de tragedia es un gran poeta" ("what may be found lacking in my sketch for a tragedy is a great poet") (TC 3:798). Elsewhere he showed himself to be a capable, if not a great, poet.[47] In this play, however, his language—intentionally stylized and suggestive of the sixteenth century—proves to be mainly pompous and labored, void of original imagery or metaphor. He claimed that on stage the poetry resides in the action, not in the language or dialogue (TC 3:810), but this argument is no defense when the language actually becomes a strident feature, an impediment rather than a neutral vehicle. The other problem underlies his question "¿Es *Corona de fuego* una tragedia estática?" ("Is *Corona de fuego* a static tragedy?") (TC 3:810). Classical tragedies, often dealing with the inevitable, avoided this pitfall by the careful use of devices like sudden reversals in the situation (peripeteia was Aritstole's term) and momentous discoveries *(anagnorisis)*. Usigli did not make the most of his opportunities. At the end of act 1, for example, the threat posed by Pax Bolón is weakened because Cortés always suspects his deviousness, while Cuauhtémoc himself has not been seen or mentioned sufficiently to have any impact. The tension is therefore minor, the conflict subdued, the suspense slight, the reversal incomplete. In act 2 a process of reasoning replaces uncertainty or threat, though the presence of an interloper during secret conversations helps to instil a modicum of uneasiness and shows Usigli's awareness of the need for more suspense. And before act 3 the principal denunciation has already occurred, Cortés has made his decision, and all that remains is the fully expected conclusion. Cuauhtémoc's spiritual survival after death constitutes a final, though perhaps tardy, reversal. Usigli was seeking something similar to Milton's effect in *Samson Agonistes,* which George Steiner justified with the argument that "the organisation of the play is nearly static . . . ; yet there runs through it a great progress toward resolution."[48] The major difference, perhaps, is that Milton was able to sustain his work with poetic language of the highest quality.

These defects were not missed by the audience and the critics during *Corona de Fuego*'s first performance in the Teatro Xola in September 1961. A particularly unfavorable review appeared in the newspaper *El Universal:* "Sólo provocó el más grande desaliento que se haya palpado, en el estreno de una pieza mexicana, de varios años a la fecha, puesto que casi pisó los linderos del fracaso" ("It only provoked the greatest disappointment that has been felt, on the first night of a Mexican play, for several years, since it closely verged on failure").[49] This reaction testifies to Usigli's greatest misconception. The basis of his endeavor was the belief that conditions peculiar to Mexico in the modern world make tragedy a feasible proposition there. The country's *sentimiento religioso* persists, and all the old myths remain a living part of the people today. Few would deny that there is an element of truth in this premise. But modern Mexico is also a technological society, and this inevitably means insuperable differences from the conditions under which the ancient Greek tragedies were written and performed. Like Europe and the United States, Mexico contains the adverse circumstances that Steiner analyzes in *The Death of Tragedy,* such as the tendency to regard drama as mere entertainment, the impact of the mass media, and the rise of the novel. Steiner asks, "Has European literature after the seventeenth century failed to produce tragic drama because European society has failed to produce the audience for it?"[50] And we might well ask whether Mexican society has produced the audiences.

In spite of these reservations, *Corona de fuego* constitutes a highly important experiment. The ambition to write a tragedy was ultimately an expression of Usigli's desire to elevate the status of Mexican theatre to a level comparable with the best in the world. It was a symptom of his aspiration for an independent, autonomous culture. One of the inherent factors, moreover, was his belief that the pre-Conquest indigenous mythology continued to exert a pervasive influence in the twentieth century. These underlying beliefs and aspirations coincide with the fundamental theme of the play itself, which is the reconciliation of antagonistic forces—Hispanic and Indian—and a consequent national unity.

One of the steps toward this end was an attempt to modify the public image of Cortés (a task considerably more difficult than that of attenuating popular antipathy for Maximilian and Carlota). In Mexico the execution of Cuauhtémoc is normally regarded as one of the paramount acts of infamy perpetrated by Cortés against the Mexican people. The Spanish point of view does not coincide, as

Salvador de Madariaga's judgment reveals: "Frío y duro cuando es necesario, pero sólo entonces y no más . . . No llevó el castigo de los conspiradores más allá del mínimo indispensable" ("Cold and hard when it is necessary, but then and only then. . . . He did not take the punishment of the conspirators beyond the indispensable minimum").[51] Although Usigli was by no means interested in exonerating Cortés in this way, he was careful to introduce an awareness of the pressures, so that the conquistador's behavior is given a rational explanation. He even showed him in a dilemma over the question of whether to act with compassion or severity. He therefore reduced the opprobrium without in any way favoring the Spanish point of view.

Simultaneously, Usigli aimed to give an extra dimension to the already heroic image of Cuauhtémoc. By making the Aztec leader conscious of his role in Mexican history, he both augmented the character's tragic dimensions and sharpened the audience's awareness that this historical episode had a bearing on the nation's future. Cuauhtémoc alludes to this future when he says to his captor:

> Sé que habrá de surgir en el futuro
> la nación mexicana por que muero.
> Quizá, quizá me equivoqué al culparte,
> y me matas al tiempo necesario;
> al tiempo de tu miedo y de la historia.

> (TC 2:834)

(I know that in the future the Mexican nation for which I die will emerge. Perhaps, perhaps I was wrong to blame you, and you are killing me at the necessary time, the time of your fear and of history.)

It has often been argued that Mexico's revolution provides the groundwork for the vindication of the Indian people. Pablo Neruda, for example, in his *Canto general* wrote:

> Ha llegado la hora señalada,
> y en medio de tu pueblo
> eres pan y raíz, lanza y estrella.[52]

(The appointed time has come, and in the midst of your people you are bread and root, lance and star.)

Usigli's idea seems different, however. Instead of suggesting that the revolution might signify the triumph of the indigenous and the defeat of the Hispanic, he gives Cuauhtémoc a speech looking forward to a time when the two strains are blended.

> Nuestros hijos, y los hijos
> de nuestras mujeres y de estos hombres a caballo
> deben vivir y nos darán el futuro. . . .
> Un día ellos serán la nación mexicana
> a la que yo quiero llegar con estos pies quemados
>
> (TC 2:813)

(Our children, and the children of our women and these men on horseback must live and will give us the future. . . . One day they will be the Mexican nation, to which I wish to come with these burnt feet)

Usigli referred to this focus in *Corona de fuego* as his treatment of *material* sovereignty. We shall see, however, that its principal idea differs only slightly from the treatment of *spiritual* sovereignty in his third *Corona*.

Corona de luz

Abandoning the artificiality of his search for tragedy, Usigli opted for a dramatic form at which he was more adept in *Corona de luz* (Crown of light). He classified the play as a "comedia anti-histórica."[53] If the form is simpler, however, the theme contains one kind of complexity not encountered in the other *Coronas*. The historical episode that the play reenacts and interprets is suffused with its own inherent ambiguities. To dramatize the miracle of the Virgin of Guadalupe is to deal with pious tradition as well as textbook history. Fraud or miracle? Separating facts from the supernatural dimension is merely the superficial aspect of the investigation. On deeper levels Usigli was interested in inquiring into the "true" quality of a miracle, in exploring the tensions between drama and truth, and ultimately in examining the nature of truth itself. By using comedy, moreover, he took full advantage of dramatic techniques to draw out the effects on stage when the truth is hidden, disguised, distorted, falsified, withheld, and suddenly revealed.

Corona de luz is based on a fact that is central to Mexican spiritual life: the pious tradition of miraculous appearances of the Virgin Mary of Guadalupe to the Indian Juan Diego on the hill of Tepeyac (just north of Mexico City) in the sixteenth century. It will be noticed that I take as historical fact, in this case, not the appearances themselves (which Usigli, as we shall see, leaves open to doubt) but the existence of a widely held belief in those miraculous appearances. The details of the pious tradition have been the subject of much scholarly debate. Usigli's work stands up well in the light of this scholarship. His anxiety was aroused when, with his play virtually completed, the historian Wigberto Jiménez Moreno informed him that modern critical opinion favored 1555 to 1531 as the date of the alleged miracle.[54] He had no need to worry, however, for in 1974 Jacques Lafaye published his considered opinion that the date 1531 "does not correspond to any established fact in an objective chronology; it appears for the first time in a work published in Spanish in 1648; this work seems to have borrowed the date from a Nahuatl manuscript whose authenticity is doubtful, but which was probably written between 1558 and 1572. According to a pious tradition which goes back to 1648, extraordinary appearances of the Virgin of Guadalupe took place in 1531. Viewed from the perspective of the history of beliefs, whether the date 1531 is correct or not is less important than its retrospective "truth" in the minds of its devotees of Guadalupe beginning in 1648."[55] Already, then, we see some of *Corona de luz*'s complexity. The play assumes the audience's familiarity with the tradition of an alleged miracle but presents as undisputed fact only the existence of the tradition, not the constituent details. Moreover, this is the substance only of the final act. In Acts 1 and 2 Usigli presents as "facts" an imaginary conspiracy by King Carlos V, Bishop Zumárraga, and other Church leaders to create a pious fraud. To complicate the matter further, the audience knows that this imaginary conspiracy is widely considered by Mexican skeptics to be the most likely practical explanation for the "miracle." The critic Roberto R. Rodríguez finds that Usigli achieves a balance between the historical and the fictitious in this play.[56] What I hope to show is that in the context of Usigli's preoccupation with history, veracity, and untruth, *Corona de luz* is the play that most severely questions the certainty of any presumed facts.

At this point it is important to draw attention to the presence on stage of historians and chronicles in all three *Coronas*. In *Corona de sombra* the fictitious historian Erasmo inquires after the truth on behalf of the author and reflects public opinion on behalf of the audience. He also provides the link between the past and the present by provoking Carlota's memories. In *Corona de fuego* the real chronicler Bernal Díaz del Castillo is reincarnated in order to foreshadow history's judgment on the other characters. *Corona de luz* places on stage no fewer than three historical figures who published books dealing with contemporary events: Sahagún, Benavente (also known as Motolinía), and Las Casas.[57] Like

Erasmo and Bernal Díaz, they introduce historical perspective. But unlike them, they do not help the eventual truth to emerge; in fact, they add to the situation's ambiguity. These Franciscan *cronistas* are all party to the conspiracy to create a false miracle—according to the play, that is—yet in reality none of their published accounts makes any reference to such a conspiracy or, indeed, casts any useful light on the cult of the Virgin of Guadalupe. (Incidentally, this detailed knowledge of their writings is surely not expected of the audience.)

Like the two previous "antihistorical" plays, *Corona de luz* contains modifications of historical reality strictly for the purpose of improving dramatic technique. According to pious tradition, the Indian Juan Diego saw visions of the Virgin on the slopes of Mount Tepeyac, was told that she wished a church to be built there in her honor, visited Bishop Zumárraga twice, and was instructed by him to produce proof. On 12 December 1531, in a third vision, the Virgin told Juan Diego to climb the hill, gather roses, and put them in his *tilma* (poncho). Among the waterless rocks on the hilltop Diego found a garden of roses, wrapped the roses in his *tilma*, and took them to Zumárraga. When he opened his *tilma*, a picture of the Virgin was seen to be imprinted on it. For dramatic effect Usigli made two alterations. In the first place, to make things neater he converted the three visits to Zumárraga into one. But secondly, the single Indian is converted into four "para implicar el número de Apariciones" ("to imply the number of Apparitions") ("Primer prólogo," 241). By arranging for his four Indians named Juan to appear one by one, Usigli achieved a useful gradation: Juan I (who speaks no Spanish) has seen a great light: Juan II (who understands Spanish but speaks none) has both seen the light and heard voices; Juan III (who speaks a little Spanish) bears a rose in the palm of his hand; Juan IV (called Juan Darío—a name tantalizingly close to the pious tradition's Juan Diego)—has seen the full vision, received the Virgin's instructions, gathered the roses, and carries the further proof of the painting on his *tilma*. The effect is one of crescendo, as the attempts by Zumárraga to shrug off the issue become slowly overwhelmed. (We shall see below what other tensions are introduced in this scene.)

Further instances were mentioned by the dramatist himself in his "Segundo prólogo." One concerns the visit of Cortés, which is imminent at the end of the play. Strictly, Cortés would not have had his palace in Coyoacán in 1531; it would be either in Cuernavaca (which would have involved an excessively long journey for him to arrive in the time available on stage) or in the Plaza Mayor of the capital (which would have enabled him to arrive too soon). In order to keep Cortés's arrival as a source of expectation and excitement, Usigli chose what proved to be the incorrect place. Learning of his factual inaccuracy, he was unrepentant: "En esto debía prevalecer, una vez más, la teoría del tiempo escénico. . . . De los nexos *históricos* que unen la figura del conquistador con Coyoacán se desprende como *probable* el trayecto requerido para el desarrollo de la acción" ("In this the theory of scenic time had to prevail once again. . . . From the *historical* links between the figure of the *conquistador* and Coyoacán, the journey needed for the action to unfold may be inferred as *probable*") ("Segundo prólogo," 259). A similar phenomenon is the dramatist's exaggeration of the speed with which the populace responded to the "miracle." Although there is no historical evidence to prove a sudden, tumultuous celebration, Usigli needed both to show the "miracle"'s effect emphatically and to end his play on a note of high emotion. Historians indicated other chronological inaccuracies in their correspondence with him. Las Casas was unlikely to be in Mexico in 1531; Motolinía's *Historia* had not been started by that year; Isabel de Portugal would not have been present in Yuste with Carlos V in 1529. But these "imprecisions" merely serve as further examples of the way in which historical facts may be subordinated to artistic necessity when their *essential* meaning is not thereby distorted.

A second type of modification has more serious implications: an alteration of the recorded facts introduced to influence the interpretation. If the three *Coronas* are arranged in some kind of gradation, it will be found that *Corona de fuego* contains the least invention (since Usigli chose carefully from the various accounts those versions that best suited his theme) and *Corona de luz* the most. The last of the trilogy goes a stage beyond anything attempted in the other plays. While part of act 3 is based on details of the pious tradition, the whole of acts 1 and 2 are based on conjecture. The main characters are historical figures, but their actions have no literal basis in historical record. There is no evidence that Carlos V issued instructions for a "miracle" to be fabricated by the Church in New Spain (act 1). Nor is there proof of a meeting of senior Franciscan missionaries to debate whether such a "miracle" should be arranged (act 2). On the other hand, it has often been conjectured by historians that, given the rational impossibility of an actual miracle occurring, the cause of the pious tradition presumably lies in a deliberate fraud. Historical record certainly offers evidence that enormous advantages might be expected to accrue from such a conspiracy: the incorporation of the Indians into the Catholic faith, the reduction of tension between Indians and conquistadores, the consequent removal of a threat to Spanish control of the New World, and even the strengthening of Spain's political position in Europe. To this Usigli added the more controversial idea that the cause of tension in New Spain was mainly a religious void among the Indians brought about by the destruction of their old faith.

A close examination of the matter shows that one of the features that most interested Usigli was the *relative* truth of the "miracle." One of the keys to the incorporation of America's Indian people into the Catholic faith was the rediscovery in the new religion of the mother-goddess of their old faith. Many countries developed a sense of independence within the emergence of the conquering people's religion by means of a cult of a national image of the Virgin. In Argentina this was the Virgen de Luján; in Ecuador, Nuestra Señora de Guálpulo; in Paraguay, Nuestra Señora de Caacupe; in old Peru, Nuestra Señora de Copacabana; and in modern Peru, Nuestra Señora de las Mercedes.[58] Apparitions of the Virgin usually had Indian physical features. Mexican nationalism (at first Indian and later *criollo*) expressed itself through the cult of the Virgen de Guadalupe. Outstripping the rival Virgen de los Remedios (symbol of Spanish rule), La Guadalupana became the banner of Hidalgo's uprising in 1811 and of Zapata's revolution a century later. Post-Revolutionary Mexico finds the cult thriving. In the 1960s—at the time of Usigli's play—Pablo González Casanova calculated that "an average of 15,648 Mexican Catholics visit the Basilica of Guadaloupe a day."[59] It is one piece of evidence that he offers for the survival of the Church through the social transformation in post-Revolutionary years. In other words, the miracle of the Virgin's appearance to an Indian on a site that was formerly associated with the worship of Tonantzin (the mother-goddess) Cihaucóatl (wife of the serpent) is clearly a phenomenon at the very core of Mexican religious faith and nationalism. Usigli would be risking great offense by questioning the supernatural aspects of the pious tradition, and this is precisely what he at first appears to be doing in the first two acts of *Corona de luz*.

The debate in act 1 reveals how tension (both military and religious) between the Indians and the Spaniards threatens future conflict in New Spain. The destruction of either party would be politically disadvantageous for Spain. The main source of tension is the Indians' religious needs. Their former traditions are unacceptable, but the sheer imposition of Christian traditions is not working. What is needed, therefore, is some way in which the Indians might be permitted a privileged view of God. The emperor feels pressure on him to "make" a miracle. Since his wife's favorite Virgin is the Virgen de Guadalupe (of Extremadura, in midwestern Spain), this will be the name for the Virgin in Mexico's "miraculous" apparitions. Act 2 takes the plan to the point where a group of Church leaders (headed by Bishop Zumárraga) agrees on the necessity to create such a "miracle." A nun has been sent from Spain to act the part of the Virgin, and a gardener to grow the roses.

At first, then, the audience is encouraged to see the action on stage as the rationalist case, the "truth" behind the unbelievable, the fraud behind the "miracle." In act 3, however, our attitude changes when we realize that events are not conforming to the plan. The appearances of the Virgin have occurred too early (they had been scheduled for a Catholic feast day) and in the wrong place (they had been intended for neutral ground, not the sanctuary of an Indian deity). Moreover, there is an element that did not figure in the plan: Juan Darío's *tilma*. With the conspirators confused (Zumárraga still suspects a human agent, though Motolinía believes it a miracle) and the instruments of the conspiracy (the nun and the gardener) overwhelmed by something seemingly beyond their comprehension, we are left to choose our preferred interpretation. Perhaps after all there is a supernatural dimension. Or perhaps there remain further rationalist explanations: a plot to "make a miracle" by Cortés or by the Indian people, or perhaps with collusion between the two parties, without the knowledge of Zumárraga and Motolinía. Despite Usigli's confessed break with the Church ("Primer prólogo," 227) and denial that he was a religious man ("Segundo prólogo," 273), it must at least be concluded that he was not advocating the rationalist line. The question—pious fraud or miracle?—is left unresolved as a powerful instance of his recurring theme that truth is difficult to perceive and that facts are not readily separable from the work of the imagination. He is not equivocal, however, on the matter of the apparitions' impact on the Indian people. Their faith is beyond dispute (that is to say, it is "true"). The means by which it was brought about may or may not be miraculous, but the outcome is precisely the one that was deemed to be necessary. Fray Juan summarizes the position: "Veo de pronto a este pueblo coronado de luz, de fe. Veo que la fe corre ya por todo México como un río sin riberas. Ése es el milagro, hermano" ("I suddenly see this people crowned with light, with faith. I see that faith now runs throughout the whole of Mexico like a river without banks. That is the miracle, brother") (TC 2:917). Usigli's innovation was to move from the idea—faith in the truth of the miracle (which he questions)—to the assertion: faith in the true miracle.

One of the assets of *Corona de luz* as theatre is that in raising these complex and profound issues Usigli still managed to be entertaining. With great ingenuity he constantly renewed the tension and maintained the suspense to the very end. He made use of well-established theatrical devices, but his particular skill was in adapting those techniques to draw out the underlying theme of ultimate uncertainty over truth and fiction. The choice of comedy proved a perfect vehicle for this theme.

At times the mystifying process is a game that has no direct bearing on the main action. Act 1 opens, for example, with a little mystery over the emperor's whereabouts, and includes—halfway through—a moment when the roles of two hidden characters are temporarily reversed and confused. Act 3 opens with a mystery over the message that has summoned Motolinía to the Obispado. (It proves to be no more than a piece of incompetence by Martincillo.) Without these episodes, the plot would proceed unharmed, but the play would develop less mysteriously. They are important contributions to the series of false situations and partial clarifications.

Often a tension is introduced by the temporary withholding of information. At the end of act 1, what has Carlos V decided? (The interval gives us time to think about it.) At the beginning of act 2, what are the instructions that Zumárraga has received? (We are tantalized by the interruptions while Fray Juan reveals them.) At the end of act 2, has Fray Juan decided to proceed with the fraud? The same question mark hangs over the beginning of act 3. (Again Usigli tantalizes us by starting to offer the information and then suspending it: "y puedo deciros que . . . [*Se abre la puerta*]" "[and I can tell you that . . . *(The door opens)*" [TC 2:895].)

Certain issues are never explained. In act 2, how much of the debate is overheard (and understood) by the young Indian eavesdropper? (He is introduced both to create uneasiness and to provide a possible explanation for events in the final act.) In act 3, what causes the nun's ecstasy? (A human foible? Madness? The experience of something supernatural?) Are the stories of Juans I, II, III, and IV genuine? How did Juan III's rose get on Tepeyácatl? How did Juan Darío get his roses and the painting on his *tilma?* (It is notable that to avoid the easy sensational effect, Usigli prevents the audience from actually seeing the painting.) Usigli's dramatic technique of creating subsidiary mysteries that are eventually solved must therefore be recognized as a means not only of increasing interest and tension but also of adding to the confusion, helping to veil the truth in the development of a situation whose full clarification does not emerge.

The master stroke was the creation of a crescendo of suspense in act 3. It begins with the matter of the origin of the roses. At first we are invited to accept the rationalist explanation that the roses are those planted by the gardener according to the plan (temporarily forgotten by Zumárraga). But then our confidence in this version is shaken: the roses were not found where the gardener was instructed to grow them. At this point, both Fray Antonio and the gardener confirm that roses were sown in the south, in accordance with instructions. Then a new revelation is made: the gardener has been visiting an Indian girl in the north, beyond Tepeyácatl, and has planted a rosebush at the door of her shack. The audience swings back to the rationalist point of view. The next ingredient is the apparition witnessed by Juan IV. Here Usigli ingeniously separates the two possible sides of the argument. Motolonía encourages belief in a miracle, while Fray Juan struggles to find a rational explanation. Then with the arrival of the Alférez to announce that Cortés is on his way, Usigli appears to have swung the pendulum in favor of rationalism again: presumably the military have taken their own initiative, preempting the clerical plan. Moreover, the nun appears on stage and, through her resemblance to the image of the Virgen de Guadalupe, strengthens the likelihood that she is the "Virgin" who has been seen. Then comes a major twist. Juan Darío denies that she is the figure of his apparition; his unfolded *tilma* reveals the image imprinted on it; and the nun collapses, as if to suggest her subordination to the image. We are therefore thrown back into the realm of the unknown. The scene is a masterpiece of dramatic suspense and shifting emphasis (surpassed only, perhaps, by the local politicians' investigation of Rubio's credentials in *El gesticulador*). At the same time, it creates a concrete representation of the vital underlying theme: the difficulty of distinguishing the real from the imaginary, the true from the false, the rational from the miraculous.

Nationalism and Universalism

The historical plays discussed in this chapter reveal an unmistakably nationalistic strain in Usigli's thought. Their artistic role was to elevate Mexican theatre to a level of high seriousness and quality. Their public function was to dramatize episodes from the past in order that the Mexico of the present might benefit. Each of them demonstrates an aspect of national sovereignty in the face of external interference, and each also emphasizes the need for harmony and reconciliation between the indigenous heritage and the Hispanic. If Usigli may be accused of advocating a compromise with Hispanic domination, he must be recognized as implacably hostile toward all foreign intervention in national affairs since Independence. An independent and united Mexico is what these historical plays teach audiences to desire, a country in which joint effort takes the place of internal strife.

It is important for us to remember that two of the *Coronas* appeared late in his production, while the earliest did not reach the public until he had already begun to make a reputation through the six works previously performed and the fourteen others already written (some of which were known in manuscript form by fellow writers, critics, and politicians). The completion of his trilogy was the fulfillment of an ambition. They testify to his determination to use the theatre as a medium for national self-awareness and regeneration. His undoubted sense of vocation for the theatre was combined with a spirit of inquiry, a critical insight, the courage to express controversial opinions, and a profound preoccupation with the character and destiny of the Mexican people.

But there is a more universal side to Usigli's theatre. Although his stated purpose in writing *Corona de luz* was to show that Mexico's spiritual sovereignty was achieved by faith in the Guadalupe miracle, the theme of rationalism in confrontation with belief also runs through the play. Our expectation that the dramatist will favor the rationalist line meets a disconcerting shift of emphasis in the final moments when we realize that the mystery has not been explained and a supernatural version of events has not been totally refuted. If anything, it is not the believer in miracles but the determined rationalist in the audience who is confounded. More than any of the other *Coronas, Corona de luz* allows the truth as perceived by the dramatic poet to take precedence over the truth as recorded by the history books (without actually contradicting them). Ultimately, however, this reflects a view of history and "truth" that we find elsewhere in his works. In the early minutes of *Corona de sombra,* Erasmo comments on the historian's role with these words: "La historia no habla mal de nadie, a menos que se trate de alguien malo" ("History does not speak badly of anyone, unless the person in question is bad") (TC 2:151). Are we not able to perceive the dramatist's ironic smile at this excessively naive belief in the objective accuracy of historians' records? Later the absurdity of Erasmo's idea is openly revealed. In the final act he lamely puts forward the excuse that an historian is a simple recorder of facts: "Yo no soy más que un historiador, una planta, parásita brotada de otras plantas—de los hombres que hacen la historia. Yo no quito ni pongo rey" ("I am only an historian, a parasitic plant springing from other plants—from the men who make history. I am strictly neutral") (TC 2:215). But this folly is immediately exposed through Carlota's retort: "Sois la mirada de México" ("You are the eyes of Mexico"). Whether his version of history is personal or the embodiment of a collective impression, it is not neutral, not fact devoid of attitude.

Usigli's interest in this theme was not confined to the context of his three *Coronas*. As was noticed in chapter 3, *El gesticulador* contains similar ideas. The fictitious historian César Rubio declares that 'la historia no es más que un sueño. . . . Los que la enseñan sueñan que poseen la verdad y que la entregan" ("history is no more than a dream. . . . Those who teach it dream that they possess the truth and that they are handing it on") (TC 1:746). The American history professor enhances events with his own melodramatic imagination, proves amazingly gullible, leaps into print before fully verifying the facts, and subordinates the search for accuracy to the opportunity of advancing his career. Between them the two historians (one inadvertently) substitute a false record of events for the "true" one (though of course General Rubio, ideal hero of the Revolution, is "true" only in the context of the play's autonomous world). And the universal dimension of these preoccupations is drawn out by Rubio's son, who longs not only for an escape from hypocrisy but for a fuller grasp of truth itself.

In his "Segundo prólogo a *Corona de luz*," Usigli discussed at length the respective positions of the historian and the dramatic poet in relation to the possibility of an objective portrayal of reality. To support his concepts he quoted the view of John Fortescue *(The Writings of History)* that the historian has to do with both kings and paupers, heroes and cowards, the complexes of individual personalities and the impact of individuals on others, and having taken everything into account, he must use his critical faculty to become an interpreter of the meaning of events. This description of the historian's task, argued Usigli, was one of the best he knew of the dramatist's art ("Segundo prólogo," 267). In *Corona de luz* he took

the investigation of reality an important step further. He showed
that a record of historical events is essentially similar to the historical—or, as he would say, "antihistorical"—work of a creative artist. But with his complex treatment of a miracle, he also cast doubt
on our ability to envisage the existence of an objective truth in
which the imagination plays no part.

8

The Wider Perspective

Despite his undoubted Mexican emphasis, Usigli never lost sight of universal themes. As early as the 1930s he focused the occasional play on the nature of reality, dramatizing its relation to imagination, fiction, and theatre. In the predominantly political, social, psychological, and historical plays examined in the preceding chapters, the context does not disguise the raising of profound issues that transcend national frontiers. Hypocrisy, insanity, sexuality, dream, ambition, resilience, aging, family bonds—these and other features of human behavior repeatedly emerge from his study of the Mexican psyche. During the 1960s, moreover, when his diplomatic career led him to Beirut and Oslo, there was a conspicuous broadening of his theatre's perspective. To ignore this dimension would be to offer a misleading impression of his overall dramatic production.

The two melodramas *Aguas estancadas* (Stagnant waters) (1938) and *Mientras amemos* (For as long as we love) (1937–1948) combine improbable plots with skillful dramatic techniques to provide entertaining and thought-provoking studies of the way fiction can be used to resolve problems with reality. There are two main points of reference in the title *Aguas estancadas*. One is Sarah, a twenty-two-year-old girl from the slums who has given up hope that the future will improve: "Nada cambiaba y yo seguía estancada. . . . Tú sabes que el agua que no corre se vuelve sucia. Así me siento yo. Sucia" ("Nothing changed, and I was still stagnating. . . . I don't have to tell you that water that doesn't flow goes dirty. That's how *I* feel. Dirty") (TC 1:634). Stagnation for Sarah means both the frustration of her potential to develop within the flow of time and the effect of being surrounded by dirt in her home. An old engraving of Porfirio Díaz hangs on one of the walls, an emblem of her parents' habit of harking back to the past. In order that the audience might share Sarah's desperation to escape from this environment, Usigli created an atmosphere of almost overwhelming squalor and oppression in act 1. The set captures the reality of a house in the slums: cramped quarters and broken furniture. Sarah's family are selfish, vulgar, and shabby. Her father and brother are idle, and only her own typing—for which she is permitted little opportunity—provides a minimal income. Her mother tacitly accepts her father's belief that women belong in the house, where they must behave as slaves. Moreover, Sarah is physically maltreated by her father. To complete this impression of unrelieved grimness, her boyfriend, Emilio, proves to be a nondescript character whose marriage proposal offers the prospect of little more than a repetition of her present conditions. "Necesito otra cosa," she tells him. "Como cuando se aleja uno de un objecto para verlo mejor. Necesito olvidar esta vida primero" ("I need something else. As when you stand back from an object to see it better. I need to forget this life first") (TC 1:635). And this is why she walks out of the slum into the house of a millionaire.

Arturo Arvide, the sixty-year-old millionaire, is the other main point of reference for the play's title: "Nuna he sentido como hoy la imposibilidad de todo esto. Nunca me produje tan completamente la impresión de ser agua sucia, estancada—para siempre" ("I have never felt the impossibility of all this as I do today. I have never had such a complete sense of being dirty water, stagnant water—for ever") (TC 1:639). Arvide's problem is that time ceased to flow for him thirty years ago, and the dirt that he feels is not physical like Sarah's but a metaphor of guilt. The brief prologue gives us a glimpse of that melodramatic event deep in the past, when Dolores, a girl from the slums who had become Arvide's mistress, was accused of infidelity and theft, and was shot. Subsequently, Arvides has become imprisoned by an uneasy conscience.

Usigli therefore created two characters whose present reality is totally unacceptable to them. Both need some kind of release. The solution is provided by a newspaper advertisement. From Sarah's point of view, this is at first no more than a modeling job, offering her good pay and the opportunity to wear fine clothes and jewelry. But for the man who placed the advertisement, Arturo Arvides, this is the opportunity to re-create the circumstances under which he killed Dolores, to reassess the girl's behavior, and to check whether the outcome was justified. Once Sarah is appointed in act 2, the situation becomes steadily more complex. Instead of simply modeling clothes, Sarah is required to spend more than twelve hours each day in Arvide's house, to join him for meals and for walks, to wear Dolores's dresses, and to speak Dolores's words (which she must memorize in advance). In short, Sarah becomes an actress in a play written by her employer. Gradually her dramatic role increases in its importance to her. When she wears the first luxurious dress, it is like being in a dream from which she does not wish to be awakened. More significantly, "es como una nueva vida en otro mundo" ("it's like a new life in another world") (TC 1:649). To lose all these refinements, she says, would be like dying (TC 1:655). In some respects, therefore, she willingly chooses theatre rather than life, and her awareness of being part of an invention does not act as a deterrent. However, she is not in full control of the situation. At times the words that she speaks—the words of Dolores—are spoken woodenly, but at other times they resound with genuine feeling. Sarah not only looks like Dolores, she comes from a similar social background, and her natural responses to the comfort and refinement of Arvide's house are the same. Before long, she has to admit an inability to distinguish between fiction and realty: "¿Y esto es el presente o el pasado?" ("And this, is it the present or the past?"), she asks in act 3 (TC 1:660).

Arvides, his secretary Pablo, and his servant Marta all share the impression that the past and present are being fused into one. At intervals the two men—both of whom had been in love with Dolores—lose their grasp on reality. And Marta becomes bewildered at the tendency for people to feel and say the same things in different generations, with the result that "ya no sé qué cosa es verdad" ("I don't know any more which thing is true") (TC 1:656). But Usigli took the situation further to suggest that external events, too, can repeat themselves The most striking moment at which past and present, fiction and reality are fused occurs when Sarah makes a determined effort to clear her mind. She insists that Pablo knows full well that Arvides has been imagining things: "Usted sabe que todo esto no existe más que en la imaginación de él—que ningún hombre nos ha seguido—que ningún hombre entrará aquí" ("You know that all this exists only in his imagination—that no man has followed us—that no man will come in here") (TC 1:662). At that very moment, Emilio comes onto the stage. Not only has he been following them, he has also been watching them in the concert hall, precisely as Dolores was watched.

The dramatic success of this situation depends on a number of elements. After experiencing the oppressive feeling of vulgarity and squalor created in act 1, the audience readily participates in the escape into a substitute world. The set itself evokes an air of opulence that is pleasing to the eye and a period atmosphere that satisfies our common yearning for evasion. From time to time the continuation of this fantasy comes under threat because of Sarah's misgivings and attempts by Emilio to discover and "rescue" her. As in the case of *El gesticulador*, where the audience is intrigued by the consolidation of César Rubio's false identity, in *Aguas estancadas*, too, the possibility of truth destroying the fabric of fiction creates a strong suspense. The greatest source of tension, however, lies in the danger to which the protagonist is exposed by her fictitious role. To all intents and purposes, Sarah is duplicating the experiences of Dolores, and the question arises whether she will unintentionally create the same circumstances under which her predecessor met her death. By chance this proves to be the case. Sarah's brother steals a bracelet, she is blamed for the theft, and Arvides attempts to shoot her.

At this point, fiction (or theatre) has become reality, and it is only Sarah's quick reflexes (and Arvides's defective aim) that save her life. In addition, however, there is a sense in which the past is changed by the present. Arvides suffers a heart attack as a consequence of the high emotions, and when he recovers consciousness, he loses any awareness of the last thirty years. Sarah is Dolores, and she has survived his attempt to kill her. As for Dolores's supposed misconduct, the record can now be corrected. The fact that Pablo and Arvides have patently made a mistake over Sarah (whose innocence is finally revealed) means that Dolores, too, may have been falsely accused. Naturally the new reality, which acts as a substitute for the old, is extremely vulnerable. It depends on Arvides's survival—and his heart is expected to last no more than a few months—and Sarah's willingness to continue playing her role. Psychologically, the latter is the more interesting case. Although she now realizes that her love for Emilio is genuine, Sarah cannot bring herself to marry him until she has purged herself of ambition and dreams of luxury. She will stay with Arvides until he dies. Eventually she will probably return to Emilio, but there is always the possibility that she will not be able to resume her old life-style. The play ends with a powerful affirmation of the human need for fantasy. When Pablo asks if she is ready to leave with Arvides, Sarah insists that he should call her Dolores. When reminded that Emilio will steadfastly wait for her, she is so engrossed in her emotional association with Dolores that she simply ignores the remark. She is dominated by "un deseo que no entiendo . . . de que Dolores viva para siempre. De que el sueño sea más que la realidad" ("a wish that I don't understand . . . that Dolores should live forever. That dream should be more than reality") (TC 1:674). To reinforce this idea of substitution, Usigli makes use of the life-sized portrait of Dolores, dressed in white, hanging above the fireplace. A beam of moonlight illuminates the figure in the painting and converts Sarah into a silhouette. We are left, however, with an emphasis not on supernatural transformation but on the human psyche. Pablo remarks that Sarah has succumbed to the prevailing madness.

> *Sarah.* ¿Por qué no? En un mundo tan cuerdo, los locos hacen más falta que nunca . . .
> *Pablo.* O en un mundo tan loco los cuerdos . . .
> *Sarah.* ¿No es lo mismo acaso? (TC 1:674)

> (*Sarah.* Why? In such a sane world, mad people are needed more than ever.
> *Pablo.* Or in such a mad world sane people . . .
> *Sarah.* Isn't it perhaps the same thing?)

It is not insanity of the kind that we encounter in *El niño y la niebla*. It is a voluntary yielding to the innate desire to escape to a more satisfying alternative reality. As the curtain falls after these final words and the theatre lights come on, the audience is drawn sharply out of the fantasy of acts 1 and 2 and thrown back into its own humdrum reality. In 1952 the audiences at the 118 performances of *Aguas estancadas* were unaware of one additional twist in the game with fact and fiction. The part of Sarah had originally been written (in the 1930s) for the actress Dolores del Río.[1] (They would have noticed, however, that on the wall of the set for act 1 hung an old engraving of the Virgen de los Dolores. And they would not, of course, have missed the connotation of pain and sorrow in the name chosen for the murdered woman.)

A more improbable melodrama based on role subsitution is *Mientras amemos* (For as long as we love). A man whose young wife is starting divorce proceedings hopes to save his marriage by paying an actor (an old friend and rival) to impersonate him. The wife pretends to be deceived and declares her love to the actor. (It is worth adding that all the meetings occur in a dimly lit room!) In love with his friend's wife, and believing her to love her husband, the actor develops a mysterious form of blindness. After a climactic meeting of all three parties, however, the truth is revealed, the actor and the wife leave together, and the husband is the one who finally remains in the room and asks for the lights to be extinguished. Several important themes are introduced into this play—though the plot is too farfetched for us to take them very seriously. Selfishness and greed, love and affection, self-discovery and redemption, blindness as the evasion of the truth about oneself. But the dominant idea concerns the use of a fictional situation as a substitute for reality, and the transformation of that invention into truth.

On 14th April 1939 Usigli broadcast a half-hour radio playlet, *Sueño de día* (Daydream), whose basic theme is a housewife's depression and her need to compensate through daydreaming. Living close to a railway station, feeling solitude, and longing for a child, she invents a romantic relationship with a radio singer. In her imagination she is pregnant. Letters that she has written to give reality to her daydream are discovered by her husband, and he, believing that she has been unfaithful, shoots her. In this playlet the emphasis is on the psychological condition of a woman whose daydreaming has developed into a nervous illness. But Usigli takes the misinterpretation of truth a little further. The singer with whom she imagines a love affair is fictitious: the company has invented him as part of a publicity exercise, and the voice is that of the Argentine tango singer Carlos Gardel (who had died some years before). The program directors are compelled to announce the death of their singer in order to avoid complicity in the murder. One subsidiary aspect of the theme, therefore, is the commercial exploitation of the human need for romance. Another is the use of radio as a facility for blending fact and fiction.

The innate instinct to create substitutes for reality is also the subject of two one-act comedies entitled *Vacaciones* (Holidays) (1940 and 1945–51). In the first, a young dramatist and a young actress hope to further their careers by seeking the help of a famous (though aging) actress. Denied permission to see Sonia, the two young people begin to enact their play. So absorbed are they in this activity that they forget the purpose of their visit, with the result that when Sonia is ready to see them, they ignore her and offend her. Finally, realizing the damage that they have done to their prospects, they decide to forget the theatre and to hunt for other employment. The daunting prospect turns their minds to holidays and to the thought that their acting was, in effect, "unas vacaciones fuera de nosotros mismos, de nuestros deseos" ("holidays outside ourselves, outside our desires") (TC 2:46). As this plot summary reveals, this playlet offers an interesting glimpse of the theme of acting as evasion. *Vacaciones II* ventures more deeply into the nature of theatre. A group of actors, their director, and their prompter argue over the play that a young author has been reading to them. Various problems arise: the vague ending, the fact that it is a Mexican play, the casting, the use of a prompter. . . . Finally, however, they are persuaded that their task is to create for the audience what the author has imagined, and that in order to achieve this, they must use their own imaginations. The theatre, they are told, lives on human substance, but to enter the theatre is to leave the world.

Once more, therefore, Usigli returned to the public's fascination with dream, imagination, fiction, and acting. The radio and theatre provided institutionalized opportunities for people to obtain a temporary escape from their humdrum lives.

These plays used the theme of theatre chiefly as a basis for studying the nature of reality. There were, however, other uses of the theme. Occasionally the intention was satirical, as in the case of *La crítica de "La mujer no hace milagros"* (The review of "A woman can't perform miracles"), which ridicules public prejudice against Mexican authors and ferociously mocks the lack of professionalism among critics. But generally the purpose was to link the topic of theatre with eternal human problems, and in particular with the anguish of aging. One of them, *La función de despedida* (The farewell performance) (1949), has the added ingredient of the cinema's threat to the theatre.

In 1948, when the actress Virginia Fábregas returned to Mexico after a successful tour of theatres in Madrid and Barcelona, Usigli was commissioned to write a play in which she would take her leave of Mexican audiences. By the time *La función de despedida* was staged in the Teatro Ideal in April 1953, Virginia Fábregas had died. To Usigli's chagrin, the theatre based its publicity on the mistaken notion that the play was a straightforward biography of the actress, ignoring the fact that the dramatist had merely used reality as a point of departure and that most of the detail was sheer invention.[2] It was a curious instance of theatre and real life becoming so confused that truth itself was—to some extent—irremediably distorted. For his part, Usigli was adamant that the director's duty was not to attempt pure realism but to create an illusion. It would appear, however, that the director and theatre manager were simply taking advantage of that gray area that exists between documentary and fiction, and Usigli could not deny that a blending of life and theatre is at the heart of the play itself.

The sexagenarian actress, Verónica Muro, has returned to her hometown in provincial Mexico with a group of actors to perform a number of her old successes. After a performance attended by only twenty people, she takes an overdose of pills. When she recovers, Verónica learns that her attempted suicide has attracted publicity and financial backing for the performances. But, adamantly refusing to move from her bed, she renews her suicide attempt. Again she survives. Various kinds of pressure fail to persuade her to perform, even though the public has packed the theatre. While she has been convalescing, memories of her career and an assessment of her life constantly preoccupy her, the lives of people around her repeatedly impinge on her thoughts, and a reencounter with her former boy-friend sharpens her judgment. Eventually she resolves not only to act in the farewell performance but to continue with many more.

There are essentially two aspects to Verónica Muro's predica-ment: theatre and life. Her deep depression allows Usigli to voice some personal complaints about the state of Mexican theatre. In a prolonged monologue in act 2, Verónica's disenchantment leads her to feel the sheer fatigue of acting a different play each week. Fine roles, and any consequent sense of fulfillment, are made unavaila-ble by the necessity of earning money. An undiscerning public attends the theatre—if at all—to see the actors and actresses rather than the works themselves. The action of *La función de despedida* reinforces this negative impression. Verónica's troupe are so short of finances that they cannot afford their train fare back to the capital. Only the sensation caused by her suicide attempt draws public attention and ensures a subvention from the local govern-ment. In contrast with this decadent state of the theatre, the cinema offers attractive prospects. Bitterly, Verónica advises an aspiring young actress to choose the cinema, where she will achieve fame in twenty-four hours, be watched by one hundred thousand people in a week, and quickly become wealthy (TC 2:312). Usigli's own sense of the cinema's relentless threat to the theatre is clearly subsumed by his character's anguish and by the despairing comments made by one of her troupe: "Se acabó el teatro" ("Theatre is finished") (TC 2:263).[3] However, Usigli's determination that the theatre will resist the challenge is also transferred to the characters in his play. A young journalist realizes the fundamental disadvantages of the cinema for a young actress: "No tendrás el contacto con el público, la emoción creadora, los aplausos que buscas" ("You won't have the contact with the public, the creative emotion, the applause that you're looking for") (TC 2:312). Verónica herself recognizes the satisfaction that such warmth has given her throughout a long career. She is aware, moreover, that she chose this career because she possessed a talent that she needed to give to the world (TC 2:294). Eventually she reverses her advice to the young actress, promises to train her for the theatre, and reminds her that "lo primero del teatro es sentir" ("the first thing about the theatre is to feel") (TC 2:322), and that it will require her to live each role with her whole being.

The other aspect of her predicament, a disenchantment with life itself, is of course inextricably connected with this preoccupation with the theatre. She can make no clear distinction between be-havior on and off the stage. In addition to her attention-drawing overdoses, she indulges in an extended act of invalidity. She herself is aware of the theatrical nature of her approach to life, as we notice when the doctor asks whether an injection is causing pain.

> *Verónica.* Otras cosas duelen más: vivir, por ejemplo.
> *Doctor.* Y ahora, ¿es usted sincera, o también actúa aquí en vez de hacerlo en el teatro?
> *Verónica.* Tengo público; tengo que actuar. (TC 3:282)

> (*Veronica.* Other things hurt more: living, for example.
> *Doctor.* And now, are you being sincere, or are you acting here too instead of in the theatre?
> *Veronica.* I have a public; I have to act.)

She expresses her death wish in terms of a call for a final curtain, and Usigli neatly finishes act 1 with a rapid curtain to meet her demand. It takes another observer—the young journalist—to highlight the egoism of mistaking her own sense of decay for the plight of the theatre as a whole (TC 2:318). By the end of act 3 a renewed zest for life leads almost immediately to a new enthusiasm for appearing on stage. It means facing the risk of whistles as well as the applause, but it ensures that she will continue to be one of the performers rather than a spectator.

Verónica's sense of failure in the theatre leads to a reassessment of her career in relation to other aspects of her life. The key to her dissatisfaction is the absence of love and marriage. In her youth she refused to marry the young man whom she loved, choosing instead to concentrate exclusively on a career. Now she is witness to two similar situations. Only when she is sure that the *novios* (whose voices are heard through the balcony window) have not repeated her own mistake can she summon the enthusiasm for renewed action. Her first priority is then to intervene in the threatened replay involving another young couple (Marina, an aspiring actress, and Emilio, the journalist). Verónica encourages Marina to express both sides of her character, combining love with the career of her choice. Indirectly, Verónica, too, will benefit. Marina is the daughter of the man whose proposal she rejected forty years ago; to train her for the theatre is to achieve a form of surrogate motherhood.

La función de despedida often makes use of technical effects to enable the reader to share Verónica Muro's point of view. The principal device is the voice of her inner thoughts. Although it would have been quite possible for Usigli to use monologues for this purpose, the advantages of a voice-over method is to allow her thoughts to be expressed while other actors are on stage. The thoughts therefore comment on other options, contradict apparent reality, and reveal the protagonist's ambivalence. Despite the proliferation of these speeches, the technique works well on the whole, particularly when it offers us an insight into Verónica's changed disposition in act 3 (e.g.,TC 2:330). A subtler and equally important indicator of her inner mind reaches the audience through the unidentified voices of a young man and woman, who are overheard in an intimate dialogue once in each act. Like Verónica, we have the feeling that we are listening to ghosts from her past, like the reenactment of painfully remembered scenes of wasted opportunity and false decision. It comes as a mild surprise to realize that there is, after all, no surrealism in this (no insane hallucinations, from Verónica's point of view), and that the couple have been meeting secretly outside the window. The result is to stress the distinction between Verónica's own life and the potential for an alternative course. The play ends, therefore, with an affirmation of life's value, a resolute determination to give the theatre a future, and a suggestion that theatre becomes richer when it is based on the full range of human experience.

In *La función de despedida* the themes of love, creative energy, career, and old age are confined more or less rigidly within the context of the theatre. They assume paramount importance, however, in *Los viejos* (Old people), one of Usigli's last plays and undoubtedly the best since the 1950s.[4] It begins as a debate about the different approaches to the theatre by two generations of dramatist, but it becomes an investigation into the process of aging, with powerful implications outside the context of drama. Although it is a one-act play, *Los viejos* has a clear development through two main phases and seven subdivisions. To facilitate analysis, I will invent a few terms and depict the structure as follows:[5]

Phase A. Theatre:	Prologue	(TC 3:162–65)	
	Take 1	(165–68)	
	Take 2	(168–73)	
	Take 3	(173–87)	
			(Overlap)
Phase B. Aging:	The Make-up	(179–92)	
	The Irreversible Reality	(192–95)	
	Epilogue	(196–97)	

A Young Dramatist (with capital letters) has published a negative review of a play written by a well-known dramatist of an older generation. The Old Dramatist visits the younger man and his wife in their apartment to propose that they collaborate in a work.

Before long, the conversation develops into a quarrel. At this point the lighting changes, and the actors return to their original positions (the Old Dramatist off stage), walking backward as though they were on the reel of a film being rewound. The scene is repeated, each actor adopting a less aggressive approach, but the outcome is a renewed quarrel and another return to the point of departure. A third "take" becomes in effect the authentic version. During this third "take" the emphasis shifts from a comparison of their attitudes as dramatists to a contrast of their conditions as men. The Old Dramatist offers his experience in exchange for the other's youth. What follows is in a sense the partial enactment of this exchange. Mockingly, the Young Dramatist applies make-up to transform his face into that of an old man while his wife gives increasingly affectionate attention to the Old Dramatist. When the make-up is completed, the lighting changes as though we were about to witness another rewind. Instead, the action continues, now with two old men on stage. A few minutes later, the Young Dramatist attempts in vain to wipe off the make-up. The play ends with the two men discussing their future now that both have been abandoned by the girl.

The conspicuous technical and structural features of *Los viejos* are careful imitations of two devices available to the cinema and television: multiple takes and rewind. At first the apparent intention is to suggest that where there is disagreement between the generations and one approach to the problem has failed, other methods may be tried. The first attempt is rejected by the Old Dramatist, the second by the Young Dramatist, and the third by the Girl. On stage, however, the effect created by a sudden imitation of the rewinding of images is different from that on a screen. The cinema or television audience receives it as a well-known mechanical process, a mere reminder of the essential unreality of the images transmitted throughout the whole performance. For the theatre audience, on the other hand, the device interferes with the illusion of *reality* created by the obviously real actors standing a few yards away. It therefore introduces a sense of *unreality* into the proceedings. This notion that the performance belongs in the realm of imagination becomes the vital preparation for the moment of tension when no rewind occurs. The Old Dramatist has already warned that the Young Dramatist is indulging in a dangerous game, and we begin to notice the signs that prove him right. When it is a matter of aging, the effects are real, not imaginary. The process of growing old takes place in a temporal flow that cannot be reversed, and there is no second or third run-through.

Asked whether he has ever given any thought to the fact that he, too, will grow old, the Young Dramatist replies (with an irony that only the audience can see) that he has never had the time (TC 3:180). This indifference is the basis of the lesson that he receives. He can conceive of age only in terms of the theatre and, therefore, as a visual effect achieved by make-up. It is impossible for him to grasp the fact that age is a reality that is not subject to his whim: "La vejez debería ser sólo una especie de maquillaje escolar que se quitara uno al volver a la realidad" ("Old age ought to be just a kind of schoolkid's make-up that you took off on returning to reality") (TC 3:180). Gradually the facts dawn on him. Once his wrinkles have been painted and his hair grayed, he begins to experience the role emotionally. His wife's kiss leaves him unmoved. He is unable to prevent her from being repelled by him. The paint, of course, cannot be removed, for he must discover that wrinkles are a real and permanent phenomenon. On learning this painful lesson he reacts with rage and frustration, at which the Old Dramatist aptly comments, "Así es como nos damos cuenta de la vejez, con esa misma desesperación" ("That is how we realize we are old, with that same desperation") (TC 3:193). The face that the Young Dramatist has made up transforms him into a grotesque monster of an old man, with visible signs of evil and hatred. It is not the elegant picture of age that the Old Dramatist offers but the expression of fears and prejudices. Now he must learn to live with the hideous truth.

A close examination of the final minutes reveals a mixture of resignation and hope, decline and resilience. The Young Dramatist is preparing to face up to his new self-awareness in complete isolation. Having discovered that love stirs no impulses in him any longer, he sends his wife away with the Old Dramatist. This action, too, proves irrevocable: like the passion of love, she will not return. But he has at least acknowledged the reality of the process of aging, and therefore accepted that the world exists not merely for the young but for people of all ages. The Old Dramatist does appear at one point to realize his ambition of recapturing his youth, thanks to the sinuous attractions of the Girl, who leads him away. But the Girl has already shown her horror at the mask of old age and the change in her husband, and when she takes the hand of the Old Dramatist, it is a disconsolate and faltering motion. Once outside, she abandons him, reinforcing the idea that there can be no full rejuvenation, as there can be no return of blood to the body once it has been shed (TC 3:196). What remains for the two men is the prospect of composing a dramatic work together, a kind of compensation for failing physical powers. Theatre—or more strictly creativity—becomes a substitute for the life and love that they have lost. In this

artistic invention there is a degree of success, but it is counterbalanced by the fact that theatre is not life itself. The Old Dramatist
therefore closes the play with an oath that is at once frustrated,
ironical, and defiant: "Exito para ella la mujer—esto es, *merde!*,
como dicen en París" ("Success for her the woman—in other
words, *merde!* as they say in Paris") (TC 3:197). This expletive
(which is perhaps a deliberate echo of the septuagenarian's exclamation at the end of Gabriel García Márquez's novel of 1959, *El
coronel no tiene quien le escriba* [*No One Writes the Colonel*], links
up neatly with the discussion on theatre in the first half of the play.
It is a term used four times to describe the plays written by both
generations. The Young Dramatist first accuses the older generation of "toda la mierda aristotélica llevada a la momificación" ("All
the Aristotelian shit taken to the point of mummification") (TC
3:163), and later of using too much unoriginal material ("mierda")
(TC 3:173). The word is a regular part of his vocabulary. But the
Old Dramatist uses it self-consciously. Not without irony, he ap-
proves of the free expression of anger and the use of an appropriate
vocabulary for insulting the older generation: "Pobre del joven que
no sabe decir ¡merde!, al hablar de sus mayores" ("It's a poor
youngster who can't say *merde!* on speaking of his elders") (TC
3:167), softening and dignifying the effect with the French version.
Although he later resorts to the Spanish form to insult the younger
generation of playwrights (TC 3:176), at the curtain he has reverted
to the foreign form and added a reference to Paris. What this implies
is that he would like to introduce some vigor and rebellion into his
work, but he has no illusions about the reception that their play will
suffer. The impact of his personal explosion is therefore cushioned
and converted into a sage and cynical, worldly-wise echoing of a
commonplace or a universal truth.

There are several indications that *Los viejos* itself could be regarded as the model for the Old Dramatist's plan. By the late 1960s
Usigli could be closely identified with the old protagonist, even to
the point of receiving hostile critical reviews (notably in the case of
Corona de fuego). During the debate on theatre the Old Dramatist
expresses a number of Usigli's own views on matters pertaining to
the theatre: the unprofessional practices of critics, the intolerance
of the young toward anything old, contemporary dramatists' lack of
attention to human qualities, the pervasive influence of Becket,
Ionesco, Albee, and—more remotely—Brecht, and the treatment of
theatre as a means to an end rather than as an end in itself. The Old
Dramatist—like Usigli himself—is compared to an anachronistic
Ibsen. Recognizing his limitations but proudly confident of his
virtues, he seeks the ideal goal of a combination of his experience

and dramatic craftsmanship with the ideas and driving force of the Young Dramatist.

Los viejos contains all the craft of Usigli at his best—conflict, suspense, surprise, transition, discovery—together with a powerful idea and a more modern and experimental technique than we usually find in his plays. One of the most striking devices, the imitation of cinematographic images moving in reverse (and the consequent imitation of multiple "takes" to correct errors) places the play squarely in the context of the 1960s, when Spanish-American dramatists joined an international vogue for exploring the borders between the different media.[6] A device that is particularly rare in Usigli's theatre is the use of a character with little more than a purely symbolic role, but the Girl in *Los viejos* is such a case. She remains utterly silent throughout the play (except for the one occasion when she utters the words "¡Así no!" [TC 3:187] in an unreal animal-like cry). She undresses, dons her ballet clothes, dances to communicate her responses and moods, serves drinks, acts as a point of reference for the two men, and always embodies an image of sensuous attractiveness. Stylized rather than natural, she is not so much a character as an emblem of youthfulness, love, and the life force. She also gives Usigli the opportunity to take advantage of the fashion for (semi-)nudity on the stage as a means of representing the aspiration toward a greater freedom (and a greater box-office appeal). It is worth mentioning that the language, too, responds to Usigli's search for a lively, forceful, and more daring form of expression. (Among his previous works, *Jano es una muchacha* is the sole notable antecedent.) The Young Dramatist expresses his vulgarity through colloquialisms and obscenities. He also helps to give the play a contemporary air by means of his appearance, which was fashionable in the 1960s: long hair, leather jacket, tight trousers, and pointed shoes.

One of the most effective devices—though by no means original—is the use of make-up to create a quasi-magic result. With his back to the audience, the actor in the role of the Young Dramatist has to perform a task that is normally confined to the dressing room. While the Old Dramatist guides him with a verbal tour of an old man's physiognomy, the actor paints wrinkles on his face and gray streaks on his hair, and turns to face the audience at the appropriate moment to produce the shock of seeing decades of aging compressed into a few minutes. A versatile use of lighting supports the surreal effects of scenes like this, the face of each speaker being illuminated alternately to suggest his isolation in the darkness of despair and emptiness. The ticking of a clock, in a crescendo of volume, powerfully evokes a sense of time's remorseless flow.

In *Los viejos* there is none of the glamour and sentimentality that Usigli attached to old age in some scenes of other plays (such as *La función de despedida*). Certain positive features are presented, it is true, through the Old Dramatist: experience, wisdom, dignity, and a determination to continue being productive. But against this must be weighed the Young Dramatist's instinctive reaction to the discovery that aging repels, dissipates, destroys, incapacitates, and isolates. Both men are forced to the conclusion that their only recourse is to *create*, but they know that creativity is undermined by the essential hopelessness of regaining lost powers. This is the closest that we ever find Usigli to the spirit of the absurd (except in *La última puerta*). In the final analysis, this may well be one reason for the play's superiority over his other late works, though it also has the virtues of combining a good universal theme with interesting techniques and of building an enigmatic situation to stimulate curiosity and thought.

"El problema del tiempo y la memoria me había fascinado siempre" ("The problem of time and memory had always fascinated me"), Isigli wrote in 1960 (TC 3:450). We have seen how he focused on the re-creation of the past in *Aguas estancadas*, the reassessment of one's life in *La función de despedida*, and the inevitability of aging in *Los viejos*. To complete the picture, we should take into account a few other plays. In *Corona de sombra* a period of sixty years separates the two sequences of the action, years in which events of historic importance acquire a clearer perspective. But as the analysis in the preceding chapter showed, Usigli divided his interest between the national events and the life of the empress as an individual. The play may be seen as the re-creation of the past through the tormented memories of Carlota, and in this aspect, time and senility are interlinked with the themes of punishment, insanity, and reassessment. *Otra primavera* is another play where—despite an apparent focus on hereditary madness—the final emphasis is on old age and the shadow of death. For the family in question, the hopes and plans, wealth and possessions have disappeared in an irretrievable past. But the aging parents will face their grim future with mutual self-sacrifice and with resolution. Usigli added two short plays to this category during the autumnal period of his career. *El encuentro* (The encounter) (1963) traces the beginning of a romance between a young girl and an older man. The difference in their ages presents an initial barrier that is gradually lowered, but a final development suggests that the impediment is ultimately insurmountable. *El caso Flores* (The Flores case)[7] deals with the way in which the past impinges on the present. In a chance meeting, two businessmen recognize each other as former contemporaries at school. As they compare their present circumstances, we realize that in the course of their lives they have both been attempting to cast off their old reputations. What the play shows is that there is no escape from the foibles already expressed in one's youth.

Although these two pieces are rather insubstantial, they illustrate the scope of Usigli's lasting preoccupation with themes associated with time and aging. They also draw our attention to the fact that during the 1960s, when his diplomatic career took him to Beirut and Oslo, there was a tendency for him to set an increasing number of his plays outside Mexico. At times he chose a non-Hispanic place, such as the transatlantic liner in the light crime melodrama *Un navío cargado de . . .* (A ship loaded with . . .) (1961), a provincial capital in northern Europe in *El encuentro,* and a small European city in *Los viejos.* Occasionally he simply indicated an unspecified or imaginary Latin American country, as in the case of *¡Buenos días, señor Presidente!* For *El gran circo del mundo* (The great arena of the world) (1968) he invented the land of "Utopia."

As noted in the study of political plays in chapters 2, 3, and 4, Usigli turned in his later years to both fantastic events and imaginary countries in an attempt to achieve a greater theoretical dimension. At the same time, he was progressing toward the more universal themes discussed in the present chapter. One of the most ambitious of all his works arose out of a combination of the two tendencies. Although in terms of theatre *El gran circo del mundo* must be judged a failure, it adds an important element to our understanding of Usigli's total output. In a brief prologue to the play[8] he refers to the last letter written by Albert Einstein before his death in Princeton in April 1955, in which the latter complained of the world's political imbecilities. Usigli reminds us that Einstein was one of the nine internationally renowned men of science who signed Bertrand Russell's "Declaration," calling on governments of the world to renounce the use of the hydrogen bomb. *El gran circo del mundo* might be described as Usigli's contribution to the campaign for nuclear disarmament.

The action takes place in the near future in the capital city of one of the world's two superpowers. Utopia is situated "en las Indias Occidentales" (best translated as the Western Indies),[9] but it appears to be a nightmare version of the United States during Senator Joe McCarthy's purges of communist infiltration, with the added characteristics of a police state like Stalin's Soviet Union. Against a background similar to that of the Cold War of the early 1950s, the president of Utopia has decided to resolve a conflict in a remote Eastern territory by dropping six "Omega" bombs.[10] However, a nuclear scientist (who committed suicide after his arrest for treason) has modified the bombs so that if improperly used they will cause the world's atmosphere to ignite. Dr. Julius Uranius, his disciple, manages to persuade the president to recall the bombers. (Fortunately we are not yet in the missiles era!) Julius is ordered to verify whether the bombs have indeed been modified in the manner described. After eight weeks he is able to confirm the alteration. In fact, he has disregarded his terms of reference and perfected a second type of bomb that, if exploded immediately after the first, will extinguish the conflagration, regenerate the atmosphere, fertilize the soil, and send people into a deep sleep from which they will awaken capable of living long lives without the effects of aging. It will even be possible to use the bomb to make other planets habitable.

This idealistic fantasy is so implausible (references to radiation look especially naive today) that its moralistic purpose is unfortunately not achieved. *El gran circo del mundo* points the way to a benevolent use for nuclear power and the abolition of nuclear weapons. Moreover, it portrays the individual's self-sacrifice for the sake of the world's population as a whole and the struggle of the man of science with his conscience. Dr. Uranius is tried for high treason and executed, but not before he has ensured that the nuclear secrets will fall into the hands of the other superpower. The president of Utopia orders the withdrawal of troops from the occupied Eastern territory and prepares a deal involving the destruction of all nuclear weapons. While the dead scientist becomes the object of public opprobrium, the president enjoys acclaim as a peaceseeker. It is not human nature that Usigli idealizes in this play but the course of human destiny. With such transparently unconvincing logic, it was clearly intended to be an allegorical rather than a realist work. Various features suggest that he planned to elevate and abstract the theme: the use of classical names (Julius, Penelope, Antonio Paulus, President Olimpio), the designation of bombs by symbolic letters (the "Omega" and "Zed" bombs are destructive, whereas the "Alpha" bomb creates a new atmosphere), and the presentation of news by radio choruses (presumably to turn our minds to Greek tragedies), not to mention the Calderonian echoes in the title.[11] One of the technical defects, however, is the attempt to create a parallel between false assumptions of betrayal at the national level and those at a domestic level. The subplot concerning Julius's supposed infidelity with a foreign spy and his wife's supposed affair with a journalist fails to integrate with the principal theme, causing instead a number of digressions and distractions. As a humanitarian gesture, *El gran circo del mundo* translates the diplomat's sincere world version into dramatic form. As theatre, it does not reflect the dramatist's genius. [12]

On the whole, Usigli's broader vision failed to inspire the same quality of theatre as his Mexican themes. In this category of plays, *Los viejos* deserves to be ranked with his best, but the majority lack either the requisite profundity or the appropriate technical efficiency. With perspective, we can see that in the Mexican plays, too, Usigli's most ambitious ventures often brought negative results. We cannot fail to admire his attempts to raise the stature of Mexican drama in international terms, but the effort to write a national tragedy *(Corona de fuego)* and the search for an allegorical mode *(Un día de éstos . . ., ¡Buenos días, señor Presidente! El gran circo del mundo)* ran into various kinds of problem. The earnest desire to communicate his profound beliefs in national unity and personal resilience, moreover, gave him an increasingly conspicuous tendency to moralize.

There is no general agreement on which titles deserve to join *El gesticulador* and *Corona de sombra* in a short list of, let us say, the six best and most representative plays. Giving particular emphasis to dramatic craft, however, and drawing from the great diversity of his production, I believe that there is a strong case for adding *Noche de estío, La familia cena en casa, Jano es una muchacha,* and *Los viejos*. Usigli was at his best when he concentrated on the actual realities of Mexico, whether political, social, or psychological. And his manner was more convincing when critical, satirical, or simply descriptive, rather than openly didactic. His most successful plays—both comic and serious—are constructed with equal attention to overall suspense and individual scenes; they do not sacrifice the dramatic merit of constituent parts for some elusive ideal in a work as a whole. In one grand ambition, however, his success is widely recognized, both in Mexico and abroad: the establishment of a national theatre. [13] He placed Mexico on the stage as a worthy theme. He created a repertory of high-quality plays, proving to audiences that foreign dramatists did not have a monopoly of the dramatic arts. [14] With honesty and boldness he allowed his characters to mock and berate his country's politicians and institutions. More than one phase of his career was blighted by unjust and uncomprehending critics, public scandals, and hostile political leaders. But whether through political commentary, social realism, psychological analysis, or historical reassessment, he ensured that his theatre became, above all, a Mexican recipe for Mexican audiences.

Notes

Chapter 1. Building a Theatre

1. In 1947 he declared, "He creado un teatro mexicano. En otras palabras, y con toda modestia, estoy seguro de que México empieza a existir de un modo redondo y crea su teatro propio a través de mí" ("I have created a Mexican theatre. In other words, and in all modesty, I am sure that Mexico is beginning to exist in a complete way and is creating its own theatre through me) ("Ensayo sobre la actualidad de la poesía dramática," *Teatro completo,* vol. 3 (Mexico, D.F.: Fondo de Cultura Económica, 1979]: 497. Two decades later he modified the claim, recognizing that "contemporáneos míos trabajaban, unidos en grupos terencianos y exclusivistas, con un objeto semejante" ("contemporaries of mine were working in Terencian and clannish groups with a similar aim") (*Anatomía del teatro* [Mexico, D.F.: Ecuador O O' O", Revista de Poesía Universal, 1967], 10. His relations with the "Contemporáneos" are discussed below.

2. "Rodolfo Usigli . . . funda el teatro dramático mexicano contemporáneo" ("Rodolfo Usigli founded the contemporary Mexican dramatic theatre") (Yolanda Argudín, *Historia del teatro en México desde los rituales prehispánicos hasta el arte dramático de nuestros días* [Mexico, D.F.: Panorama Editorial, 1986], 135); "Proclamado por muchos como el redentor del teatro mexicano . . ." ("Proclaimed by many to be the redeemer of the Mexican Theatre . . .") (John B. Nomland, *Teatro Mexicano contemporáneo* [Mexico, D.F.: Instituto Nacional de Bellas Artes, 1967], 263). A more cautious view holds that Usigli did not succeed in saving the Mexican theatre from its continuing crisis but acknowledges that he was described for many years as the principal Mexican dramatist (Carlos Monsiváis, "Notas sobre la cultura mexicana en el siglo XX," in *Historia general de México,* ed. Daniel Cosío Villegas, 3d ed. [Mexico, D.F.: El Colegio de México, 1981], 1542).

3. Rodolfo Usigli, *México en el teatro* (Mexico, D.F.: Imprenta Mundial, 1932). Translated as *Mexico in the Theater* by Wilder P. Scott (Mississippi University Press: Romance Monographs, 1976).

4. Usigli, *Anatomía del teatro,* 18, 28, 31, 33, 34, 36. In summarizing the comments on drama critics, I have given the gist of Usigli's ironical circumlocutions.

5. Monsiváis, "Notas sobre la cultura mexicana," 1532–33.

6. Argudín, *Historia del teatro en México,* 67; and Frank Dauster, "La generación de 1924: El dilema del realismo," *Latin American Theatre Review* 18, no. 2, (1985): 13.

7. Usigli, *Teatro completo,* 3:599. Usigli's "Prólogos, epílogos y otros textos" are collected on pp. 279–844 of this volume. References will be given in parentheses within the text and will follow the model: (TC 3:599).

8. The seven members of this group were: Francisco Monterde, José Joaquín Gamboa, Carlos Noriega Hope, Víctor Manuel Díez Barroso, Ricardo Parada León, Lázaro Lozano García, and Carlos Lozano García.

9. Dauster, "La generación de 1924," 13. The play was Carlos Díaz Dufoo's *Padre mercader.*

10. Argudín, *Historia del teatro en México,* 79; Monsiváis, "Notas sobre la cultura mexicana," 1539.

11. The founders of the Teatro de Ulises were Xavier Villaurrutia, Celestino Gorostiza, Salvador Novo, Gilberto Owen, and Antonieta Mercado.

12. Some confusion arose over the presence or omission of the word *de.* Usigli explained that the correct form for the group (as opposed to the theatre) includes the preposition (TC 3:601).

13. Quoted by Margarita Mendoza López, "Teatro de las Bellas Artes de la Ciudad de México," *Latin American Theatre Review* 18, no. 2 (1985): 9.

14. Ibid., 10.

15. Antonio Magaña Esquivel, "Exégesis de Rodolfo Usigli," program notes for the production of *El gesticulador* by the Compañía Nacional de Teatro del INBA, at the Teatro Jiménez Rueda, August 1983.

16. Argudín, *Historia del teatro en México,* 161.

17. A note added in 1962 to the original version of Usigli's *Anatomía del teatro* reflects his disappointment: "Y me pregunto si en realidad el cuarto de siglo transcurrido desde la *Anatomía* ha operado verdaderos cambios de fondo" ("And I wonder whether in fact the quarter of a century that has passed since the *Anatomía* has really brought about any basic changes") ("Acotación," *Anatomía del teatro,* 12).

18. Quoted by Mendoza López, "Teatro de las Bellas Artes," 11.

19. Kirsten F. Nigro, "Entrevista a Luisa Josefina Hernández," *Latin American Theatre Review,* 18, no. 2 (1985): 102.

20. It had not yet become the Instituto Nacional de Bellas Artes (as is implied by W. P. Scott in his introduction to *Mexico in the Theater,* 9.)

21. While *El gesticulador* was on at the Palacio Nacional de Bellas Artes, Usigli's childhood friend and long-standing rival Salvador Novo assaulted him in the dark on the theatre steps, bringing their enmity to a climax and severing whatever ties remained between Usigli and the former "Contemporáneos."

22. *El niño y la niebla* earned the theatre 200,000 pesos, and *Jano es una muchacha* earned 225,000 pesos for the first hundred performances (Usigli received 120 pesos for each performance) (TC 3:722, 723).

23. Usigli, *Anatomía del teatro,* 19.

24. *Ibid.,* 25–26.

25. The idea came to him around 1932, and the title around 1935–37, though he did not mention it again until 1945. T. S. Eliot responded appreciatively to the project; G. B. Shaw was totally indifferent (TC 3:653).

26. The question of realist drama is resumed with greater detail in chapter 5.

27. The clearest and most forthright expression of these views appears in Usigli's essay "Primeros apuntes sobre el teatro," *El Universal Ilustrado* 15, no. 748 (10 September 1931): 187–91.

28. Rodolfo Usigli, "La novela disuelta en el cine," *Número,* Primavera 1935. Reproduced in *Revistas literarias mexicanas modernas* (Mexico, D.F.: Fondo de Cultura Económica, 1980), 435.

29. Rodolfo Usigli, "Primer ensayo hacia una tragedia mexicana," *Cuadernos Americanos* 52, no. 4 (1950): 102–25. The subject of tragedy is briefly mentioned in chapter 3 and fully discussed in chapter 7.

30. *Conversaciones y encuentros de Rodolfo Usigli* (Mexico, D.F.: Organización Editorial Novaro S.A., 1974), 15–65.

31. See in particular, "Una comedia shaviana *Noche de estío*" (TC 3:303–6); "El Gran Teatro del Nuevo Mundo," (TC 3:651–53); "*Jano es una muchacha.* Prólogo*" (TC 3:696–742); and "Análisis, examen y juicio de *¡Buenos días, señor Presidente!*" (TC 3:820–44).

32. Usigli, *Conversaciones y encuentros,* 69.

33. *Ibid.,* 38.

34. Bernard Shaw, *Complete Plays with Prefaces* (New York: Dodd, 1963), 3:4. Quoted in Charles A. Berst, *Bernard Shaw and the Art of Drama* (Urbana, Chicago, London: University of Illinois Press, 1973), 3.

35. "Primer prólogo a *Corona de luz,*" in *Corona de sombra, Corona de fuego, Corona de luz* (Mexico, D.F.: Editorial Porrúa, 1973), 231 (this prologue is not included in *Teatro completo,* vol. 3).

36. *The Complete Plays of Bernard Shaw* (London: Constable and Co. Ltd., 1931) contains thirty-nine titles; the same is true of *Teatro completo de Rodolfo Usigli.* This remarkable (and admittedly trivial) similarity was achieved only by the inclusion of some Usiglian works of relatively slight merit in the first and third volumes. Shaw, of course, subsequently wrote more plays, but for Usigli the 1931 collection—appearing at the start of his career—may well have set an irresistible target.

Chapter 2. The Legacy of the Revolution

1. "Una comedia shaviana *Noche de estío*" (TC 3:303–416) is an indispensable source of information for his political opinions of that period. In this chapter I have adapted and augmented material first published in my article "Usigli's Political Drama in Perspective," *Bulletin of Hispanic Studies* 66 (1989): 251–61.

2. Usigli's were not the only plays to suffer prohibition around that time. Juan Bustillo Oro's trilogy *San Miguel de las Espinas* was banned in 1933 after its first night, and Carlos Díaz Dufoo's *Sombras de mariposa* suffered a similar fate in 1936 (TC 3:475).

3. He resigned from his post after six months because he intended to publish and stage the *Tres comedias impolíticas,* which could have created problems for at least one well-known secretary (TC 3:600).

4. Usigli's dispute with contributors to *Plural* is discussed in G. O. Schanzer, "Usigli, Calderón and the Revolution," *Kentucky Romance Quarterly* 26 (1979): 193, 200.

5. See, for example, Thomas E. Skidmore & Peter H. Smith, *Modern Latin America* (New York and Oxford: Oxford University Press, 1984), 252.

6. Judith Adler Hellman, *Mexico in Crisis* (New York: Holmer and Meier Publishers; London: Heinemann, 1978), 156.

7. The Partido Nacional Revolucionario of 1929 was reformed as the Partido de la Revolución Mexicana in 1937 before its further change to the Partido Revolucionario Institucional in 1946.

8. José Agustín, "The Intellectual and Freedom of Expression: Censorship in Latin America," in *Three Lectures: Literature and Censorship in Latin America Today: Dream Within a Dream,* ed. John Kirk and Don Schmidt, Occasional Papers, No. 1, Department of Foreign Languages and Literatures, 36 (Denver: University of Denver, 1978).

9. Hellman, *Mexico in Crisis,* 100.

10. César Rubio in *El gesticulador,* act 3 (TC 1:775).

11. For reasons not entirely dissimilar to the first of these, Usigli applied the label *antihistórica* to each of his historical plays.

12. A rereading of Bernard Shaw's *Heartbreak House* apparently acted as a direct source of inspiration for the composition of *Una noche de estío* (TC 3 : 303). Although there are superficial similarities—diverse social elements brought into political intercourse within one house—Usigli's characters, plot, and purpose owe little (if anything) to Shaw.

13. Ramón Layera, "Mecanismos de fabulación y mitificación de la historia en las 'comedias impolíticas' y las *Coronas* de Rodolfo Usigli," *Latin American Theatre Review* 18, no. 2 (1985): 51.

14. The increase in the number of strikes at that moment was spectacular: 33 in 1933; 202 in 1934; 642 in 1935. After 1936 the number gradually declined. See Pablo González Casanova, *La democracia en México,* 14th ed. (Mexico, D.F.: Serie Popular Era, 1983), 233.

15. John Edwin Fagg, *Latin America: A General History,* 3d ed. (New York: Macmillan Publishing Co.; London: Collier Macmillan Publishers, 1977), 544, 548.

16. "Carta a Xavier Villaurrutia," preceding the text of *La última puerta* (TC 1 : 404).

17. See J. García Lora, "Usigli 'esperó a Godot,' " *Papeles de Son Armadans,* no. 269/70 (1978): 129–47.

Chapter 3. The Revolution, Politics, and Hypocrisy: *El gesticulador*

1. D. L. Shaw, "Dramatic Technique in Usigli's *El gesticulador,*" *Theatre Research International* (Oxford) n.s. 1, no. 2 (1976): 125.

2. J. W. Kronik, "Usigli's *El gesticulador* and the Fiction of Truth," *Latin American Theatre Review* 11, no. 1 (1977): 5.

3. "Epílogo sobre la hipocresía del mexicano" (TC 3 : 460).

4. Kronik, "Usigli's *El gesticulador,*" 14.

5. D. W. Foster reinforces this interpretation in the chapter "Dos ejemplos de metateatro" in his book *Estudios sobre teatro mexicano contemporáneo: Semiología de la competencia teatral* (New York, Berne, Frankfurt, Nancy: Peter Lang, 1984), in particular p. 14.

6. See Berta Ulloa, "La lucha armada (1911–1920)," in Cosío Villegas, *Historia general de México* 2 : 1136.

7. Ibid., 1147.

8. Guillermo Schmidhuber de la Mora, "El teatro mexicano y la provincia," *Latin American Theatre Review* 18, no. 2 (1985): 27.

9. An essentially similar criticism is made by César to Elena in act 1 (TC 1 : 754–55).

10. It should be noted that in this essay Usigli traces the origins of this hypocrisy from Independence to the twentieth century.

11. Fagg, *Latin America,* 548.

12. Lorenzo Meyer, "El primer tramo del camino," in Cosío Villegas, *Historia general de México* 2 : 1245.

13. Hellman, *Mexico in Crisis,* 37.

14. See Peter Calvert, *Mexico* (London: Ernest Benn, 1973), table 3, p. 261. Since 1940 the trend has changed drastically, with candidates from the core dominating the presidency.

15. González Casanova, *La democracia en México,* 24.

16. Adolfo Gilly, *La revolución interrumpida* (Mexico, D.F.: Ediciones "El Caballito," 1971), summarizes the proletariat and Marxist conception by explaining that in the absence of a proletariat leadership and a workers' program, the revolution was twice interrupted: in 1919–20 and in 1940. Lorenzo Meyer, dealing with the whole of Mexican history since 1920 ("El primer tramo del camino," and "La encrucijada," in Cosío Villegas, *Historia general de México* 2:1183–1355) divides the period into two, describing the years before 1940 as a time focused on the formation of the political and social system, and the years since 1940 as a time of political stability and rapid economic growth and diversification (1275). Michael C. Meyer and William L. Sherman, in *The Course of Mexican History* (New York: Oxford University Press, 1979), make a similar division, using "The Constructive Phase" and "The Revolution Shifts Gear: Mexico Since 1940" as their chapter headings.

17. This was in fact the second revision of the Departamento de Bellas Artes (formed by José Vasconcelos within his Secretaría de Educación Pública).

18. See Margarita Mendoza López, "El teatro en la ciudad de México durante cincuenta años," *Plural* (segunda época) 17–19, núm. 201 (1988): 43; and Monsiváis, "Notas sobre la cultura mexicana," 1544.

19. It appeared in installments in the first three numbers of *El Hijo Pródigo* (1943). The edition published by Letras de México (1944) included the essay "Doce notas."

20. Usigli believed the opposition to be orchestrated by a few influential figures, some of whom were senior members of the INBA (TC 3:541–44).

21. On the day that the play's run was ended, 30 May 1947, Usigli summarized these charges in his article "El caso de *El gesticulador*" (TC 3:532).

22. José Emilio Pacheco names the official as Vicente Lombardo Toledano (in the prologue to *Rodolfo Usigli: Tiempo y memoria en conversación desesperada*, Textos de Humanidades 26, Difusión Cultural [Mexico, D.F.: Universidad Nacional Autónoma de México, 1981], 14). Lombardo Toledano—whose ascendancy was promoted by President Cárdenas—was the first leader of the Confederación de Trabajadores Mexicanos after the political restructuring of 1937.

23. Carlos Fuentes, *La muerte de Artemio Cruz*, 4th ed. (Mexico, D.F.: Fondo de Cultura Económica, 1968), 277.

24. Kronik, 'Usigli's *El gesticulador*," 5.

25. D.L. Shaw, "Dramatic Technique," 126.

26. Kronik, 'Usigli's *El gesticulador*," 5.

27. Foster, *Estudios sobre teatro*, 14.

28. See Lionel Abel, *Metatheatre* (New York: Hill and Wang, 1963).

29. Kronik, "Usigli's *El gesticulador*," 14.

30. William Shakespeare, *Julius Caesar*, act 2, scene 2 in *The Complete Works of William Shakespeare* (London: Gawthorn Press and Bruce Publishing Co., n.d.), 727–28.

31. A notable example was the production by the Compañía Nacional de Teatro del INBA at the Teatro Jiménez Rueda, directed by Rafael López Miarnau, in August/September 1983.

32. There is no sanction anywhere in Usigli's text for the shooting of Rubio to occur on stage. It is interesting to note, however, that the playwright did offer what he considered to be a more concise and intense version of the very last scenes in a note entitled "Apostilla" in the first volume of his *Teatro completo* (TC 1:799–802). The amendment does not affect the plot in any way, since it consists only of a slight modification of the order of events. But there is a minor change in the mood a few minutes before the end of the play. Instead of having Navarro burst in on the

family's grief, Usigli's alternative version has his voice drifting into the room while he is addressing the crowd outside. The spectacle of a grieving family is prolonged a little, and at the same time the audience is able to watch the gradual impact of his hypocritical speech on the family and to share with them a sense of the remorselessness of this triumph of crime and corruption. It is as the demagogue and not only as the assassin that we eventually see him return to the stage.

33. Leach, *Tragedy,* 32.
34. D. L. Shaw, "Dramatic Technique," 129.

Chapter 4. Politics and Fantasy

1. Pacheco, "Prólogo," in Usigli, *Tiempo y memoria,* 15.
2. Even Lázaro Cárdenas might be deemed to emerge from the play in an ambiguous light. There are hints of him in the figure of former President General Avalos (expropriator of mineral reserves). Although Usigli endows him with many admirable attributes, such as integrity, unselfishness, patriotism, and loyalty to his ideals, and although he alone among the former presidents has no accumulated wealth, General Avalos could be implicated in political assassinations.
3. Pedro Calderón de la Barca, *La vida es sueño* (Life's a Dream), 1635.
4. Hellman, "The Student Movement of 1968," in *Mexico in Crisis,* 131–45.
5. Calvert, *Mexico,* 321.

Chapter 5. Social Drama: The Family at Home

1. "*Medio tono:* Discurso por un teatro realista" (TC 3:439).
2. In the context of Usigli's production as a whole, the concept of cannibalism suggests the situation in a theatre, where Mexicans—particularly bourgeois Mexicans, to maintain Julio's point of view—devour the image of their own selves. Destruction is not the key to this fuller context.
3. Usigli complained that the performance in the Palacio de Bellas Artes on 13 November 1937 made it "una familia cualquiera, borrosa, desagradable" ("just any family, indistinct, unpleasant") (TC 3:441).
4. Marco Aurelio, "Teatralerías," *El Universal Ilustrado,* 15 November 1937, 27.
5. Ibid.
6. "Introducción a *La familia cena en casa.* Carta a un dramaturgo novel" (TC 3:613).
7. Ovid's version of the myth depicts Pygmalion as the sculptor of an ivory statue of a young woman, which the goddess Venus brings to life. Pygmalion and his sculpture are then united in marriage.
8. Berst, *Bernard Shaw and the Art of Drama,* 198.

Chapter 6. Psychological Drama: Two Faces of Usigli's Success

1. The observation was made in his "Introducción a *La familia cena en casa:* Carta a un dramaturgo novel," written in 1942. To take later plays into account, historical and universal themes would need to be added.

2. *Ensayo de un crimen* has a plot full of intricacies and ironies. The protagonist, Roberto de la Cruz, twice makes careful plans to commit a wholly gratuitous murder but fails in both cases because his intended victims are killed by other people. When eventually he does murder somebody, it is the result of a loss of self-control, and the person killed is not the expected victim but his wife. There is a neatness in the structural use of two motifs: Cruz's dizzy spells and a music box. At the opening of the novel he suffers dizziness while he is shaving, and it is while shaving that he finally commits his murder. A particular music box seems to exert some hold over him, and it is while his wife is bending over the box that he loses control and kills her. Toward the end of the novel we learn about the two quite separate predetermining factors in Cruz's ambition to commit a murder and his fascination with this music. As a youth, he boasted to a girl that he was marked out to be somebody special: either a great criminal or a great saint. But as a child, he witnessed a gratuitous shooting during the Revolution, while a nearby barrel organ was playing the piece of music later reproduced by the music box. In the end, Roberto de la Cruz, desperate to be considered a great criminal, is committed to a mental asylum, feeling like a cornered animal and incapable of destroying the public's belief that he has merely committed a crime of passion.

3. Most of these plays are studied in chapter 8.

4. William A. R. Thomson, *Black's Medical Dictionary,* 31st ed. (London: Adam and Charles Black, 1976), 774.

5. See S. H. Tilles, "Rodolfo Usigli's Concept of Dramatic Art," *Latin American Theatre Review,* 3, no. 2 (1970): 31–38.

6. In his "Noticia" to the play Usigli calls this a "revolución o revelación" (TC 2:436).

7. Usigli's definitions coincide in their essential details with authoritative accounts of Janus. H. R. Hays writes that "Janus . . . , who gave his name to January, looked both ways. He acquired an image with a face before and behind. He was both the spirit of doorways and the object of a domestic cult. In the city of Rome he had charge of gateways. He was probably linked up with rites de passage, a threshold, going from one state to another, a time of magic peril" (*In the Beginning: Early Man and His Gods* [New York: G. P. Putnam and Sons, 1963], 189). The idea of Janus as a girl appears to be Usigli's own, though it is worth noting that Robert Schilling feels the need to refute the theory that this god was derived from the goddess Diana in his *Rites, cultes, dieux de Rome* (Paris: Editions Klincksieck, 1979), in the chapter "Janus: Le dieu introducteur. Le dieu des passages," 220–62. An additional point to bear in mind is that the nickname Janus may be applied to any person who acts with duplicity.

8. Usigli's extensive and important prologue to *Jano es una muchacha* serves as his justification for writing the play.

9. See "Addenda después del estreno" (TC 3:718–42).

10. Arthur Ganz, *George Bernard Shaw* (London and Basingstoke: Macmillan, 1983), 91. There are, of course, another *two* acts to follow in Shaw's play.

Chapter 7. History and Sovereignty

1. For Europeans, the daughter of King Leopold of Belgium was Charlotte or Carlotta; for Mexicans, Carlota. I use the Hispanic spelling for both the historical figure and the dramatic character. In the sections below I have adapted and augmented material in three of my articles, each of which has a different purpose

and emphasis from the present chapter: "Insanity and Poetic Justice in Usigli's *Corona de sombra*," *Latin American Theatre Review* 10, no. 1 (1976): 5–14; "Usigli and the Search for Tragedy: *Corona de fuego*,", in *Hispanic Studies in Honour of Frank Pierce*, Ed. J. P. England (Sheffield: University of Sheffield, 1980), 1–15; and "Los niveles de la verdad en *Corona de luz* de Rodolfo Usigli," *Anales de Literatura Hispanoamericana*, núm. 12 (1983): 13–27.

2. Rodolfo Usigli, "Advertencia," in *Corona de sombra*, ed. Rex Edward Ballinger (London: Harrap, 1965), xv.

3. Ibid., xv–xvi.

4. See Hayden White, *Metahistory: The Historical Imagination in Nineteenth-Century Europe* (Baltimore and London: John Hopkins University Press, 1973), 15, quoted in Layera, 'Mecanismos de fabulación y mitificación," 55. Layera's article, though void of textual analysis, is the best commentary on the three *Coronas*.

5. Usigli, "Advertencia," xv.

6. A. A. Parker, "History and Poetry: the Coriolanus Theme in Calderón," in *Hispanic Studies in Honour of I. González Llubera*, Ed. Frank Pierce (Oxford: Dolphin Book Co., 1959), 211.

7. Richard O'Connor, *The Cactus Throne: The Tragedy of Maximilian and Carlota* (London: Allen & Unwin, 1971).

8. Ibid., 245–48.

9. José Luis Blasio, *Maximilian: Memoirs of his Private Secretary*, (trans. R. H. Murray) (New Haven: Yale University Press, 1934).

10. O'Connor, *Cactus Throne*, 273.

11. See for example Lilia Díaz, El liberalismo militante," in Cosío Villegas, *Historia general de México* 2:857–58, 874–75.

12. Ibid., 2:895.

13. O'Connor, *Cactus Throne*, 177, 147.

14. Ibid., 180.

15. Díaz, "El liberalismo militante," 882.

16. O'Connor, *Cactus Throne*, 228.

17. Blasio, *Maximilian*, 84.

18. Arnold Blumberg, *The Diplomacy of the Mexican Empire, 1863–1867*, (Philadelphia: American Philosophical Society, 1971), 106.

19. O'Connor, *Cactus Throne*, 268.

20. Blasio, *Maximilian*, 107.

21. Peter Hays, *New Horizons in Psychiatry* (Harmondsworth: Penguin Books, 1964), 19.

22. Ibid.

23. O'Connor, *Cactus Throne*, 345.

24. Ibid.

25. Ibid., 344.

26. Ibid., 345.

27. Ibid., 343.

28. Blasio, *Maximilian*, 187.

29. Díaz, "El liberalismo militante," 872–96.

30. Lesley Byrd Simpson, *Many Mexicos* (Berkeley and Los Angeles: University of California Press, 1966), 282.

31. O'Connor, *Cactus Throne*, 250.

32. In an article on the Mexican dramatist Juan Ruiz de Alarcón, G. W. Ribbans quotes A. A. Parker's definition of poetic justice as "the satisfaction or appropri-

ateness felt when a deserving man should meet with good fortune or an undeserv-
ing man with ill fortune, whether or not the particular recompense is directly
connected with his desserts. . . . The 'punishment' of the character who has erred
. . . need not be punishment by any outside agent; it may only be a failure or a
frustration brought about by events; but the failure must be felt to be fitting"
("Lying in the structure of *La verdad sospechosa,*" in *Studies in Spanish Literature of the Golden Age Presented to Edward M. Wilson,* Ed. R. O. Jones [London:
Tamesis, 1973], 211–12). A similar concept was applied to the historical events that
I am discussing by the French radical politician Georges Clemenceau when, after
Maximilian's execution, he remarked: "His wife is mad, you say. Nothing more
just. This almost makes me believe in Providence. Was it not her ambitions that
incited the fool? I regret that she *has* lost her reason and cannot realize that she
killed her husband and that a people are avenging themselves" (quoted by O'Connor, *Cactus Throne,* 333). Usigli's intention was clearly to apply a less harsh
standard once Carlota had suffered more than he deemed appropriate.

33. Dennis Perri, "The Artistic Unity of *Corona de sombra,*" *Latin American
Theatre Review* 15, no. 1 (1981): 17.

34. To be precise, Usigli stipulated that the setting should be the double room
with only the left-hand side of the stage used. The Harrap edition of the play
misleadingly omits Usigli's careful instruction: "La acción de esta escena se
desarrolla en el salón de la izquierda" ("The action of this scene unfolds in the
room on the left") (TC 2:210).

35. See Usigli, *Conversaciones y encuentros,* 62.

36. *La exposición,* a "comedia divertimiento en tres actos," is also in verse.

37. For a good indication of these versions see in particular Hernán Cortés,
Letters from Mexico, trans. and ed. by A. R. Pagden, (London: Oxford University
Press, 1972), n. 52 to "Fifth Letter," 518; and Josefina Muriel, "Divergencias en la
biografía de Cuauhtémoc," *Estudios de Historia Novohispana* (Mexico) 1, (1966):
53–114. In addition to these sources, the remarks that I make below are based on
Bernal Díaz del Castillo, *Historia verdadera de la conquista de la Nueva España*
(Mexico, D. F.: Porrúa), 1960.

38. Díaz del Castillo, *Historia verdadera* 2:205.

39. See Hernán Cortés, *Cartas de relación de Fernando Cortés sóbre el descubrimiento y conquista de la Nueva España: Carta quinta* (Madrid: Biblioteca de
Autores Españoles, 1877), 22:126–27. The son of Pax Bolón stayed with Cortés
two days in Tiçatepal; they then traveled five leagues to Teutiacar (Tuxakha),
where Cortés heard of Pax Bolón's deceit; the following day (i.e., the fourth) Pax
Bolón visited Cortés, and the next Cortés moved on with him to Itzamkanac.
There is some doubt concerning the actual town in which Cuauhtémoc was
executed. Both Teotilac and Itzamkanac have been named. In any case, clearly at
least one more day must be added.

40. See A. R. Pagden's detailed note 52 in Cortés, *Letters from Mexico,* 518,
and my note 43, below.

41. Cortés, *Letters from Mexico,* n.52, 518.

42. Díaz del Castillo, *Historia verdadera* 2:206.

43. Cortés, *Cartas de relación,* 127; Francisco López de Gómara, *Conquista de
México: Segunda parte de la historia general de las Indias* (Madrid: Biblioteca de
Autores Españoles, 1877), 22:143; Díaz del Castillo, *Historia verdadera,* 205.
Other sources (cited by Pagden in Cortés, *Letters from Mexico*) are: *Obras
históricas de Don Fernando de Alva Ixtlilxóchitl,* publicadas y anotadas por
Alfredo Chavero (Mexico, 1891); S. G. Morley, *The Inscriptions of Peten* (Wash-

ington D.C.: Carnegie Institute of Washington, 1937–38) publication no. 437; and France V. Scholes and Ralph L. Roys, *The Maya Chontal Indians of Acalan-Tixchel: A Contributor to the History and Ethnography of the Yucatan Peninsula* (Washington D.C.: Carnegie Institute of Washington, 1948) publication no. 560. See also Muriel, "Divergencias," 107–14.

44. Usigli, 'Primer ensayo hacia una tragedia mexicana," 102–25.

45. George Steiner, *The Death of Tragedy* (London: Faber and Faber, 1961), 323.

46. *The Works of Aristotle,* ed. W. D. Ross, vol. 11, *De Poetica* (Oxford: Clarendon Press, 1924), chap. 6, 1449b.

47. Usigli, *Tiempo y memoria.*

48. Steiner, *Death of Tragedy,* 31 (quoted in Spanish by Usigli in "Notas a *Corona de fuego*" [TC 3:810]).

49. "Las coronas y los ripios," *El Universal,* 15 September 1961, 3a sección, p. 7.

50. Steiner, *Death of Tragedy,* 113.

51. Salvador de Madariaga, *Hernán Cortés* (Buenos Aires: Sudamericana, 1941), 589–90.

52. Pablo Neruda, *Obras completas,* 3d ed. (Buenos Aires: Losada, 1968), 2:381.

53. Usigli used the Spanish term *comedia* without the specific connotations associated with the theatre of Lope de Vega or Calderón. In his essay "Una comedia shaviana: *Noche de estío,*" he alluded to the wide variety of forms that he admired: "la comedia de Aristófanes, de Moliere o de Shaw" (TC 3:304). In the case of *Corona de luz,* he was applying the most traditional sense of a play with a mixture of comic and serious elements.

54. See Usigli's "Segundo prólogo a *Corona de luz,*" in *Corona de sombra, Corona de fuego, Corona de luz* (Mexico, D.F.: Porrúa, 1973), 259–65. This and the "Primer prólogo" are not included in the third volume of *Teatro completo.* In this section all references are to the Porrúa edition and are made within the text in the following way: ("Segundo prólogo," 259–65).

55. Jacques Lafaye, *Quetzalcóatl and Guadalupe: The Formation of Mexican National Consciousness, 1531–1813,* Trans. Benjamin Keen (Chicago and London: University of Chicago Press, 1976), 3. The original version is *Quetzalcóatl et Guadalupe* (Paris: Gallimard, 1974).

56. Roberto R. Rodríguez, "La función de la imaginación en las *Coronas* de Rodolfo Usigli," *Latin American Theatre Review* 10, no. 2 (1977), 42. For other aspects of the play, see Layera "Mecanismos de fabulación y mitificación"; and Francisco A. Luneli, "Los mitos de la mexicanidad en la trilogía de Rodolfo Usigli," *Cuadernos Hispanoamericanos* 333 (1978): 466–77.

57. Bernadino de Sahagún, *Historia general de las cosas de Nueva España;* Toribio de Benavente (Motolinía), *Historia de los indios de la Nueva España;* Bartolomé de Las Casas, *Brevísima relación de la destrucción de las Indias.*

58. See Lafaye, *Quetzalcóatl and Guadalupe,* 226–27.

59. Pablo González Casanova, *Democracy in Mexico,* trans. Danielle Salti (New York: Oxford University Press, 1970), p. 41.

Chapter 8. The Wider Perspective

1. Dolores del Río was subsequently to become an internationally famous film star, but she was never to play this role in *Aguas estancadas.* See "*Mientras amemos y Aguas estancadas.* Breve noticia" (TC 3:449).

2. The suicide attempts, the specters from the past, and the central anecdote were all fiction.

3. Usigli's reaction to the cinema and his faith in the theatre's capacity to survive are discussed in chapter 1.

4. No date is given in *Teatro completo,* but A. Rodríguez-Seda states 1971 in "Las últimas obras de Usigli: Efebocracia o gerontocracia," *Latin American Theatre Review* 8, no. 1 (1974): 45.

5. My presentation of the structural arrangement has no authorial sanction in the textual format.

6. See S. C. Pearce and D. G. B. Piper, eds., *Literature of Europe and America in the 1960s* (Manchester: Manchester University Press, 1989), and in particular Peter Beardsell, "Spanish America," chap. 4, 116–42.

7. No date, but 1968–1974 is suggested by its penultimate position in *Teatro completo.*

8. This "Prólogo" of 1968 immediately precedes the text of the play (TC 3:102). Another of 1950 is collected with his "Prólogos, epílogos y otros textos" (TC 3:684–95).

9. In Spanish the usual term for the West Indies is "las Antillas."

10. The play's composition spanned the period 1950–1968, making both the Korean and Vietnam wars possible models. Most details, however, more closely resemble the former.

11. Calderón's play is entitled *El gran teatro del mundo.* Usigli chose the term *circo* (arena) to suggest the idea of mankind's struggle. See "Prólogo de *El gran circo del mundo*" (TC 3:695).

12. When he was working on early plans for the play in 1950, he foresaw some of the problems: "Con lo que no sé si acertaré es con el tono, con la medida, con el contacto que requiere la pieza" ("What I am not sure whether I will manage is the tone, the proportion, the contact that the play requires") (TC 3:695).

13. See chap. 1, n. 2.

14. The limits of his influence on the commercial theatre are discussed in chapter 1.

Bibliography

Three indispensable sources for a detailed study of Usigli's theatre are Wilder P. Scott. "Toward an Usigli Bibliography (1931–1971)," *Latin American Theatre Review*, 6, no. 1 (1972): 52–63; A. Mendoza López, *Boletín sobre Usigli*, México, D.F.: Bellas Artes, 1983; and *Teatro completo de Rodolfo Usigli*, México, D.F.: Fondo de Cultura Económica, vol. 1, 1963; vol. 2, 1966; vol. 3, 1979. The following bibliography is selective and, in the case of critical essays, mainly limited to items since 1971. The list of plays adheres to the order in the *Teatro completo* and includes Usigli's subtitle, the date of composition, and (in parentheses) the year of the first performance.

Plays by Rodolfo Usigli

El apóstol (Comedia en tres actos), 1931.

Falso drama (Comedieta en un acto), 1932.

4 Chemins 4 (Pièce en quatre scènes), 1932

Alcestes (Moraleja en tres actos), 1936.

Noche de estío (Comedia en tres actos), 1933–35.

El Presidente y el ideal (Comedia sin unidades. Prólogo, tres actos divididos en dieciséis cuadros y breve epílogo), 1935.

Estado de secreto (Comedia en tres actos y cinco cuadros), 1935 (1936).

La última puerta (Farsa impolítica para hacer dividida en dos escenas y un ballet intermedio), 1934–36.

El niño la niebla (Pieza en tres actos), 1936 (1951).

Medio tono (Comedia en tres actos), 1937 (1937).

Mientras amemos (Estudio en intensidad dramática en tres actos), 1937–48.

Aguas estancadas (Pieza en tres actos), 1938 (1952).

Otra primavera (Pieza en tres actos), 1937–38.

El gesticulador (Pieza para demagogos en tres actos), 1938 (1947).

La mujer no hace milagros (Comedia de malas maneras en tres actos), 1938 (1939).

La crítica de "La mujer no hace milagros" (Comedieta en un acto), 1939.

Sueño de día (Radiodrama en un acto), 1939 (1939).

Vacaciones I (Comedieta en un acto), 1940 (1940).

Vacaciones II (Comedieta en un acto), 1945–51.

La familia cena en casa (Comedia en tres actos), 1942 (1942).

Corona de sombra (Pieza antihistórica en tres actos y once escenas), 1943 (1947).

Dios, Batidillo y la mujer (Farsa americana en tres escenas), 1943.

La función de despedida (Comedia en tres actos), 1949 (1953).

Los fugitivos (Pieza en tres actos), 1950 (1950).

Jano es una muchacha (Pieza en tres actos), 1952 (1952).

Un día de éstos . . . (Fantasía impolítica en tres actos), 1953 (1954).

La exposición (Comedia divertimiento en tres actos), 1955–59.

Las madres (Las madres y los hijos) (Pieza en tres actos), 1949–60.

La diadema (Comedieta moral en un acto y tres cuadros), 1960.

Corona de fuego (Primer esquema para una tragedia antihistórica americana) 1960 (1961).

Corona de luz (La Virgen. Comedia antihistórica en tres actos), 1963 (1969).

Un navío cargado de . . . *(o Ultima noche a bordo)* (Comedieta marítima en un acto), 1961.

El testamento y el viudo (Comedieta involuntaria en un acto), 1962.

El encuentro (Comedieta en un acto para la primavera y para el tedio), 1963.

Carta de amor (Monólogo heterodoxo en tres pliegos y un post scriptum), 1968.

El gran circo del mundo (Magnus circus mundi) (Tres actos), 1950–1968.

Los viejos (Duólogo imprevisto en un acto).

El caso Flores (Comedieta amargosa en un acto y tres evocaciones).

¡Buenos días, señor Presidente! (Moralidad en dos actos y un interludio según *La vida es sueño*), 1971–72.

Principal Nondramatic Works by Usigli

ESSAYS

México en el teatro, Mexico, D.F.: Imprenta Mundial, 1932. Translated by Wilder P. Scott as *Mexico in the Theater*. Mississippi University Press: Romance Monographs, 1976.

Itinerario del autor dramático. Mexico: La Casa de España en México, 1940.

"Primer ensayo hacia una tragedia mexicana." *Cuadernos Americanos* 52 (1950): 102–25.

Anatomía del teatro. Mexico, D.F.: Ecuador 0 0'0", 1967. Consists mainly of essays first published in *El Universal*, 6 April–11 May 1947.

"Prólogos a *Corona de luz*." In *Corona de sombra, Corona de fuego, Corona de luz*. Mexico, D.F.: Editorial Porrúa, S.A., 1973. Not included with other prologues in *Teatro completo*. See below.

Conversaciones y encuentros de Rodolfo Usigli. Mexico, D.F.: Organización Editorial Novaro, S.A., 1974.

"Prólogos, epílogos y otros textos." In *Teatro completo de Rodolfo Usigli*, 3:279–844. Mexico, D.F.: Fondo de Cultura Económica, 1970. Includes prologues, etc., originally published in journals, and many unpublished addenda.

NOVEL

Ensayo de un crimen. Mexido, D.F.: Editora Nacional, 1944. Republished by Secretaría de Educación Pública. Lecturas Mexicanas, Segunda Serie, 39, 1986.

VERSE

Conversación desesperada, poemas. Mexico, D.F.: Cuadernos de México Nuevo, 1938.

Tiempo y memoria en conversación desesperada. Prólogo de José Emilio Pacheco. Textos de Humanidades, 26, Difusión Cultural. Mexico, D.F.: Universidad Nacional Autónoma de México, 1981.

Critical Studies of Usigli's Works

Ballinger, Rex Edward, ed. *Corona de sombra.* London: Harrap, 1965.

———, ed. *El gesticulador.* London: Harrap, 1965.

Beardsell, Peter R. "Insanity and Poetic Justice in Usigli's *Corona de sombra.*" *Latin American Theatre Review* 10, no. 1 (1976): 5–14.

———. "Usigli and the Search for Tragedy: *Corona de fuego.*" In *Hispanic Studies in Honour of Frank Pierce,* 1–15. ed. J. P. England. Sheffield: University of Sheffield, 1980.

———. "From the Mexican Revolution to *El gesticulador.*" *Vida Hispánica* vol. 32, no. 2 (Spring 1983): 12–20.

———. "Los niveles de la verdad en *Corona de luz* de Rodolfo Usigli." *Anales de Literatura Hispanoamericana,* núm. 12 (1983): 13–27.

———. "Usigli's Political Drama in Perspective," *Bulletin of Hispanic Studies* 66 (1989): 251–61.

Beck, Vera. "La fuerza motriz en la obra dramática de Rodolfo Usigli." *Revista Iberoamericana* 18 (1953): 369–83.

Di Puccio, Denise M. "Metatheatrical Histories in *Corona de luz.*" *Latin American Theatre Review* 20, no. 1 (1986): 29–36.

Finch, M. S. "*Corona de sombra, Corona de fuego, Corona de luz:* The Mythopoesis of Antihistory." *Romance Notes* 22, no. 2 (1981–82): 151–54.

Foster, David William. "*El gesticulador:* El Gran Teatro de México." In *Estudios sobre teatro mexicano contemporáneo: Semiología de la competencia teatral,* 13–26. New York, Berne, Frankfort on the Main, Nancy: Peter Lang, 1984.

Garcí, Lora, J. "Usigli 'esperó a Godot.'" *Papeles de Son Armadans* no. 269/70 (1978): 129–47.

Gates, Eunice J. "Usigli as Seen in his Prefaces and Epilogues." *Hispania* 37 (1954): 432–39.

Kronik, J. W. "Usigli's *El gesticulador* and the Fiction of Truth." *Latin American Theatre Review* 11, no. 1 (1977): 5–16.

Labinger, A. G. "Age, Alienation and the Artist in Usigli's *Los viejos.*" *Latin American Theatre Review* 14, no. 2 (1981): 41–47.

Larson, Catherine. " 'No conoces el precio de las palabras': Language and Meaning in Usigli's *El gesticulador.*" *Latin American Theatre Review* 20, no. 1 (1986): 21–28.

Layera, Ramón. "Mecanismos de fabulación y mitificación de la historia en las 'comedias impolíticas' y las *Coronas* de Rodolfo Usigli." *Latin American Theatre Review* 18, no. 2 (1985): 49–56.

Luneli, F. A. "Los mitos de la mexicanidad en la trilogía de Usigli." *Cuadernos Hispanoamericanos* 333 (1978): 466–77.

Martínez Peñalosa, P. "Sobre el poeta R. Usigli." *Abside* 39, no. 4 (1975): 429–36.

Nigro, Kirsten F. "Rhetoric and History in Three Mexican Plays." *Latin American Theatre Review* 21, no. 1 (1987): 65–73.

Pacheco, José Emilio. "Prólogo. Rodolfo Usigli: La indignación y el amor." In *Rodolfo Usigli: Tiempo y memoria en conversación desesperada.* Textos de Humanidades, 26, Difusión Cultural. Mexico, D.F.: Universidad Autónoma de México, 1981.

Perri, Dennis. "The Artistic Unity of *Corona de sombra.*" *Latin American Theatre Review* 15, no. 1 (1981): 13–19.

Peterson, G. W. "El mundo circular de Rodolfo Usigli." *Explicación de textos literarios* (Sacramento) 6, no. 1 (1977–78): 105–8.

Ragle, Gordon. "Rodolfo Usigli and his Mexican Scene." *Hispania* 46, no. 2 (1963): 307–11.

Rodríguez, R. R. "La función de la imaginación en las *Coronas* de Rodolfo Usigli." *Latin American Theatre Review* 10, no. 2 (1977): 37–44.

Rodríguez-Seda, A. "Las últimas obras de Usigli: Efebocracia o gerontocracia." *Latin American Theatre Review* 8, no. 1 (1974): 45–48.

Savage, R. Vance. "Rodolfo Usigli's Idea of Mexican Theater." *Latin American Theatre Review* 4, no. 2 (1971): 13–20.

Scarano, Laura Rosana. "Correspondencias estructurales y semánticas entre *El gesticulador* y *Corona de sombra.*" *Latin American Theatre Review* 22, no. 1 (1988): 29–38.

Schanzer, G. O. "Usigli, Calderón and the Revolution." *Kentucky Romance Quarterly* 26 (1979): 189–201.

Schmidhuber de la Mora, G. "El teatro mexicano de la provincia." *Latin American Theatre Review* 18, no. 2 (1985): 23–27.

Scott, Wilder P. "A Critical Study of the Life and Dramatic Works of Rodolfo Usigli." Ph.d. diss., University of Georgia, 1968.

———. "Roldolfo Usigli and Contemporary Dramatic Theory." *Romance Notes* 11 (1970): 526–30.

———. "Female Characters in Two Plays of Usigli." *South Atlantic Bulletin* 39 (1974): 31–37.

———. "French Literature and the Theater of Usigli." *Romance Notes* 16 (1974): 228–31.

———, trans. *Rodolfo Usigli: Mexico in the Theater.* Mississippi University Press: Romance Monographs, 1976.

Shaw, D. L. "Dramatic Technique in Usigli's *El gesticulador.*" *Theatre Research International* n.s. 1, no. 2 (1976): 125–33.

Tilles, S. H. "Rodolfo Usigli's Concept of Dramatic Art." *Latin American Theatre Review* 3, no. 2 (1970): 31–38.

General

Abel, Lionel. *Metatheatre: A New View of Dramatic Form.* New York: Hill and Wang, 1963.

Agustín, José. *Three Lectures: Literature and Censorship in Latin America Today: Dream Within a Dream.* Edited by John Kirk and Don Schmidt. Occasional

Papers, no. 1, Department of Foreign Languages and Literatures. Denver: University of Denver, 1978.

Argudín, Yolanda. *Historia del teatro en México desde los rituales prehispánicos hasta el arte dramático de nuestros días.* Segunda Edición en Español. Mexico, D.F.: Panorama Editorial, 1986.

Beardsell, Peter. "Spanish America." In *Literature of Europe and America in the 1960s,* edited by S. C. Pearce and D. G. B. Piper, 116–42. Manchester: Manchester University Press, 1989.

Berst, Charles A. *Bernard Shaw and the Art of Drama.* Urbana, Chicago, London: University of Illinois Press, 1973.

Blasio, José Luis. *Maximilian: Memoirs of his Private Secretary.* Translated by R. H. Murray. New Haven: Yale University Press, 1934.

Blumberg, Arnold. *The Diplomacy of the Mexican Empire, 1863–1867.* Philadelphia: American Philosophical Society, 1971.

Bravo-Elizondo, Pedro. *Teatro hispanoamericano de crítica social.* Madrid: Playor, 1975.

Calvert, Peter. *Mexico,* London: Ernest Benn, 1973.

Cortés, Hernán. *"Cartas de relación de Fernando Cortés sobre el descubrimiento y conquista de la Nueva España. Carta Quinta."* In *Historiadores primitivos de Indias,* by Enrique de Vedia, vol. 1, Madrid: Biblioteca de Autores Españoles, 1877, vol. 22.

———. *Letters from Mexico.* Translated and edited by A. R. Pagden. London: Oxford University Press, 1972.

Cosío Villegas, Daniel, *coordinador. Historia general de México.* 3d ed. Mexico, D.F.: El Colegio de México, 1981.

Dauster, Frank. *Historia del teatro hispanoamericano: Siglos XIX y XX.* Mexico, D.F.: De Andrea, 1973.

———. *Ensayos sobre teatro hispanoamericano.* SepSetentas, 208. Mexico, D.F.: Secretaría de Educación Pública, 1975.

———. *"La generación de 1924: El dilema del realismo." Latin American Theatre Review* 18, no. 2 (1985): 13–22.

Díaz, Lilia. "El liberalismo militante." In Cosío Villegas, *Historia general de México* 2:819–96.

Díaz del Castillo, Bernal. *Historia verdadera de la conquista de la Nueva España.* Mexico, D.F.: Editorial Porrúa, 1960.

Eidelberg, Nora. *Teatro experimental hispanoamericano, 1960–1980: La realidad social como manipulación.* Minneapolis, Minn.: Institute for the Study of Ideologies and Literature, 1985.

Fagg, John Edwin. *Latin America: A General History.* 3d ed. New York: Macmillan Publishing Co.; London: Collier Macmillan Publishers, 1977.

Fuentes, Carlos. *La muerte de Artemio Cruz.* 4th ed. Mexico, D.C.: Fondo de Cultura Económica, 1968.

Ganz, Arthur. *George Bernard Shaw.* London and Basingstoke: MacMillan, 1983.

Gilly, Adolfo. *La revolución interrumpida.* Mexico, D.F.: Ediciones "El Caballito," 1971.

González Casanova, Pablo. *La democracia en México.* 14th ed. Mexico, D.F.: Serie Popular Era, 1983. Translated by Danielle Salti as *Democracy in Mexico.* New York: Oxford University Press, 1970.

Hays, H. R. *In the Beginning: Early Man and His Gods.* New York: G. P. Putnam and Sons, 1963.

Hays, Peter. *New Horizons in Psychiatry.* Harmondsworth: Penguin Books, 1964.

Hellman, Judith Adler. *Mexico in Crisis.* New York: Holmes and Meier Publishers; London: Heinemann, 1978.

Lafaye, Jacques. *Quetzalcóatl and Guadalupe: The Formation of Mexican National Consciousness, 1531–1813.* Translated by Benjamin Keen. Chicago and London: University of Chicago Press, 1976.

Lamb, Ruth. *Bibliografía del teatro mexicano del siglo XX.* Mexico, D.F.: Studium, 1962.

―――. *Mexican Theater of the Twentieth Century.* Claremont, Calif.: Ocelot Press, 1975.

Leech, Clifford. *Tragedy.* London: Methuen, 1969.

López de Gómara, Francisco. *Conquista de México: Segunda parte de la historia general de las Indias.* Madrid: Biblioteca de Autores Españoles, 1877, vol. XXII.

Lyday, Leon F., and George W. Woodyard, eds. *Dramatists in Revolt: The New Latin American Theatre.* Austin: University of Texas Press, 1976.

Madariaga, Salvador de. *Hernán Cortés.* Buenos Aires: Sudamericana, 1941.

Magaña Esquivel, Antonio. *Teatro mexicano del siglo XX.* Mexico, D.F.: Fondo de Cultura Económica, 1970.

Mendoza López, Margarita. "Teatro de las Bellas Artes de la Ciudad de México." *Latin American Theatre Review* 18, no. 2 (1985): 7–11.

―――. "El teatro en la Ciudad de México durante cincuenta años." *Plural* (Segunda Epoca) 17–19, núm. 201 (1988): 42–53.

Meyer, Lorenzo. "El primer tramo del camino." and "La encrucijada." In Cosío Villegas, *Historia general de México* 2 : 1183–1355.

Meyer, Michael C., and William L. Sherman. *The Course of Mexican History.* New York: Oxford University Press, 1979.

Monsiváis, Carlos. "Notas sobre la cultura mexicana en el siglo XX." In Cosío Villegas, *Historia general de México* 2 : 1375–1548.

Muriel, Josefina. "Divergencias en la biografía de Cuauhtémoc." *Estudios de Historia Novohispana* 1 (1966): 53–114.

Neruda, Pablo. *Obras completas.* 3d ed. Buenos Aires: Losada, 1968.

Nigro, Kirsten, ed. *Latin American Theatre Review* 18, no. 2 (1985). Special Issue on Modern Mexican Theatre.

―――. "Entrevista a Luisa Josefina Hernández." *Latin American Theatre Review* 18, no. 2 (1985), 101–4.

Nomland, John B. *Teatro mexicano contemporáneo.* Mexico, D.F.: Instituto Nacional de Bellas Artes, 1967.

O'Connor, Richard. *The Cactus Throne: The Tragedy of Maximilian and Carlota.* London: Allen and Unwin, 1971.

Oliver, William I. *Voices of Change in the Spanish American Theatre.* Austin: University of Texas Press, 1971.

Parker, A. A. "History and Poetry: The Coriolanus Theme in Calderón." In *Hispanic Studies in Honour of I. González Llubera,* ed. Frank Pierce. 211–24. Oxford: Dolphin Book Co., 1959.

¿Qué pasa con el teatro en México? Mexico, D.F.: Organización Editorial Novaro, S.A., 1967.

Revistas literarias mexicanas modernas. Mexico, D.F.: Fondo de Cultura Económica, 1980.

Ribbans, G. W. "Lying in the Structure of La verdad sospechosa." In Studies in Spanish Literature of the Golden Age Presented to Edward M. Wilson, ed. R. D. Jones, 193–216. London: Tamesis, 1973.

Rojo de la Rosa, Grínor. Orígenes del teatro hispanoamericano contemporáneo. Valparaíso: Ediciones Universitarias de Valparaíso, 1972.

Ross, W. D., ed. The Works of Aristotle. Vol. 11, De Poetica, trans. Ingram Bywater, chap. 6, 1449b. Oxford: Clarendon Press, 1924.

Saz, Agustín del. Teatro social hispanoamericano. Barcelona: Labor, 1967.

Schilling, Robert. Rites, cultes, dieux de Rome. Paris: Editions Klincksieck, 1979.

Shakespeare, William. The Complete Works of William Shakespeare. London: Gawthorn Press and Bruce Publishing Co., n.d.

Shaw, George Bernard. The Complete Plays of Bernard Shaw, London: Constable and Co., 1931.

Simpson, Lesley Byrd. Many Mexicos. Berkeley and Los Angeles: University of California Press, 1966.

Skidmore, Thomas E., and Peter H. Smith. Modern Latin America. New York and Oxford: Oxford University Press, 1984.

Solórzano, Carlos. "El teatro de la posguerra en México." Hispania (Lawrence) 48, no. 4 (1964): 693–97.

———. El teatro latinoamericano en el siglo XX. Mexico, D.F.: Editorial Pormaca, 1964.

Steiner, George. The Death of Tragedy. London: Faber and Faber, 1961.

Thomson, William A. R. Black's Medical Dictionary. 31st ed. London: Adam and Charles Black, 1976.

Trífilo, S. Samuel. "The Contemporary Theater in Mexico." Modern Language Journal 46 (1962): 153–57.

Ulloa, Berta. "La lucha armada (1911–1920)." In Cosío Villegas, Historia general de México 2: 1073–1182.

Warren, S. A. "In Search of Contemporary Theatre on Mexico." Review 75, no. 14 (1975): 48–53.

White, Hayden. Metahistory: The Historical Imagination in Nineteenth-Century Europe. Baltimore and London: John Hopkins University Press, 1973.

Woodyard, George W. "Studies on the Latin American Theatre, 1960–1969." Theatre Documentation 2 (1969–70): 49–81.

Woodyard, George W. and Leon F. Lyday. A Bibliography of Latin American Theater Criticism, 1940–1974. Austin: University of Texas, 1976.

Index